"Enemies"

"Enemies"

WORLD WAR II ALIEN INTERNMENT

by John Christgau

to the Smiths,
with thanks for your
interest in this issue —

John Christgau

Authors Choice Press
San Jose New York Lincoln Shanghai

Enemies
World War II Alien Internment

All Rights Reserved © 1985, 2001 by John F. Christgau

Authors Choice Press
an imprint of iUniverse.com, Inc.

For information address:
iUniverse.com, Inc.
5220 S 16th, Ste. 200
Lincoln, NE 68512
www.iuniverse.com

Originally published by Iowa State University Press

ISBN: 0-595-17915-0

Printed in the United States of America

CONTENTS

PREFACE

A number of years ago, an elderly neighbor was reminiscing about World War II, and remarked in passing that he had spent the war years as a guard for Germans at a prison camp in North Dakota. My ears perked up, since, as a writer of fiction, I was then in search of a familiar setting for an escape story.

Later, when I interviewed my neighbor for the details of his experiences, he made it clear for the first time that it was German *aliens* he had guarded, not POWs, at a place called Ft. Lincoln Internment Camp, just south of Bismarck. But before he could get too far into the details of the camp, his wife, who had nervously busied herself serving coffee, stopped his reminiscing cold when she interrupted, "You signed an oath that you would never discuss this."

Whether by virtue of secrecy oaths, or more probably simple historical oversight, the subject of American enemy alien camps is an area of World War II history about which little has been written. As far back as 1798, Congress established provisions for the arrest and internment of enemy aliens in the event of war or threatened invasion. After President Franklin D. Roosevelt proclaimed on December 7 and 8, 1941, that invasion was real or threatened by Japan, Germany, and Italy, he immediately promulgated the regulations to be followed for the arrest and detention of aliens residing in the United States who were deemed dangerous to the public peace and safety.

Thus was instituted an Enemy Alien Internment Program which was to span six years from 1941 to 1946, ultimately imprison 31,275 enemy aliens, and involve the efforts of thousands of administrative and guard personnel from principally four agencies. The FBI was charged with investigating the subjects. The Border Patrol of the Immigration and Naturalization Service was given the job of running the camps where the enemy aliens were imprisoned. The Alien Enemy Control Unit of the Justice Department took on the responsibility of creating and running the Hearing Boards to determine release, parole, or deportation. Finally, the War Relocation Authority (WRA) got involved peripherally when five thousand Japanese Americans held in WRA relocation centers renounced their American citizenship and were judged enemy aliens.

Not long after I began the initial research into the story, I recognized that the documentary resources surrounding the history of the program are staggering: INS records for the eight internment camps it operated total almost 400 feet of cartons in the National Archives; FBI files on enemy alien subjects amount to 28,000 pages. Short of a decade of research, and an inevitably dry summary of the mountains of documents, the "complete history" was never going to be told.

Finally I returned to the very site which had first sparked my interest: Ft. Lincoln Internment Camp in Bismarck. The men who passed through it, the men who ran it, and the procedures by which it was run were characteristic of the larger Enemy Alien Internment Program. From the focus of Ft. Lincoln then, "Enemies" is the dramatic story of that program.

SOURCES AND ACKNOWLEDGMENTS

Personal correspondence and diary entries for the section entitled "Kurt" were provided courtesy of Kurt Peters. All official memos, correspondence, reports, hearing board recommendations, and orders pertaining to his case are in his alien enemy case file in the Washington National Records Center located in Suitland, Maryland. INS central office records and Ft. Lincoln administrative files, which provide the details of the creation of the Enemy Alien program, and the operation of Ft. Lincoln, are also in the Suitland archives.

The FBI "Reports" on Edgar Friedman, Dr. Arthur Sonnenberg, Wolfgang Thomas (and Thomas's father-in-law, Carl Kroll) are kept in the FBI's voluminous Alien Enemy Case Files. Memos, hearing board recommendations, and orders relating to *Die Wanderkameraden* come from their INS case files at Suitland. Copies of the letters which Friedman and Wolfgang Thomas wrote pleading to be released are in their individual files. Official alien enemy correspondence between the INS, the attorney general's office, the FBI, the Security Defense Unit, and the Alien Enemy Control Unit is in the Suitland archives, INS central office records. All documents relating to the principal subjects of this book were released to them, and to me, under the provisions of the Privacy Act and the Freedom of Information Act.

The activities and difficulties surrounding "The Railroaders" at Ft. Lincoln were reconstructed from Ft. Lincoln administrative files at Suitland, and through interviews with former Ft. Lincoln guards and administrative personnel. Copies of letters from internee spokesmen for the railroaders to INS officials are in the central office records. Reports and investigations into the escape of Karl Heinz Alfred Fengler are among the Ft. Lincoln administrative files and INS central office files at Suitland. McCoy's log of events and the letter to him from Fengler are in the Ft. Lincoln administrative files. Records of the activities of Fengler before his escape from Ft. Lincoln were obtained from the Illinois Department of Corrections, Information Services Unit, Springfield, Illinois, and the Cook County Clerk's Office, in Chicago.

Ft. Lincoln administrative records of the escape attempt of Hermann Cordes and Albert Gregeratzki are among the records at Suitland. Included in those records are verbatim transcripts of interviews with Cordes and Gregeratzki, and John Schultz's handwritten notes to McCoy. Selected copies of *The Bismarck Echo*, the internees' newspaper, are in the Ft. Lincoln administrative files. FBI reports on investigations into the activities of the eastern branch of the German-American Bund provide the details of Hermann Cordes's arrest in Union City, New Jersey.

Hiro Tanaka's internment story was reconstructed from several documentary sources, all in the Suitland archives: his WRA case file; his Wartime Civil Control Administration file; and his INS case file, kept when he became an enemy alien. Ft. Lincoln administrative files and INS central office records contain the correspondence and memos relating to the removal of the renunciants from Tule Lake to Ft. Lincoln. The Federal Archives and Records Service (FARC) in San Bruno, California, is the repository for the district court records of *Abo* v. *Clark,* and Hiro Tanaka's affidavit in that case is among those records. The personal files of Wayne Collins, attorney for the Japanese American renunciants in *Abo* v. *Clark,* are in the Bancroft Library, University of California, Berkeley.

In each episode, all dialogue from hearings and interrogations was reconstructed from verbatim transcripts. In the absence of transcripts, I encouraged my interview subjects to reconstruct critical aspects of the proceedings from memory. Where memory failed after forty years, the episode was dealt with only in summary.

A complete listing of source material can be found in the bibliography. It will reveal that "Enemies" is a collective effort, and I am grateful to the principal contributors:

Kurt and Evelyn Peters, Eddie and Liesl Friedman, Dr. Arthur Sonnenberg, Wolfgang Thomas, and Hiro and Aki Tanaka—for poignant and difficult recollections;

Albert Gregeratzki and Hermann Cordes, whose memories were so complete they even sent a tunnel chart, with distances reckoned down to centimeters;

Phyllis Johnson, who finally found Albert and Hermann, and skillfully recorded (with Klint Johnson's help) and then translated their stories;

Hisao Inouye, Alfred Henzler, Richard Birkefeld, Paul Mueller, Victor Petereit, and especially Robert Nebel, whose background information helped create a foreground;

"Red" Selland and Will Robbins, who dug enthusiastically into their memories and picture albums;

Bill Cook and Boyd Kimmins, who took the time to write at length about events at Ft. Lincoln;

Edg Fennessey, who first alerted me to a "camp for Germans in North Dakota," and then to Norm Meltzer, who told me who to see once I got there;

Cliff Peck, Ray Lenihan, Ed Pendray, Frank Alshouse, George and Hattie Kashino, Carl Lee, and Rita Rene, who also agreed to my interviews;

Edward J. Ennis, for his frank recollections to me, and before the Commission on Wartime Relocation and Internment of Civilians;

Peg Homan, for her inside view of the Ft. Lincoln headquarters, and Carol Laidlaw, for her details of the operations of the Alien Enemy Hearing Boards;

Kevin Sweeney, Kathleen Devaney, Dan Keefe, and Jess Nierenberg, research gumshoes who found bits and pieces that proved fascinating;

Bill Lewis and T. Lane Moore, for the keys to the Suitland archives; David Cook, for valuable assistance at the FBI's Records Management Division;

Stella Yim, for making INS central office records available to me;

Bill Tsukida, who first told me about the renunciants;

Officials at the State Historical Society of North Dakota, and *The Bismarck Tribune,* for providing photographs from their files;

Sarah Sharp of the Regional Office of Oral History at Berkeley, whose interview of Judge Alfonso Zirpoli provided background on the Hearing Boards;

Chris Fritz, of the Federal District Court in San Francisco, who directed me to the court records of *Abo* v. *Clark* at the Federal Archives in San Bruno, where Robyn Dondero graciously made those records available to me;

Judith Gildner, of the Iowa State University Press, for guidance in tightening the story;

Paul Cook and Erick Christgau, for helping me to overcome my pathological fear of computers;

My wife Peggy, and my children Erick, Sally, and Jenny, for tolerating my periodic disappearances, physical and mental, in pursuit of the story.

Finally, my thanks to many others who listened patiently as I tried to explain what I was about. If it still isn't clear, blame me, not the contributors.

The Ft. Lincoln compound, summer of 1941 Taken from the northwest tower North fence, along which *Die Wanderkameraden* walked, to the left. *Center right,* Captains' bungalow with pants hanging on the clothesline Internees' brick barracks in background behind soccer field (Courtesy of *The Bismarck Tribune.*)

"Enemies"

Ft Lincoln Internment Camp, Bismarck, North Dakota, winter 1941–42 View west along north fence (Courtesy of Will Robbins)

Kurt

GERMAN SEAMEN AND THE BEGINNING OF THE INTERNMENT PROGRAM

Arriving seamen internees are loaded into trucks for transport to Ft Lincoln, May 31, 1941 (Courtesy of Will Robbins)

View from inside compound of northwest surveillance tower Entrance to Ft Lincoln in background (Courtesy of Red Selland.)

Above left, Ft Lincoln Headquarters Building, outside compound Administrative offices downstairs, censor's office upstairs *Above right*, Ft. Lincoln Control Center Guardhouse, where Cordes and Gregeratski were kept, was in the rear of this building

Mess hall scene, German seamen internees, summer of 1941 (Courtesy of Will Robbins)

1941

INTERNIERTE
DEUTSCHE
SEELEUTE

German sailors carving memorial stone at Ft Lincoln, 1941 (Courtesy of Will Robbins) The erected memorial is shown above (Courtesy of *The Bismarck Tribune*)

Ft Lincoln, summer 1941, just outside the south fence of the compound Chief Patrol Inspector A S Hudson inspecting laying of floor of Barracks T13, in a separate compound which would eventually house the Japanese internees in 1942, and later German internees The crawl space and foundation partitions which figured in the Cordes-Gregeratzki tunnel escape attempt are visible (Courtesy of Will Robbins)

German ship captains outside their bungalow, 1941: *front left*, Captain Fred Stengler, first internee spokesman (Courtesy of Will Robbins)

Above, internee Kurt Peters, *left*, teaching his course in English and American citizenship (Courtesy of Kurt Peters) *Left*, Peters instructs another class at Ft Lincoln, winter 1941–42 (Courtesy of Will Robbins)

Above, Bungalow T94, summer 1941, which housed Kurt Peters and other ships' officers, in southwest corner of compound (Courtesy of Will Robbins)

Right, ships' officers in quarters T94, summer 1941 Kurt Peters in far corner in front of stove Alfred Henzler on bunk in front of Peters. (Courtesy of Will Robbins)

Christmas gathering of detained seamen, inside T94, December 1941 *Third from left,* Kurt Peters *Fourth from left,* Alfred Henzler. *Second from right,* Johann Marquenie, who attempted to escape by floating down the Missouri River (Courtesy of Will Robbins)

Kurt

By six o'clock the evening of May 31, 1941, several hundred curious citizens of Bismarck, North Dakota, lined the Northern Pacific railroad tracks along Main Street as if awaiting the arrival of some political figure. However, it was no American politician they had come to greet. Menacing canvas-topped olive drab Civilian Conservation Corps trucks were backed up to the tracks. Dozens of soldiers wearing garrison hats and Border Patrol inspectors in Sam Browne pistol belts stood in groups beside the trucks, talking quietly, exchanging what meager information they had on the new arrivals.

For almost two months, *The Bismarck Tribune* had been running stories anticipating the internment of foreigners in Bismarck. Italian sailors, the paper wrote, who were taken off ships in American ports, were on their way to Bismarck to be held in what the newspaper called romantic Ft. Lincoln.

If there was romance associated with the fort, it was because of the legend of George Armstrong Custer, who had headed out from Old Ft. Lincoln for his last stand. Not long after Custer perished, Old Ft. Lincoln was abandoned and dismantled by settlers. In 1900 a new fort was constructed on the east side of the Missouri River, just south of Bismarck, and garrisoned by infantry regiments until 1939. Only a handful of men occupied it from then until early 1941, when the government decided to use it to intern seamen considered to be a threat to United States security.

The first report in the *Tribune* (April 12, 1941) that it was Italians headed for Ft. Lincoln sparked only a mild ethnic reaction in the Bismarck community, which was heavily populated with German Americans. One woman remarked sardonically, "It'll be poetic justice to unload these Italians at a town named Bismarck." Another woman claimed, "I suppose we'll be pulling Italian fugitives out of the coal bin." But when it was finally established that "potentially dangerous Germans" were to be interned at the fort, the citizens of Bismarck were very curious.

7

At seven o'clock a photographer stepped out of the crowd, crouched down next to the tracks, and directed his camera eastward, as if to snap a picture of the train as it hove into sight. But at that moment the train bearing 220 German and 162 Italian seamen was stopped outside Bismarck on a siding next to the North Dakota State Prison. For the first time the men inside were permitted to raise the window shades to look out the barred windows of the old prison train which had been pressed into use. The men had been on the train three days, enough time to get all the way across Europe. Now, as they raised the curtains, they half expected to see the Pacific Ocean. Instead, they discovered they were in the midst of a green, rolling, treeless prairie.

The twenty-two car train was cut in two at the railroad siding, and the Italians were sent on their way west for internment at Ft. Missoula, Montana. The German seamen were then told for the first time they had arrived at Bismarck, North Dakota, which was to be their final destination. Looking out the windows again they spotted the ominous, high walls of the state prison and assumed the worst. It wasn't until the train started up again and reached the site of the trucks and the huge crowd, just at 8:00 p.m., that the men understood they were bound for somewhere else.

The forty-five German officers were unloaded from the train first. One by one they were ushered from the railroad cars and through a tight alley of guardsmen and patrol inspectors which led to the CCC trucks. Inside the cars, waiting their turn to be unloaded, the crewmen affected hilarity as they waved through the barred windows of the train. One crewman kept flashing a broad smile which revealed several missing teeth. Someone in the crowd shouted a German greeting to him. He shot back an English hello.

Meanwhile few of the officers smiled as they climbed ladders up into the trucks. None waved. In contrast to the crewmen, they were grave and serious—none more so than a twenty-year-old ship's radioman named Kurt Heinrich Rudolf Peters.

Kurt was born in Hamburg, Germany, on October 15, 1920, the only child of Frieda and August Peters. As a schoolboy, Kurt began to receive a Nazi political indoctrination which set him against the social-democratic ideals of his parents. Then one evening when he was fifteen, his parents sat him down in the kitchen of their Hamburg apartment to explain their beliefs.

"This is going to be a very serious evening," his father began. "And we hope you're grown enough to understand what we're trying to do."

After closing the windows, his mother and father laid out for him in lowered voices the twenty-year history of the social-democratic movement in Germany. "We still believe in it," his father finished. "And we want you to realize what our ideals are."

Quietly but eagerly, the Peters disputed the National-Socialist dogma their son had learned. By the time he was eighteen, Kurt rejected the Nazi philosophy entirely. To avoid service in the *Wehrmacht,* Kurt attended radio school in Hamburg, then went to sea as a radioman aboard various passenger-freighters in the Atlantic.

On August 24, 1939, Kurt was aboard the Standard Oil tanker *Peter Hurll* when it docked in New York. Germany attacked Poland a week later, and Kurt found himself stranded in the Yorkville area of New York City when Standard Oil replaced its German crewmen with American sailors. Standard Oil officials apologized to the German crewmen and explained that the company accepted full responsibility for returning the sailors to Germany when it was perfectly safe to do so. Meanwhile the men were to remain in the New York area.

Kurt promptly moved into an apartment in Astoria, and in a few weeks he had seen enough of America to be certain that he wanted to become an American citizen. He enrolled in an American literature course at Columbia University to learn the literature of the country. His instructor was a forty-year-old black professor who soon took Kurt aside and explained that it was obvious Kurt wanted to Americanize himself quickly. Addressing himself to Kurt's two accents, German and British, the instructor demonstrated the proper jaw movements for the English *th* and *w,* which Kurt was to study with a hand mirror.

As 1939 drew to a close, Kurt practiced his English for hours in front of a mirror, gradually mastering the inflections and phrasing of American speech. By November he was beginning to feel that his European characteristics were growing less conspicuous. One night late in November he was invited to attend a party in Yorkville, hosted by one of the Standard Oil seamen he had associated with during his brief stay in that area of the city.

Kurt was still happy to have moved out of Yorkville, but he agreed to go to the party because he felt the opportunity to circulate again among Germans would give him something against which to measure his own Americanization. Then, too, since he had moved to Astoria, he had had little news of what new circumstance had developed concerning official efforts to get the stranded sailors back to Germany. Moreover, his host promised the company of American women.

So he went off to the party with enthusiasm, eager to mingle and socialize. It was not long into the evening before he saw that, even with what little American speech he had mastered, he was obviously more comfortable in the setting than the other sailors there, who stood in the corners and chatted in German.

Shortly, a bushy-haired, middle-aged man took Kurt aside, introduced himself as Edward John Kerling, and presented a bizarre proposal. He explained to Kurt that he was familiar with the efforts of the stranded seamen to return to Germany, and he launched into a lively explanation of plans he was making to sail to Germany aboard a yacht, crewed by experienced sailors like Kurt. Once back in Germany, they would be trained as saboteurs, after which they would secretly return to America to carry out sabotage assignments.

Kurt was invited to join Kerling's plot as the yacht's radio operator. Hoping to find a reason beyond the madness of the plan for declining the invitation, he proceeded to ask a series of technical questions concerning the radio equipment. His questions had the opposite effect, however, and several days after the party broke up he was persuaded to travel to Baltimore, where the yacht was berthed, to inspect the radio equipment. Following his inspection, Kurt refused to join the crew, offering as an excuse that the yacht was not fit for an Atlantic crossing. After this incident, Kerling dropped from sight.

Kurt busied himself with his classes at Columbia, but he was careful thereafter about which, if any, sailors he associated with. Mainly he read and studied in his Astoria apartment, emerging from that solitude only for his classes, or an occasional opera or symphony performance.

From initial courses at Columbia in American literature and English composition, Kurt progressed through the year to English literature, short story writing, American history and government, and finally philosophy. In the summer of 1940, he began to keep a journal in English, jotting down ideas from his philosophic readings that impressed him. By September of 1940, he was so absorbed in his studies that the worldly news of the Battle of Britain seemed irrelevant to him, and he had almost ceased to worry about deportation. He felt that he and the other seamen, whom he saw little or nothing at all of, were forgotten nobodies who would be permitted to go their own way while the rest of the world went to war.

However, complaints about alien espionage were coming into the Justice Department at the rate of three thousand a day. First charged in 1939 with the responsibility of investigating sabotage and espionage, the FBI now hummed with activity. According to Earl G. Harrison, INS director, the U.S. alien population in 1940 was only 3.5 percent of the total population. But Congress nevertheless feared that alien propagandists would undermine the democratic institutions of the United States. Consequently, the Alien Registration Act was passed in the spring of 1940. President Roosevelt signed the act in June, setting in motion the procedures for the registration and fingerprinting of more than three million aliens.

Mere registration of aliens was not the end of it, however. In September of 1940, the Justice Department began drawing up arrest warrants to be served on the German seamen still stranded in New York City. The reason was, technically, that the sailors had overstayed their visas and remained in the country longer than the sixty days permitted under immigration laws. But in fact the arrest warrants were served to reassure the country that proper precautions were being taken against potential fifth column activities in the United States.

On September 21, 1940, Kurt Peters received an arrest warrant in the mail, which granted him a hearing to show cause why he should not be deported. His hearing was set for January 16, 1941. While waiting for the opportunity to clear himself and avoid deportation, Kurt registered as an alien in accordance with the legislation enacted that spring.

He also remembered Henry Uterhart. Kurt had met Uterhart at a party almost a year before, when he had first been stranded. Uterhart and his wife, old enough to be Kurt's grandparents, were obviously taken by Kurt's youth and intelligence. Uterhart, a lawyer, had offered to help Kurt, and it was Uterhart who had pulled strings to get Kurt enrolled at Columbia. Deportation was of fleeting concern to Kurt then, as he dove into classwork convinced that he had been forgotten by the U.S. immigration authorities.

Even with an arrest warrant in his hand, Kurt decided to postpone seeing Uterhart until he had had his hearing, which he was sure would be the opportunity he needed to explain that he fully intended to become an American citizen. Having been in the United States almost a year and a half, he would shortly be able to file a declaration of intention to gain his citizenship. He felt that once he had an opportunity to explain his plans, the whole business of his deportation would be dropped.

Kurt rose early the morning of January 16 for a day that would leave him confused and alarmed. He rode the subway to the Barge Office at the foot of Battery Street, fully expecting to be alone. However, seventy-five seamen were already gathered there when Kurt arrived, and together they were ferried out to Ellis Island. In the Great Hall of Ellis Island, the seamen were fingerprinted and photographed, then led back through various hallways and corridors to a large room where several hearings were in progress at once. Each hearing was presided over by an inspector of the Immigration and Naturalization Service who sat behind a long table, accompanied by a secretary who took notes.

Kurt was sworn by an immigrant inspector who formally warned him against perjury. The official shuffled through a stack of papers to find Kurt's arrest warrant, and read aloud that Kurt was in the United States in violation of the Immigration Act of 1924. He then asked if Kurt understood the charge.

Kurt nodded and answered "yes" in crisp and clear English which he hoped would suggest that he was already very much an American.

"This warrant provides for your parole under suitable arrangement," the inspector explained. "Do you understand?"

"I do," Kurt smiled. Checking in periodically with an INS parole office would be no trouble. It would be a minor inconvenience among a long list of freedoms he would otherwise have.

The inspector next asked if Kurt wished to be represented by a lawyer.

Kurt shook his head again, pleased with himself for having foregone calling on Mr. Uterhart. The presence of a pushy attorney might well make this inspector more serious than he already is, Kurt thought.

There followed a list of quick biographical questions which Kurt answered confidently. How old was he? Where was he born? Married? How long had he been in the United States? And then, "What was the reason you remained in the United States since August 24, 1939?"

"I was compelled to stay in the United States because I am a German, and the Standard Oil Company is paying me $18.41 a week as I was a ship's officer." Kurt forced himself to pause then, to avoid a rush of clumsy language which would betray him.

"At the time of your last entry," the inspector pushed ahead, "was it your intention to remain permanently in the United States?"

"No," Kurt had to admit. He wanted to go on and explain that he couldn't possibly have foreseen being suddenly stranded in New York.

But the inspector promptly launched into another series of questions which he read in a dry, formal voice from a paper he held before his face: Had Kurt ever been deported from the United States? Where did his parents live in Germany? What was his religious faith? And finally, "Have you registered under the Alien Registration Act of 1940?"

Kurt answered each question with as much authority and English grace as he could muster. Yet he began to grow anxious for an opportunity to answer questions he felt were more to the point of his case: When did he decide to become a U.S. citizen? Why did he decide? What was it about Germany that had caused him to leave it to go to sea?

He had rehearsed his answers, fully intending to explain the secret kitchen lectures on democracy his parents had given him in Nazi Germany. But the inspector suddenly put aside the paper from which he had been reading questions. "Have you any further statement you wish to make as to why the government should not deport you?"

Kurt was dumbfounded. Deportation? Further statements? He hadn't even had a chance to begin his appeal. But it was clear now that his hearing was about to be concluded.

"I do not want to be deported!" he blurted out suddenly. "It is in the contract that I signed with the Standard Oil Company that they should return me to Germany," he was almost whining now. It wasn't *his* idea to go back to Germany. "As soon as the war is over they will return me to Germany." Kurt stared at the inspector. Return to Germany meant that he would be drafted into the *Wehrmacht!* "But I want to remain in the United States!" he finished. "I want to become a citizen."

The inspector asked only if Kurt would appear at Ellis Island when the time came for deportation.

"Yes," Kurt answered.

Then the hearing was closed.

Following his hearing at Ellis Island, Kurt retreated to the privacy of his apartment in Astoria. He had no interest in his classes now, and the concentration he had once used to disentangle philosophic arguments was now applied to the confusing circumstances of his own life: Why had he been given a deportation hearing when the government and Standard Oil had already agreed that international circumstances prevented deportation? How could they carry it out? Had circumstances changed? If anything, Kurt felt, they'd grown worse. The news daily was of skirmishes and ships sinking in the Atlantic. Whatever ship tried to take him back to Germany would have to run the gauntlet of British cruisers and then perhaps German submarines. So what was the point of threatening him with deportation? Yet, if it was an idle threat, it still seemed to hang over his head like a death sentence.

He waited around his apartment for weeks for some clarification of his status from the INS. Once or twice he thought to call them, but decided against it on the slim hope they would forget about him if he didn't remind them.

Then late in February he received notice of the findings and conclusions of his Ellis Island hearing. He read the official notice over and over, anxious to learn at last what was to happen to him. Instead, the legal sounding document only confused him more. It had been found that he was in the United States illegally. He was deportable to Germany at the government's expense. Yet, since he was of good moral character, and willing to depart at his own expense without the issuance of a deportation order, he was eligible to do so. Therefore, it was ordered, "The respondent is accorded permission to depart from the U.S. in lieu of deportation, at his own expense."

He hadn't asked to depart from the United States at the government's expense, his own, or anybody's. Where could he go? Who would accept him? "I do not want to be deported!" he had almost shouted at his hearing. It had obviously made no impression on the officious immigrant inspector. It would take, he decided, somebody with a louder, more authoritative voice than his to penetrate the bureaucratic deafness. Again, he remembered Henry Uterhart's offer to help him. With the confusing government document jammed in his pocket, he set out for Uterhart's house on West Thirty-sixth Street in Manhattan.

At the Uterharts Kurt was quickly invited inside where he explained the predicament he was in. Kurt protested that he did not want to leave either voluntarily or through deportation proceedings. Uterhart assured Kurt that as a practical matter, neither could be done at the moment, because of the war conditions. The entire proceedings involved complicated legal questions which could be resolved only through court action.

For Kurt, all legal complications were beside the point. He merely wanted to declare his intentions to become an American citizen. However, to even apply for citizenship, he had to be a legal resident. It meant therefore that he would have to depart the United States voluntarily, then reenter legally, whereupon he could apply for citizenship. Yet, as Uterhart explained, departure under any circumstances was impossible. He was stranded. In the meantime, he remained a deportable alien.

It was a relief to Kurt to be able to turn over to Henry Uterhart the responsibility of arguing his case with the INS. Uterhart had practiced law in New York for forty years, and was well known as general counsel for the Long Island Railroad. His first legal maneuver was to file promptly a formal exception to the order of voluntary departure which Kurt had received. He felt that the INS would take note of the exception he had filed, and therefore Kurt would be "officially" ignored until the conflict ended. Then, the unusual circumstances of the case would be recognized, and Kurt would be permitted to file for citizenship.

Still, Kurt worried that the worsening war news meant he would be in limbo longer than he or Henry Uterhart realized. The expansion of the so-called Battle of the Atlantic alarmed him. The conflict had widened beyond European waters to include U.S. ports.

As March 1941 ended, the INS moved suddenly to seize sixty-five German, Italian, and Danish ships. Officially, the ships were seized to prevent them from being sabotaged to block U.S. ports. Government communiqués cited as justification the fact that twenty of twenty-eight seized Italian ships had been sabotaged by their crews. However, other reports suggested that, since Great Britain had already lost eight million tons in the Battle of the Atlantic, the seizure of ships in U.S. ports was meant to make up for those losses.

The German government quickly protested the ship seizures, calling it an act of "historic importance" (*San Mateo Times,* March 31, 1941). And to prevent further seizures of merchant ships which could be used in the conflict, the Axis powers began to order ships scuttled to avoid capture. In Houston, the captain of the Italian freighter *Mongolia* said he had been ordered by the Italian naval attaché in Washington to sabotage his ship's engines. "We tried to carry out those orders completely," he said when the Coast Guard arrested him. "I presume we will be interned now for the duration of the war" (*San Mateo Times,* March 31, 1941).

Internment for the duration of the war was an eventuality Kurt Peters hadn't even considered until reading of these events. Since he hadn't committed a crime, the government had no reason to lock him up. Despite his brief encounter with Kerling, he did not consider himself a saboteur. Nor had the Standard Oil crew members scuttled any of their ships. Surely, Kurt hoped, the government would make a distinction between him and the Axis crew members who in fanatical defiance were setting their ships on fire to avoid seizure.

On April 1, the German government declared that American seizure of shipping constituted an absolute violation of German rights. The ships' crews were entitled to damage their ships in any way they saw fit, German sources maintained, as long as they didn't block harbors. The German government forwarded an official note of protest to the U.S. State Department demanding immediate release of the detained seamen. The U.S. government responded by explaining that the crewmen would be held in custody pending deportation hearings or prosecution for sabotage.

Meanwhile, the international cat-and-mouse game of scuttling before seizure escalated: seven German and Italian tankers were sunk by crews in South American ports when South American governments indicated they might follow U.S. leads in seizing ships. The French liner *Normandie* was placed under surveillance by the U.S. Coast Guard, to avoid scuttling. Axis tankers and freighters in Venezuela and Peru were reported to be smoldering hulks.

On Wednesday, April 2, Germany delivered a second note of protest over ship seizures to the U.S. government. Axis demands included immediate release of the ships and the 875 crew members who were now being detained on Ellis Island. The U.S. response came when a federal grand jury in Boston indicted the captain and four officers of the German tanker *Pauline Frederich* on charges of sabotaging their vessel before it could be seized by the Coast Guard in Boston Harbor. The United States also demanded recall of the Italian naval attaché because of his implication in acts of sabotage on Italian ships in U.S. harbors. U.S. officials let it be known that they were considering doing the same for the German naval attaché. Germany's response to the news was to arrest and jail eight Americans in Berlin, while German police announced they expected to arrest more Americans soon.

In Washington, the Italian naval attaché was considered persona non grata and Italy was ordered to withdraw him immediately from the United States. In Italy crowds in Venice Square rallied in an anti-American demonstration. Mussolini appeared on the balcony of his residence to give a Fascist salute to the crowd.

On April 4, 1941, Secretary of State Cordell Hull officially rejected the Nazi protests of ship seizures. "In the first place," Hull's note said, "you do not state upon which principle of international law. . .you rely; and in the second, you. . .disregard the plain provisions of our statutes which make it a felony. . .to cause or permit the destruction or injury of a vessel's motive power" (*San Mateo Times*). Hull's note concluded with the explanation that U.S. statutes permitted authorities to seize any vessel and remove officers and crew when it was necessary to prevent sabotage.

The German government clearly indicated its anger by making April the worst month since Dunkerque for Allied shipping losses: Nazi raiders sank 106 British, Allied, or neutral ships. Closer to home, it was reported that the U.S. fleet consisted of only forty-six merchant vessels available for foreign trade. Because of insufficient ships to move them, materiel and goods were piling up around the world. Not incidentally, Axis sailors were piling up at Ellis Island, where some 1,500 men were then in government custody.

Kurt Peters followed closely the developments involving the Axis sailors, well aware that the eventual disposition of their cases might well bear on his. Despite Henry Uterhart's assurances that no matter what happened there were legal counter-measures which could be undertaken, Kurt worried that the deportation order outstanding against him would be executed before Uterhart could even react. It would be an exercise in futility to have Uterhart eloquently arguing his case before U.S. authorities, while he was already goose-stepping in the *Wehrmacht*.

Kurt's fears of being deported despite wartime complications were not unfounded. In fact, while Henry Uterhart did what he could to block Kurt's deportation, the government was already moving against the young German radioman.

The first step had been taken by Attorney General Robert Jackson, who in early May had ordered arrest warrants drawn up for those seamen who had been found guilty of overstaying their leaves. The arrest warrants were then forwarded by Jackson to various INS district directors around the United States, in whose jurisdictions the stranded seamen were known to be residing.

The majority of the men, numbering some 133 sailors, including Kurt Peters, were still in the New York City area. To insure that no one escaped because of advanced warning, plans for a mass arrest were laid. In that first week of May a strike force of INS men was quietly assembled in the New York City area. Thirty Border Patrol men were brought down from the Canadian border. *The New York Times* reported that on Tuesday, May 6, Byron Uhl, District Director of the INS for New York and northern New Jersey, notified New York Police Commissioner Valentine of his plans. Valentine immediately assigned one hundred detectives and twenty-five police officers to the strike force. There were several training sessions involving the entire force of men, during which it was emphasized that the sailors were possibly violent and dangerous Nazis and that all necessary precautions should be taken. Step-by-step procedures for the arrest action were rehearsed. At precisely 4:00 a.m., May 7, armed with warrants, pictures of the seamen, and addresses supplied by Standard Oil Company, the authorities set out in three-man teams to make the arrests.

They awakened Kurt Peters by knocking quietly on his door.

Kurt sat up slowly, having only just fallen into a deep sleep. "Who is it?" he managed to raise his voice.

A voice answered, almost in a whisper, "You have a telegram from your mother."

Kurt swung his feet to the floor quickly. His mother! He tried to clear his head and focus on why she would be telegramming him in the middle of the night. What had happened to her?

He stood up, stumbled across the dark room, and stood facing the door. "I'm not going to open the door," Kurt was suspicious now.

"Well, you can. We just have a telegram here from your mother," the voice reassured him.

He turned the lock finally and opened the door just enough to see there were three of them, one in a police uniform. They asked if he was Kurt Heinrich Rudolf Peters. He said he was. The three of them stepped into his apartment quickly and explained nervously that he was under arrest. "Pack a suitcase for one night," they directed him.

"Gentlemen," he interrupted, "it's the middle of the night. This cannot be easy for you. Shall we have a cup of coffee?"

Feeling resigned but still cooperative, Kurt was taken from his apartment to the station house of the Astoria police precinct. From there, he was loaded into a patrol wagon with half a dozen other sailors, and driven to the Barge Office at the Battery. There, groups of arrested sailors, surrounded by a police cordon, huddled silently in the morning light until they were put aboard a Coast Guard ship and transported to Ellis Island.

That afternoon the roundup of what the newspapers called "Nazi sailors" spread to Chicago, Minneapolis, Kansas City, Baltimore, Philadelphia, and San Francisco. The same day the House of Representatives demonstrated its support for ship seizures by voting 266 to 120 to empower the government to take control of foreign ships tied up in U.S. ports. Congress's action made it quite clear what steps the United States intended to take to augment allied shipping. Yet, it remained unclear just what was to be done with the seamen left stranded by the seizures and now detained at Ellis Island. As reported in *The New York Times* of May 12, Hugh deLacey, chairman of the American Committee for Protection of Foreign Born, charged in a letter to Attorney General Robert Jackson that the "spectacular" arrest of aliens (which now included Italians who had remained in the United States illegally after the New York World's Fair) was done to influence Congress into "enactment of a concentration camp bill." In a nationwide radio speech, Jackson denied that mass arrests were a prelude to a general roundup of aliens.

Despite Jackson's speech, the population at Ellis Island swelled to some two thousand men. Rumors of concentration camp confinement began to circulate among the detainees when it was announced that in order to relieve the crowding, the Italian detainees were being sent to somewhere in Montana.

At the same time that rumors of internment for the duration circulated, there were conflicting reports of immediate deportation. For Kurt Peters, those reports became more credible when his "Permission to Depart Voluntarily" was replaced by a formal deportation order, which was served on him at Ellis Island on May 15, 1941. Kurt saw little difference between being told to leave voluntarily, and merely being told to leave. Still, he contacted Henry Uterhart and asked him to file an exception to the new deportation order. Uterhart agreed, but not without assuring Kurt that inasmuch as the international conditions were less favorable now for his return to Germany, the deportation order could not possibly be carried out.

So, Kurt wondered, what could he expect to happen? Was he destined to spend months, perhaps years on Ellis Island, packed with as many as twenty men in a little room off the balcony of the Great Hall? All day long the voices of newly arrested aliens echoed in the hall with an irritating shrillness. Where would he ever again find an opportunity for solitude and privacy? In Montana? One day not long after rumors of relocation to that state began to circulate, one of the aliens in his room obtained a contraband road map of the United States. Kurt inspected the map carefully, hoping to discover something of what was in store for him by studying the place-names and highway numbers in Montana. Finally, he had to admit that any inferences he drew from the map would probably be erroneous. He passed the map on to somebody else, and abandoned himself to an uncertain, vague future.

The stay on Ellis Island ended unceremoniously. Before dawn on the morning of May 29, the door of Kurt's dormitory room flew open and a uniformed INS guard shouted, "Pack everything you have. We are going to take you out West."

Two days later, the train loaded with German and Italian sailors arrived in Bismarck, North Dakota. Kurt Peters and the 220 alien German sailors were driven by truck convoy to Ft. Lincoln, on the flat bottomland of the Missouri River, two miles south of town.

The haste with which Ft. Lincoln had been made ready that spring to receive German aliens was misleading. In fact, several other detention centers had been planned and implemented during the previous year and a half.

On December 14, 1939, while Kurt Peters was rehearsing his English in front of a mirror, the SS *Columbus,* third largest ship of the German merchant fleet, was scuttled by its crew while trying to escape seizure by the Allies off Cape May, New Jersey. After the scuttling, the American ship *Tuscaloosa* picked up the crew members. The next afternoon they were taken to Ellis Island, thence shipped across country to Angel Island, a wooded island lying just north of Alcatraz in San Francisco Bay. Five *Columbus* crewmen escaped in transit. Nevertheless, the German sailors were frequently permitted to come ashore in San Francisco during the year they were on Angel Island, to the apparent dismay of city residents. In time a jittery San Francisco made it known through newspaper accounts that the so-called dangerous sailors were not welcome in their city.

Finally, the Justice Department decided that detention facilities were necessary in a more remote area. In 1940 the first World War II alien detention facilities were laid out at Ft. Stanton, New Mexico, which was the site of an old frontier post established in 1856 to contain Apaches. In January of 1941, 410 distressed seamen from the *Columbus* arrived to be detained for the duration.

Subsequently, there were nine unsuccessful escape attempts from Ft. Stanton. The authorities cited those escape attempts, and the lessons learned from Ft. Stanton, when it became quite clear by April of 1941 that permanent detention facilities were needed for the increasing number of Italian and German sailors who were left stranded by ship seizures. Overall responsibility for the new detention camps was given to the Immigration and Naturalization Service, which was then run by Commissioner Earl G. Harrison, a Philadelphia lawyer and a progressive Republican who had been appointed by President Roosevelt. From his INS offices in Philadelphia, Harrison promptly assigned the immediate task of running and staffing the camps to the Border Patrol, under Chief Supervisor Willard F. Kelly. On May 9, 1941, Harrison and Kelly opened a second detention facility at Ft. Missoula, Montana, which was a site as remote as Ft. Stanton.

The first arrivals at Missoula that spring were 125 Italian sailors who were also skilled mechanics, sent as an advance complement to ready the camp for later distressed seamen. They left Ellis Island the day before the mass arrest of the Standard Oil crewmen, which caught Kurt Peters in his sleep in Astoria. By mid-May, Missoula was ready to receive more detainees, and an additional four hundred Italian sailors were removed from Ellis Island to Montana, sparking the rumor which led Kurt Peters to pore over a map of the state.

Meanwhile, efforts to turn Ft. Lincoln into a detention camp were in full swing. A double-wing wooden mess hall was constructed, as well as a large scullery. A Bismarck dairyman received queries from the government concerning his ability to supply Ft. Lincoln with milk for eight hundred men. Director Kelly began to order the transfer to Bismarck of patrol inspectors from various Border Patrol posts around the country. Guards, recruited from the civilian men in Bismarck and around North Dakota, were hired and briefly trained.

Whether it was Germans or Italians who were to be detained at Ft. Lincoln, no one seemed certain, least of all Attorney General Jackson. "If facilities at Ft. Missoula, Montana, are sufficient for housing detained Italians," he explained in a letter to Governor John Moses of North Dakota, "it is contemplated that only German sailors will be kept at Ft. Lincoln." His assurance to the governor, "Everything possible will be done to safeguard the interests of North Dakotans," was reported by *The Bismarck Tribune* (May 13, 1941).

Safeguarding mainly involved the construction of a secure enclosure, and as May drew to a close, workmen began erecting a ten-foot cyclone fence around part of Ft. Lincoln, enclosing three, two-story red brick barracks, several wooden buildings, and a portion of the parade ground in a 500 by 1,300 foot compound. Floodlights were installed outside the fence to surround the compound with a wide corridor of light at night.

On Wednesday, May 28, Attorney General Jackson finally revealed that it was Germans who would be detained at Ft. Lincoln. They would begin their journey to Ft. Lincoln the next day, he announced. That news created a last-minute rush to complete the cyclone fence, and all available Border Patrol personnel were pressed into service to finish the job. Still, a twenty-foot gap remained in the fence when Kurt Peters and the 220 Standard Oil seamen rolled through the main gate to the Fort and were unloaded at the entrance to the small compound.

The men were led into the fenced area and marched past the three red brick buildings to the parade ground. There, they were organized into rank and file, counted, then addressed by a small, slight-of-build man with wire frame glasses, cowboy boots, and a wide-brimmed Western hat.

"This is Ft. Lincoln," he began in a sharp loud voice which belied his size. "My name is Mr. Hudson. What happens inside the camp, that's pretty much up to you. But I expect you to comply with the rules. You will be treated as if you were in boot camp. . . . Officers are to billet there!" He pointed to a group of small wooden bungalows immediately south of the parade ground. "Crewmen billet there!" He indicated the red brick barracks to the east. "Dis-missed!"

A man who preferred warm weather, A. S. Hudson reluctantly accepted assignment to Ft. Lincoln as its first Chief Patrol Inspector. He brought with him a Border Patrol reputation for tough discipline. In the first few days of 1940, when the Border Patrol had been doubled, Hudson was in charge of the Del Rio, Texas, station. Rookie patrol inspectors arriving for duty at the station had heard stories of what a tough disciplinarian he was. Because of Hudson's pompous bearing and often abrasive manner of speech, the reputation for toughness stuck. Dressed in Western boots and a light grey, Western-style hat, Hudson seldom gave praise to his men and was quick to criticize. He could be reasonable enough, the guards felt, so long as the work got done. However, to the detainees who shuffled off across the parade ground in search of their billeting, Hudson remained a disappointing and unsympathetic figure.

The crewmen located themselves in the various dormitory-sized rooms of the brick barracks. Factions were formed on the basis of friendships developed at Ellis Island or political convictions that were only now beginning to emerge. Ardent Nazis, who up to that point had remained discreetly quiet in hopes of avoiding imprisonment, now spoke their minds openly and stuck together in the same barracks rooms. Meanwhile, the captains and officers settled in the wooden bungalows south of the parade ground, and Kurt Peters found himself in bungalow T94 with approximately twenty other deck officers and engineers.

Among the men in T94 was a twenty-seven-year-old radio officer named Alfred Henzler from Duisberg, Germany. He and Peters had met several times in Yorkville in the early days of their stay. Even though Henzler was six years older than Kurt, they were both considered young for ship's officers. They also shared an interest in radio and athletics. Although Henzler wore wire frame glasses and had about him the look of a quiet intellectual, he was a natural athlete who, because of his speed and coordination, enjoyed playing librero (free man) at soccer. Despite the fact that they took a liking to each other in New York, Kurt had moved to Astoria and Henzler had been anxious to return to Germany to take care of his aging mother, and the two men didn't meet again until they found themselves occupying adjacent bunks in the corner of T94.

Kurt and Henzler tried to make their barren corner of the barracks as cozy and comfortable as they could. They found a lampshade for the bare ceiling bulb over their heads. Kurt put up makeshift bookshelves at the head of his bed, where he could store his small library of books on American history and literature. Finally, they secured a small writing table from the supply office and situated it between their bunks, so that each could write on it from his side.

Despite the new predicament Kurt found himself in, his intentions were stronger than ever to become an American citizen. After informing Henry Uterhart of his whereabouts, Kurt began filling out several required documents which had been distributed to the men. He listed August Peters of Hamburg, Germany, as the person to be notified in the event of sickness or death. And with bold strokes of his pencil, he printed *not interested in repatriation* across a "Petition for Repatriation" form each alien had received.

Henzler, on the other hand, remained committed to a return to Germany in order to aid his mother. The renewed friendship between Henzler and Peters might have ended right there, since it was obvious the two men were making separate plans for themselves. But Henzler enjoyed listening to Kurt read or paraphrase dramatically from American literature and English books, and he insisted he too would return to America some day. In turn, Kurt considered Henzler a worldly man who was still young enough to be free of the self-importance which the older officers possessed. Kurt realized they would one day go their separate ways. Yet, for the time being, circumstances had put them side-by-side at Ft. Lincoln, and he was determined to make the most of Henzler's friendship.

Seeing the improvements which Kurt and Henzler made in their corner of the barracks, the other men in T94 did likewise, and the barracks began to take on a decorated, lived-in look. Draperies and pictures were hung. A separate lounging room at the entrance to the barracks was equipped with chairs and a davenport. Each man did his best to give his living-sleeping area a unique personality.

A solitary holdout to the beautification project was Johann Theodor Heinrich Marquenie, a handsome twenty-eight-year-old third officer from the German ship *Clio*. Marquenie occupied the corner bunk directly across from Kurt and Henzler. He had been arrested by the FBI on the East Coast after sabotage was suspected aboard the *Clio*. Now, while the rest of the men busied themselves making the barracks as livable as possible, Marquenie spent the day stretched out on his bunk, staring morosely at the ceiling. They soon learned that his brooding was caused by separation from a fiancée in New York. In hopes of snapping him out of it, other men related their own forced partings from girlfriends. But Marquenie refused to be drawn into these confessions and was soon left to suffer alone.

The day after their arrival in camp, Mr. Hudson posted "Crew Memorandum #1," which laid down the first rules for running the camp. It included mess hall hours and mail privileges. It also granted to the men the right to set up a "Detainees' Canteen," the profits from which could be retained by the men. Finally, the memorandum revealed that Captain Fred Stengler would be in charge of the detainees inside the compound.

Reading the news of Stengler's appointment, the men in T94 were immediately angry. Of the four captains who were in the camp at that time, Stengler was the only one from a German merchant vessel, in this case the *Arauca*, a modern turboelectric ship which Stengler had tried to scuttle before it was seized. On the train ride from Ellis Island to Ft. Lincoln, the accompanying German counsular representative had hand-picked Captain Stengler to lead the men and keep up their German loyalties. But Stengler's idea of ship discipline was too strict for most of the men, whose Standard Oil tankers were run without military formalities. Among other things, Stengler insisted that the men stand watch, and that crewmen wait on officers in the mess hall.

By the end of the first week in June, most of Captain Stengler's attempts to militarize the camp had met with failure. Still, Stengler managed to create for himself a loyal cadre of National Socialists who considered him an Adolph Hitler surrogate, and who therefore were eager to display their Nazi loyalties in any way they could. Several of these men, led by two sailors who had been apprentice stonecutters in civilian life, began carving a small stone monument to their internment. When completed finally and erected on the edge of the parade ground like a tombstone, it read: "1941—*Internierte Deutsche Seeleute*" ("To the memory of the interned German sailors"). A bold swastika was carved in relief above the inscription, and small stones around the base of the tombstone marked the various shipping lines from which the sailors had been seized. Once erected, all the internees waited anxiously to see what the reaction of the guards and Mr. Hudson would be. However, Hudson saw it as a symbolic grave for Nazi rule, and he instructed the guards to let the memorial stone remain.

Just after dark on the evening of June 13, the lovesick seaman Johann Marquenie slipped away from Ft. Lincoln desperate to be reunited with his New York sweetheart. A nearly hysterical A. S. Hudson set into motion a manhunt which involved most of North Dakota. Marquenie was finally caught three days later trying to float down the Missouri River in a flat-bottomed boat. Hudson, much relieved, ordered Marquenie driven into Bismarck to be locked up in the Burleigh County Jail. Hudson then telegrammed W. F. Kelly that he had captured the escaped detainee and that routine had been restored to the camp.
     In an effort to find out Marquenie's destination, Hudson interrogated him extensively, but the handsome ship's officer would only admit to having been bound for St. Louis, or perhaps to Mexico. In his statement of June 16, 1941, he claimed his desire was "just to be free." He never mentioned his fiancée in New York. Finally, when Marquenie was returned to his barracks after thirty days confinement in the jail, he thanked his fellow officers in T94 for not revealing where he was headed. He claimed that the mosquitoes and the cold had softened him up, but that he would know what to do next time. He did not, however, have a next time.

Hudson promptly set about trying to prevent more escapes by his prisoners. The chain link fence around the camp was topped with three-strand barbed wire, angled into the compound to discourage climbing. Thirty-foot high guard towers were constructed at the four corners of the compound. Each tower was outfitted with a telephone connection to the Control Center switchboard, and the guards in the towers were required to report into the switchboard every half hour. Finally, Hudson had a message delivered to a two-day meeting of the North Dakota Peace Officer's Association, asking for its cooperation in the event any detainees should make their escape.
     A further precaution was to organize the guard force into two divisions. The Surveillance Division was charged with manning the towers and patrolling the fences. Casting about for the right man to head

up the Surveillance Division, Hudson selected "Charlie" Lovejoy, a muscular senior patrol inspector who had developed his toughness working lumber mills in northern Minnesota. Hudson also created a Liaison Office inside the compound. Located in the old brick firehouse just inside the main gate to the detention area, the office was charged with the responsibility of billeting the detainees, processing paperwork, and overseeing work, entertainment, and educational and recreational activities within the enclosure. Furthermore, it was expected to keep a close eye out for any internee activity of a suspicious nature that might be an indication of an escape attempt. Leadership of the Liaison Office was given to Senior Patrol Inspector Will Robbins, also a Minnesotan. Robbins had shown no outward resentment toward the internees. He seemed fair, intelligent, impartial, just the man who could gain the men's confidence and therefore be tipped off on any escape attempts before they occurred.

Seeing his office more a support service than an undercover operation, Robbins selected as his assistant a likeable North Dakota native named Edwin J. "Red" Selland. Selland, Robbins noted, had a special, easy way with the detainees and often chatted with them when on guard duty.

The two men, Robbins and Selland, were immediately given a complement of eight guards, recruited from the civilian population of North Dakota. For the most part older men not eligible for military service, these guards carried only gas billies and were responsible for walking the interior compound day and night, keeping alert for any suspicious activities.

Kurt Peters watched these new security measures with disappointment. It was clear that he was considered just another potentially dangerous alien. When a group of thirty-seven outspoken Nazi merchant seamen arrived in late June, their presence in camp further convinced Kurt that there would be no easing of security measures. Calling themselves *Schlageter*, a term literally translated "strikers" that was used in the early 1930s to characterize Nazi party members, these seamen quickly made it known throughout camp that they considered themselves POWs in an enemy country.

Kurt was soon convinced that he had to do something dramatic in order to secure his American citizenship. On June 26, 1941, he wrote directly to Attorney General Francis Biddle, explaining the circumstances under which he had left Germany, then become stranded in New York: "Several times," Kurt wrote, "I was given the opportunity to return to Germany, but I refused because I did not want to fight for National Socialism." He went on to point out that if the outstanding

deportation order against him was ever executed and he was forced to
return to Germany, he would be considered a criminal because of his
democratic beliefs. He pleaded to be permitted to remain in the United
States. Then he disclosed a hope he had been secretly entertaining ever
since his English and writing courses at Columbia. "I have often been
told...that I have literary ability. This as yet undeveloped talent could
never be developed in Germany." But in America, he finished, he could
write what he wanted and "openly cherish my faith in humanity and
individualism."

On August 2 a letter arrived from Henry Uterhart explaining that
he was in need of a character reference from Mr. Hudson. Kurt's appeals
for a stay of his deportation order, and his citizenship application would
be much stronger, Uterhart said, with a character reference from somebody in the government. Kurt promptly sent a note to Hudson and
gently requested the recommendation. However, since Marquenie's escape, Hudson was in no mood to bear witness with respect to any
detainee's character, so he turned Kurt's note over to Patrol Inspector
Bert Fraser, who was assistant supply officer for the camp.

Fraser had been transferred to Ft. Lincoln from the Border Patrol
station in San Antonio. He was a well-educated, career officer who
immediately recognized that Kurt Peters was an articulate young man
with serious citizenship ambitions. It was Fraser, then, who on August
9, 1941, wrote Uterhart a glowing recommendation on behalf of Kurt:

> I know he is a sincere, honest and industrious young man and that
> he has a real desire to become an American citizen.... Now is the
> time for we Americans to really show our belief in freedom and
> democracy by helping those who are deserving.

Fraser's letter concluded with a warning that if Kurt Peters were
ever deported back to Germany, it would mean "a long prison term, or
even death. There are Nazi agents confined here who watch, listen and
report every man whom they regard as traitors to Germany."

Uterhart forwarded the recommendation to the chairman of the
Board of Immigration Appeals in New York. He requested that Fraser's
glowing letter be taken into consideration by the Board, which had yet
to respond to Uterhart's appeal back in May that the deportation order
be lifted.

There was nothing else to do then but wait, Uterhart concluded.
He wrote Kurt that he would telegram Ft. Lincoln the moment the
Board notified him of its decision. Meanwhile, Kurt decided that the
only way to make the time pass swiftly while waiting was to further
occupy himself with whatever enterprises he could inside the compound.

First, he proposed to Will Robbins and Red Selland in the Liaison Office that he be permitted to begin instructing a course for the detainees in English and citizenship. They agreed immediately, but not without requesting that if any of the *Schlageter* attempted to intimidate him, he was to report it to the Liaison Office.

Having gained staff approval, Kurt promptly wrote the Library of Congress and requested material for the courses in English and American government he intended to teach. The materials arrived shortly and in a matter of weeks, Kurt's instruction was in full swing in an unused second-story room of one of the barracks. Interest in the English instruction was much greater than Kurt had anticipated, and over one hundred men were soon enrolled in four levels of English, from basic to advanced instruction for the men who, like Kurt, were seeking American citizenship.

The classes occupied Kurt's entire day, and were sometimes followed in the evenings by discussion sessions in the seamen's barracks, where conversation flowed in English on the books that were being read. It was the same dormitory room in which the *Schlageter* had their bunks, and they often made abusive remarks within earshot of Kurt. He met the insults head on, however, and was therefore regularly engaged in political arguments with these men.

Every Sunday night Kurt walked over to the seamen's barracks and spent the evening with a small group of fellow admirers of operatic music, listening to the "Longines Wittnauer Hour," featuring Richard Crooks and Vivian della Chiesa. The often romantic music appealed to those who, like Johann Marquenie, had been smitten in New York and now were isolated from their women. Meanwhile, from another room of the barracks, the faint sounds could be heard of someone playing German folk tunes on an accordion, accompanied by the boisterous *Schlageter*, whose homesick voices drifted out of the barracks to the four corners of the compound.

By midsummer, the men in T94 had a full garden of flowers in bloom in front of their bungalow. While Kurt waited for some news on his plans for naturalization, he busied himself gardening or teaching his courses in English. Then, since he had become well known by the camp staff for his fluent English and his intelligence, he was approached by Mr. Hudson and asked to sit in on the weekly staff meetings, which were also attended by Captain Stengler.

It was clear that Hudson was fed up with Stengler, whose anti-American views made him increasingly balky and unmanageable. Stengler's daily rosters had already proved more trouble than help, and he insisted on involving himself in every decision Hudson made, no matter how trivial.

Kurt agreed to attend the Monday staff meetings. It would be an opportunity, he felt, to further demonstrate his pro-American views, in hopes of speeding up the processing of his naturalization petition. Furthermore, Kurt sensed that the meetings might give him a chance to persuade Hudson that the seamen weren't saboteurs and spies. Perhaps in time Hudson could be encouraged to relax the "boot camp" atmosphere he felt he had to create.

Those hopes disappeared one day in mid-July when trucks began to roll through the main gate into the compound. Their assignment was to haul off cement chunks from old cavalry tent floors being broken up just inside the south fence. Word soon spread throughout camp that the area was being cleared in preparation for the construction of temporary wooden barracks to house an anticipated increase in detainee population.

At 4:00 p.m., July 17, one of the trucks carrying out the broken slabs sank to its axle in the rain-soft ground south of the mess hall. Efforts to jack the truck up caused more earth to collapse around the sunken wheel, revealing a tunnel running straight south toward the fence. Guards were summoned, a search was conducted, and the tunnel head was located beneath the floor of the mess hall scullery. Immediately, a small group of men who worked in the kitchen came under suspicion. Even though no one confessed, Hudson finally confined five men to the Ft. Lincoln guardhouse for thirty days for what he felt was their part in the tunnel.

Two weeks after the tunnel discovery, on July 31, an editorial appeared in the *Ambrose Herald*, a small North Dakota paper. "We don't like to think that the guards (at Ft. Lincoln) are all deaf, dumb and blind, but how those Nazis could dig out that amount of fresh earth and dispose of it...and not be detected just bewilders us." The critical editorial was forwarded to Hudson by W. F. Kelly, with a stinging warning not to let further escape attempts become public matters. Hudson warned his newly created Surveillance Force to be especially on the alert for "skulduggery" and escapes, and to refrain from making public comments about such matters. It was an order that some of the guards took so seriously that even forty years later, they were reluctant to talk about what had gone on at Ft. Lincoln.

With the discovery of the tunnel, and renewed fears of escape, Hudson intensified his efforts to secure bloodhounds to assist the guard force at Ft. Lincoln. For almost a month, since the escape of Johann Marquenie, Hudson had been badgering the Border Patrol for at least two animals. Director Kelly's offer to transfer trained German shepherd dogs from the Bureau of Prisons in Atlanta seemed unacceptable to

Hudson, so he made inquiries himself to several bloodhound breeders in North Dakota. Those inquiries brought offers of the loan of tracking bloodhounds in the event of future escapes. But Hudson wanted his own tracking dogs permanently quartered at Ft. Lincoln, and he finally accepted Kelly's offer of the two police dogs.

The two German shepherds named Hooch and Waven arrived at Ft. Lincoln, but despite the daily spectacle of the training in an open field north of the compound, there were two more escape attempts that fall which made it plain to Hudson that he could not relax the strict security measures he had instituted.

On September 3, a detainee named Erich Asshauer walked away from the hospital, where he had gone with two dozen other detainees for dental work. He was captured some two hours later walking south on a road leading to the Missouri River. The quick apprehension of Erich Asshauer did not stop rumors of another escape from circulating in Bismarck. But when reporters called for verification of the story, Hudson flatly denied that any such thing had happened. Life at Ft. Lincoln was routine, he insisted.

Then on Saturday, October 18, Bernard Binczyk and Gottfried Kruger, two trustees who had been permitted to work outside the compound, reported for work at 8:00 a.m. in the supply department. Kruger was a seventeen-year-old mess boy whose last ship had been the *Pauline Frederich*. Binczyk, two years older than Kruger, was an ordinary seaman from the *Prometheus*. Since agreeing to work in the supply office, both men had been threatened with violence by *Schlageter* who considered their action treasonous. Convinced the *Schlageter* meant business, the two men decided to escape, and on the morning of October 18, as a light rainfall began, they walked east along the county road, then caught a ride north with Frank Czczok, a farmer headed toward U.S. Highway 10 in his truck. Czczok let the two detainees out east of the North Dakota State Penitentiary at the intersection of Highway 10. Binczyk and Kruger followed the railroad tracks east again, hiding in a haystack from noon until nightfall. At 9:00 p.m. they arrived in the tiny town of McKenzie, six miles east of Bismarck on Highway 10. In McKenzie, they entered a restaurant-filling station owned by Mr. and Mrs. George Watson. The two men ordered four hot dogs and sat drinking coffee while they planned how they would work their way toward Mexico.

However, they never got out of the restaurant. Alerted by a radio station KYFR bulletin which broadcast a description of the escapees, Mrs. Watson recognized the two men as soon as they entered, and she instructed her husband to phone the authorities. As the phone call was made, she calmly poured another cup of coffee for them, smiled pleasantly, and then asked if they were the Ft. Lincoln escapees. They confessed they were, and she told them there was a fifty dollar reward for their capture.

Learning from Mrs. Watson that a statewide manhunt was under way, Kruger and Binczyk were discouraged from further attempts to flee, and they surrendered without resistance when patrol inspectors arrived at the restaurant. Back at Ft. Lincoln, Kruger explained in interrogation that they had merely been trying to escape from the *Schlageter,* but he predicted there would be more escapes from the camp. When Hudson pressed him to elaborate, Kruger refused to talk anymore. Both men were confined then for sixty days in the guardhouse, where they received no mail and only two meals a day.

By late summer construction had begun on fourteen temporary barracks which were set in a row on raised foundations along the south line of the camp. At the same time that the framing went up, the detainees converted one of the wooden buildings outside of the compound into a bakery, which delivered its first loaves of fresh pumpernickel bread in a bizarre parade ceremony. Led by a guitar, banjo, and accordion, the little parade entered the compound through the main gate, then moved down the main street. A dozen marching detainee bakers carried the hot loaves of bread to the mess hall, where the men cheered and whooped.

While the detainee bakers and cooks learned to prepare mess hall fare which would gratify the sailors' tastes for heavy German foods, a small group of men organized to provide the camp with dramatic and musical entertainment which would capture the spirit of the homeland. An empty wooden barracks in the southeast corner of the compound was converted into a theater and a stage, and there were regular performances by a choir, an orchestra, and a group of seamen who put on short, usually comic skits. During the week, the same makeshift theater was used to show old American films, which half of the camp turned out to see, even though many of the men couldn't follow the English dialogue.

Kurt Peters seldom attended the movies, preferring to stay in his quiet, empty barracks and enjoy again the peace and solitude he had come to value in New York. It was during one of those quiet evenings alone in his barracks that he decided to resume keeping a journal in English of his thoughts and activities. He saw it not only as an opportunity to speed up the development of his English, but also as an excellent chance to begin acting upon his ambition to become a writer.

At first Kurt's journal was merely a collection of philosophic and political reactions to the worsening world news. "Europe's countries have always been ruled by men who took upon their shoulders responsibilities they were unable to carry," Kurt wrote on August 28. But, he continued, "America alone is able to make the world happy and peaceful. Its great fault," he observed ruefully, "is that it has not awoken to the fact yet."

Notwithstanding whether America was ready yet to make the whole world happy, she took a step in the direction of gratifying Kurt Peters by finally notifying him on October 7, 1941, that the Board of Immigration Appeals in New York had agreed to rehear his case in order to determine the advisability of releasing him from custody. Then, a week later on October 15, Kurt received a telegram from his lawyer in New York. "Congratulations and best wishes and many happy returns," Henry Uterhart said. Since it was Uterhart who had presented Kurt's case to the Appeals Board, the telegram might have been mistaken as merely an acknowledgment of the good news. It was, however, not just news of a rehearing that needed celebrating. It was Kurt's birthday. He was twenty-one years old.

By November, Kurt's efforts to Americanize himself were well known inside the compound. Condemned now by the *Schlageter* for his citizenship ambitions, he wondered, "What on earth makes them feel that way?" Despite their profound hatred, Kurt vowed "not to look left or right or be swerved" from his purpose. "You will receive gratitude eventually," he prophesied in his journal on November 24.

A hearing at Ft. Lincoln was ordered by the chairman of the Board of Appeals to give Kurt an opportunity to testify on his own behalf. Also, provisions were made to gather statements from Ft. Lincoln staff who would attest to Kurt's loyalty. First to step forward and again vouch for Kurt's character was Bert Fraser, who wrote a five-page confidential report. In it he attested that Kurt "very definitely does not believe in a dictator, Naziism, Fascism, or Communism. He does believe in and appreciate our country and form of government. He states that the only thing wrong with Americans is that we do not love our country enough." Will Robbins and Red Selland, the two patrol inspectors who ran the Liaison Office, also came forward in early November to speak in Kurt's favor. Finally, several guards who had observed Kurt's classes on Americanization forwarded their strong recommendations to the Appeals Board.

It remained only for Kurt to appear before Inspector Boldin (hearing records do not give Boldin's first name), a hearing officer who was sent to Ft. Lincoln from the district INS office in St. Paul. In an upstairs office of the headquarters building, Boldin met with Kurt in November and December 1941.

Because of the excellent character recommendations which accompanied Kurt to the hearings, he felt a favorable atmosphere prevailed during the two proceedings. He was only pressed by Boldin to account for all his acquaintances, both male and female, during the time he had been stranded in New York City. Because other detainees sought parole on the excuse they were engaged to American women, Kurt was asked whether he intended to marry once he was released. "Most decidedly not before my future is clear," he told Boldin and related in a letter to a friend on November 17. "And anyway, I am only twenty-one and would have to secure (a) position before I would even think of matrimony."

Inspector Boldin seemed pleased by Kurt's assurances that he had no desire to get married if paroled. Still, Kurt wondered just what had been the point of Boldin's fishing for the names of all of his New York City acquaintances? If Boldin was aware of Kurt's brief encounter with the fanatical Nazi Edward J. Kerling, he gave no indication of it. They would surely have confronted him with the incident at his Ellis Island hearing. Furthermore, why would half a dozen Ft. Lincoln guards risk their integrity by vouching for an enemy alien whose past was in any way suspicious? It seemed obvious to Kurt, then, that Boldin's questions were just routine probing, as if Boldin was just going through the motions of a hearing on a matter that had already been decided. Favorably, Kurt could only hope!

After the hearing, Kurt returned to teaching his English and citizenship classes, confident that he would be receiving his own citizenship before long. Meanwhile, Inspector Boldin forwarded his hearing report to the New York Appeals Board, along with the statements on Kurt's loyalty. In the evenings, Kurt continued to write in the quiet of T94, concentrating now on short stories and imaginative vignettes rather than mere journal entries.

Kurt Peters and the men in T94 received the news of the Japanese attack on Pearl Harbor on a little shortwave radio which one of the men had fashioned from commercial radio parts and then concealed beneath the floor. All that Sunday and the following Monday, the men discussed the news and speculated over the grave consequences the war would have for them personally. But Kurt remained hopeful that his release was imminent, and he refused to see dire personal consequences in the war.

Kurt's hopes were still high when, on December 17, A. S. Hudson finally forwarded a recommendation to the New York Appeals Board on the question of releasing Kurt Peters. In his statement, Hudson conceded that Kurt was intelligent, loyal, and cooperative. "Under ordinary circumstances I would recommend his release from custody. However," Hudson went on, "since this country is at war with Germany, I believe the best interests. . . would be served by keeping him in detention until after the termination of the hostilities." At that time, Hudson concluded, consideration should be given to not deporting him.

On December 20, the population at Ft. Lincoln jumped to 410 with the arrival of 110 German alien enemies. Most of the new arrivals had been arrested on the West Coast on the heels of Presidential Proclamations 2525, 2526, and 2527, which stipulated that all German, Japanese, and Italian citizens residing in the United States were alien enemies and therefore subject to arrest and detention. It was only natural to turn over these so-called alien enemies to the Border Patrol for detention in their existing facilities. At the same time, however, responsibility for hearing and reviewing individual cases of apprehended alien enemies was turned over to the newly created Alien Enemy Control Unit operating out of the War Division of the Justice Department. Under the direction of Edward J. Ennis, the Alien Enemy Control Unit was charged with the responsibility of creating hearing boards to determine whether an alien would be released, paroled, or interned. Immediately Ennis began drafting the rules by which the hearings would be conducted.

Meanwhile, with the arrival of the new civilian enemy aliens at Ft. Lincoln, there was now a much wider range of ages, political loyalties, and professional interests than had existed among the seamen. Consequently, inside the compound the militant rule of Captain Stengler was challenged and rejected by those who looked to their own civilian leadership to represent them in whatever negotiations were necessary with Hudson and the camp staff.

Two days after Christmas, the INS Appeals Board in New York finally issued its findings and conclusions with respect to the deportation of Kurt Peters. Kurt received the long-awaited letter at a noon mail call in T94 in late January of 1942. There were a dozen pages of documents inside the thick envelope. Kurt flipped through the next few pages, noting that they merely summarized the facts of his case and the recommendations in his favor by Robbins, Selland, and others. The last document, dated January 22, was a warrant from W. W. Brown, Chief of the Warrant Branch of the INS. "Whereas," it began, "after due hearing. . . ." Kurt jumped ahead again. "An order has been duly made that the alien Kurt Heinrich Rudolf Peters. . . who has remained in the U.S. for a longer time than permitted. . . ." Kurt dropped his eyes to the last lines on the page. "I, the undersigned officer of the United

States, by virtue of the power and authority vested in the Attorney General...do hereby command to deport the said alien to Germany."

It was days before Kurt's initial bitterness diminished enough so that he could admit to his students that he had been ordered deported by a country whose democratic ideals he had been celebrating. It was, he confessed, a deep disappointment, but he regarded it as merely a bureaucratic mistake which he insisted would be corrected. Meanwhile, on January 6, 1942, Henry Uterhart had filed an official exception to the deportation order. Kurt tried to remain confident that Uterhart's efforts would ultimately correct the error.

Kurt wrote feverishly that winter, reconciling himself to a long confinement which he tried to look upon as an opportunity to "think upon the vastness, the contradictions, the deep intricacies, and deep buried goodness of man.... Here I am in absolute solitude," he wrote, "detained from reality, free to read and think and learn."

However much Kurt tried that spring to remain isolated in the contemplative world of his journal, the real world of war and detention kept forcing its way into his consciousness. On February 9, 415 West Coast Japanese aliens arrived at Ft. Lincoln at dawn while an icy wind blew in from the Northwest. "Ringed by a cordon of federal immigration patrolmen armed with submachine guns," *The Bismarck Tribune* reported on February 9, 1942, "the little yellow men scrambled out of the coaches twenty-five at a time, were put in guarded trucks, and rushed out to the internment camp." Kurt and the men in T94 watched as the Japanese were then unloaded from the trucks and billeted in the newly constructed row of fourteen barracks to the immediate south of the existing German compound. The Japanese and German compounds were separated from each other by a ten-foot wide alley between barbed wire fences, inside which the guard dogs Hooch and Waven were permitted to run loose at night to discourage fraternization between German and Japanese detainees.

On February 26, a second group of 715 Japanese alien enemies arrived, swelling the camp population to over 1,500 men, more than a thousand of whom were Japanese. Immediately after the arrival of the Japanese alien enemies, a team of immigrant inspectors appeared in order to interrogate the new detainees with an eye to untangling their complicated immigration status in the United States.

As those interrogation sessions progressed, the Alien Enemy Control Unit under Edward Ennis finished drafting the procedures for alien enemy hearings. Several three-man Alien Enemy Hearing Boards arrived at Ft. Lincoln to conduct hearings. Each Board's recommendation for release, parole, or internment was to be forwarded to Attorney

General Francis Biddle, who would make the final determination. Most of the Germans who appeared before these hearing boards were granted release or parole. It irritated Kurt that some of these people, detained for only two months, obtained their release so quickly. Meanwhile, the German seamen who had been stranded in the United States and had inadvertently broken immigration laws were considered *illegal* aliens, whose cases were not subject to review by the Alien Enemy Hearing Boards. Like Kurt Peters, most of them had been ordered deported. An INS hearing was accorded only to those few who filed exceptions to the deportation order, and it appeared to Kurt that the INS officials who would decide his fate were stricter and less sympathetic in their deliberations than the civilians who sat on Alien Enemy Hearing Boards.

There were other developments that spring which Kurt followed with interest. A. S. Hudson, who had advised against Kurt's release, was replaced as OIC of the camp by I. P. "Ike" McCoy. Conflicting rumors as to the reason quickly spread throughout the camp. One report had it that the excitable Hudson had been fired for permitting too many escapes. On the other hand, some felt that the dour Hudson had ruled with too much of an iron hand. (The fact was Hudson effected his own transfer to a position in a warmer climate.) The men in camp considered Hudson's departure a positive sign of change in the government's attitude toward the internees. If the tall, likeable, easygoing, snuff-chewing McCoy could be put in charge, it perhaps meant that the government no longer considered them dangerous saboteurs and spies.

Then Captain Fred Stengler, whose military-type rule inside the compound had irritated most of the detainees more than Hudson's behavior, was deposed by McCoy. But with Stengler's removal, his supporters, the *Schlageter,* felt that they had lost their Nazi voice in camp affairs. They began to resort to beatings and clandestine threats against those detainees whose pro-American actions were too strong. Kurt began to avoid political arguments with some of these men. The grim news of Allied bombings in the interior of Germany and Axis losses in Italy had so incensed the *Schlageter* that most of them were beyond the grasp of reason anyway.

The deep North Dakota snows slowly receded to occasional spots of ice with thin, translucent lips beneath which water trickled quietly toward the drains. By June, tulips and daffodils were growing in the little garden in front of T94. Kurt enjoyed sitting again in the white lawn chair and daydreaming, as elsewhere in camp the cheering voices of a German-Japanese softball game, organized by his friend Alfred Henzler, symbolized the existence of a microcosmic Axis alliance in the heart of the country some of the men hated.

Kurt requested and received from McCoy approval to have a radio
of his own in T94, permitting him to listen by himself on Sunday night
to the operatic voices of Richard Crooks and Vivian della Chiesa. On
June 28, Kurt was suddenly jolted out of his dreamy world by startling
news. Eight saboteurs, among them Edward John Kerling, had been
caught after having been put ashore on the East Coast by a German U-
boat. Ultimately, the saboteurs were captured by the FBI, and tried
before a military tribunal. Meanwhile Kurt feared that he would somehow be implicated. The brief, foolish association with Kerling haunted
him and he continued to chastise himself for not having had the
courage to refuse the trip to Baltimore when it had first been proposed.
Too afraid of offending Kerling and his gang, he had gone along almost
as an act of stupid courtesy. Then in August Kerling and five others
were executed, and Kurt ceased worrying about being implicated in
their plot. Still, Kurt sat wondering now if his tactful arguments with
the *Schlageter* weren't also foolish acts of courtesy to men who should
be openly denounced. Kurt broke off entirely with the *Schlageter* a few
weeks later.

McCoy had received a request for harvesting help from short-
handed North Dakota farmers. At the same time, Kurt had launched a
weekly, mimeographed camp newspaper called the *Bismarck Echo*. Mc-
Coy asked him to run the announcement that men were needed to work
in the fields. Kurt agreed, but went a step further by adding a front
page editorial that encouraged the detainees, for nutrition's sake, to
raise their own vegetables. In the minds of the *Schlageter*, Kurt's editorial proposed treason, and even though many of the detainees went out
in the fields to harvest crops or raise vegetables, the Nazi loyalists in
camp refused to speak to Kurt now.

The execution of the saboteurs, the grave war reports that summer,
and the fanatical devotion of the *Schlageter* had the effect of burying
once and for all any hope Kurt had for peace in the world. It was clear
to him now that the principle of democracy, which his parents had first
laid out for him in their Hamburg kitchen, was under seige in Egypt,
the Solomon Islands, Russia, even at Ft. Lincoln where some of the men
hurled insults and threats at him when he passed. Kurt decided he
must help the cause of democracy by taking part in the American war
effort in some way beyond merely writing editorials.

At the same time, a letter arrived in Ike McCoy's office from Bert
Fraser, who had written such glowing recommendations for Kurt and
was now in charge of the detention camp for Italians in Missoula, Montana. Fraser offered Kurt the chance to work on a farm in Montana,
where they were also desperately in need of men to harvest the crops.

Kurt promptly wrote Fraser that he was eager to come if arrangements could be made.

Nothing further was heard from Fraser, however, and Kurt assumed the INS in Philadelphia had objected. So on September 22, he sent a long letter to the INS reminding them gently that it had been eight months since Uterhart had filed exception to the deportation warrant outstanding against him. While it wasn't his intent to be meddlesome, he wrote that he did want to "inquire now as to my status." Offering himself to the American war effort, Kurt wrote, "I believe that the best proof of my loyalty would be if an opportunity were given to do my share in the war." Kurt mentioned Bert Fraser's request as a possibility. Better still, Kurt felt, would be to use his radio skills. As a licensed radio operator, he was "willing to join the American merchant marine, where at present more benefits could be derived from my abilities."

Kurt then wrote directly to Admiral Emory S. Land of the U.S. Maritime Commission appealing to him for an opportunity to serve the United States as a merchant seaman. Two weeks later, the answer came, not from the Maritime Commission, but the War Shipping Administration. "We regret that under present circumstances," they wrote, "it is impossible to make use of your services." It was a rejection which stung Kurt deeply.

By October of 1942, most of the German enemy aliens who had been detained since Pearl Harbor were either paroled or transferred to Army POW camps for "internment," the government considering internment more permanent than temporary detention. Since FDR had already signed the infamous Executive Order 9066, "relocating" Japanese Americans from the West Coast, it would have been awkward to have American citizens of Japanese descent behind barbed wire while *aliens* were free. Therefore, most of the Japanese aliens at Ft. Lincoln and elsewhere were transferred to War Relocation Authority camps. That left approximately three hundred men at Ft. Lincoln, all but a handful of whom were seamen like Kurt Peters, who had now been temporarily "detained" for a year and a half.

At the same time that the German seamen at Ft. Lincoln were growing weary of their temporary detention, Attorney General Francis Biddle broke the news in a Columbus Day speech that Italian citizens in the United States were no longer to be automatically considered alien enemies. Following Biddle's speech, Ugo Carusi, executive assistant to the attorney general, delivered a radio address of his own that celebrated the news "that our government understands how devoted the Italian people are to the principles of liberty.... It must be especially heartening to you Italian aliens," Carusi finished, "to know that you have the friendship and confidence of the government."

Whatever joy Italians felt in having the cloud of suspicion lifted from them by the Justice Department's decision, it only left the German seamen feeling more embittered.

With the arrival of 1943, a few of the crewmen worked off their restlessness and irritation in stick-clattering hockey games on a newly flooded rink on the soccer field. However, the bitter cold drove most of the men to sleep or read in the barracks all day. Kurt's English classes grew with men desperate to find some activity.

During the two-hour lunch break, Kurt wrote in his journal or composed letters to his parents in Hamburg. He also reminded the INS that he was still expecting a decision regarding the lifting of the deportation order against him. To I. P. McCoy he sent a note asking if it would be appropriate to appeal his case to the Committee on Immigration and Naturalization of the House of Representatives, or to the Committee on Immigration in the Senate, or even directly to the attorney general.

Before McCoy could respond, the St. Paul District Office of the INS finally communicated the decision that had been made. In a two-sentence letter dated January 28, District Director E. E. Adcock wrote, "Your application for release has been denied by the Department, and an order has been issued for your deportation to Germany."

Angered more than depressed, Kurt went straight to Mr. McCoy's office with the news that his deportation order had been upheld. It was time, Kurt felt, to take his case directly to Congress! McCoy disagreed, advising Kurt to appeal one more time to the Board of Immigration Appeals. Kurt reminded McCoy that he had already done that, *twice.* But this time McCoy promised he would include his own powerful letter of recommendation.

Kurt wrote a persuasive letter to Thomas G. Finucane, chairman of the Board of Immigration Appeals in Washington. In the letter, he confessed he was saddened and disappointed by the fact that "a man whose admiration for America (is) purely ideological is being denied the privilege to fight and work for it, whereas men whose reasons are material have been granted the opportunity to do so."

He went on to explain that some of the graduates of his Americanization course at Ft. Lincoln had been released from detention, while he, "who taught the spiritual and idealistic aspects of America...am arbitrarily forbidden to earn the noblest title any man can bear—American citizenship."

The letter to Finucane was accompanied by McCoy's recommendation. Describing Kurt as an "intellectual type, of frail nature, clean-cut in appearance," with a mild disposition, McCoy summarized all that

Kurt had done while at Ft. Lincoln: his English classes, the Americanization course, which had almost a dozen students, his work on the camp newspaper. McCoy's recommendation concluded, "I feel that it is through the efforts of detainees like Peters that we have been able to sell a good deal of our democracy to some of the more rabid anti-Americans at this station."

For a third time, Bert Fraser wrote his superiors on behalf of Kurt. "If released or paroled," Fraser testified, "and I am absolutely convinced that he should be, I know this boy would in no way endanger the internal security of this country."

Having dispatched his third appeal, Kurt began what he was sure would be another long wait for the decision. He tried to keep his spirits up all through the cold North Dakota winter, but the record of past denials kept him from even admitting to the men in T94 that he had appealed his case again.

Then, beginning in March, to make room for POWs, the government started moving civilian alien enemies back to INS control from the Army POW camps. It meant that with the arrival of civilian internees from POW camps in Wisconsin, Tennessee, and Ohio, Ft. Lincoln's population swelled to almost 1,500 men, most of whom were alien enemy "internees." Therefore to be consistent with previous hair-splitting between detention and internment, the government now officially categorized Ft. Lincoln as an "internment camp."

There would ultimately be eight such INS "internment" facilities in operation. They were: Ft. Missoula, Montana, for Italians; Ft. Lincoln for Germans and some Japanese; Kooskia Internment Camp in Idaho and Santa Fe Internment Camp in New Mexico, for Japanese; Kenedy Internment Camp, Texas, for Latin American Germans, Italians, and Japanese; Seagoville Internment Camp, Texas, for female alien enemies; Crystal City Internment Camp, Texas, a Japanese conjugal camp; and Ft. Stanton Internment Camp, New Mexico, a segregation camp for the most rabid Nazis.

In an effort to segregate in one camp the majority of definitely pro-Nazi seamen, eighty-three *Schlageter* were transferred from Ft. Lincoln to Ft. Stanton Internment Camp. At the same time, a handful of pro-American crewmen at Ft. Stanton were sent to Ft. Lincoln in the interest of harmony. The movement of men between camps that spring left Kurt and the seamen "detainees" wondering if they hadn't been lost in the shuffle. So on March 10, Kurt wrote again to Finucane. It was the farm season, Kurt reminded Finucane. Help was needed in the fields. "I urge you...in the interests of America," Kurt pleaded, "to grant me the opportunity (to participate) in the war effort."

By mid-March, just when the men in T94 had thought the icy winter was releasing its grip, a ferocious, five-day blizzard struck North

Dakota, piling snow to the eaves of the barracks and producing an eerie wind-whistle through the camp. It seemed to Kurt that he was especially isolated now, removed forever from the war, ice-bound and wind-whipped and forgotten on the North Dakota plains. Nevertheless, at the height of the blizzard, the mail clerk entered T94, clomped the snow off his boots, and barked Kurt's name.

Kurt received the letter casually and glanced at the official INS envelope. It was from Finucane, chairman of the Appeals Board.

Quickly, Kurt went to his bunk corner, sat down, and ripped open the letter. It was dated March 15.

"In regard to the matter of your release," he read hastily, "the Alien Enemy Control Unit is undertaking a survey of all detainees in your class and will direct the release of those where such action is considered advisable."

It seemed partial good news. Surely a reexamination of his case would bring the long-awaited release. However, the last paragraph of Finucane's letter struck a familiar, frustrating note:

> In regard to your wish eventually to become a citizen of the United States, it will be necessary for you first to secure lawful admission to this country for permanent residence. Your voluntary departure from this country, the securing of an immigration visa and legal reentry are necessary before you will be in a position to seek citizenship.

Voluntary departure. Legal reentry. It was the same impracticable combination of events which he had first been offered at Ellis Island almost two long years ago. Except that now there was even less possibility of voluntary departure. Again, he wondered, where would he depart to? What country would accept him? The only place where it would ever be "practicable" for him to depart to was Germany, and not unless she was defeated. It would even be difficult to return to a defeated Germany. The cloud of internment and Fascism would hang over him, and he'd be at the mercy of Germans who hated Nazis and who perhaps wouldn't look beyond the fact that the Americans had obviously considered him dangerous.

Kurt was saddened by the realization that so little had changed after almost two years of pleading his case. Still, Finucane's letter implied that at long last the government had recognized the unusual circumstances of the detained seamen. There was some comfort in the announcement from McCoy that the Alien Enemy Control Unit was about to institute proceedings for releasing some of the seamen. A Hearing Board would appear at Ft. Lincoln in early April to hear their cases. Every man who desired a hearing would get one, even if deportation orders were pending. The Board would decide whether to release a man on parole until such time as he was ordered to appear for deportation.

Early in April, McCoy notified Edward Ennis of the Justice Department's Alien Enemy Control Unit that he had put together a list of prospective Hearing Board members chosen from North Dakota citizens who were selected for their loyalty, judgement, and ability to spare time. Next, McCoy distributed to the seamen a form asking them to declare whether they did or did not want hearings set to begin April 20. Out of 226 seamen still at Ft. Lincoln, 182 including Kurt Peters, indicated that they wished to be included. In order to establish the particulars of each case, those who desired hearings were asked to fill out a thirty-page Alien Enemy Questionnaire, which the Hearing Board needed when it began its deliberations.

Shortly before the first hearings, Edwin J. Clapp arrived from the Justice Department to direct and coordinate the procedure. Clapp immediately held an orientation session in a courtroom of the Federal Building in Bismarck for the fifteen citizens who had agreed to be Board members. In order to expedite the hearings, the volunteers were then divided into several Boards of three each, which would hear cases simultaneously.

On April 20 four cases were heard before the first Board to be convened. Then on April 21 several Boards were convened at once to hear the cases of seventeen men, one of whom was Kurt Peters.

Kurt cancelled his classes that day, too anxious to put his mind to the business of anything but presenting his own case as persuasively as he could. Shortly after lunch he reported to the second floor of the headquarters building, where he was ushered into a small room with a large conference table at which sat the three men who would hear his case. Chairman of the hearing was William C. Hunter, a professor from Fargo. Hunter was flanked by William D. Graham, a retired Bismarck journalist, and A. E. Brown, a retired grocer.

Hunter smiled at Kurt, greeted him by his first name, and invited him to be seated. The friendly greeting surprised Kurt, and as he took a seat across the table from the three men, Hunter introduced himself and his two colleagues.

Pointing to personal documents on Kurt which were now laid out on the table, Hunter congratulated Kurt on the fine work he had done with his students. Then he explained that the Board had merely wanted to meet the young man they'd heard so much about.

Invited to say anything he wanted for the record, Kurt offered again an explanation of his background in Germany and his flight to avoid conscription in the *Wehrmacht*. Next, he explained that even before he had been interned, he had told them at his Ellis Island hearing, "I'm not like the others around here. I want to stay in the United States." Kurt made it clear to Hunter and his two colleagues that he hadn't said that as an expedient to gain his freedom. It was an honest expression of his belief in democracy.

Kurt went on to express the obligation he felt to keep alive the ideal which his parents had passed on to him. "If I am not free to express it here, perhaps it will die. . . . So I want to be free to become an American citizen. I want to be free to continue my education in this country. . . . I want to be free to become a writer."

It was a speech Kurt had rehearsed a dozen times in his mind, and Hunter's response to it was to ask, "Would you take up arms?"

"Yes," Kurt nodded, he would take up arms.

"We're asking you that not in the sense of ever sending you to Germany. You would go somewhere else. But that is the pledge you must give if you want to become a citizen during wartime. You must say, 'Yes, I will!' "

Since Kurt had already offered in writing his services to both the merchant marine and the military — offers that had been rejected — his pledges before the Hearing Board came as no surprise. After a short, fifteen-minute hearing, Hunter dismissed Kurt with the friendly remark that the Board was rushing to hear other cases less cut-and-dried than his. A recommendation for Kurt's parole would be forwarded promptly to the Justice Department, Hunter promised.

In the weeks immediately following his hearing, Kurt was reluctant to discuss the promise of parole which the Board had given him. Things had seemed "cut-and-dried" before. Then the rejection had come and made him look like a naive fool in the eyes of the other men. This time, he would wait until he had his parole orders in hand before he spoke.

While Kurt waited for his promised parole, other seamen in the camp who had had hearings remained skeptical. Among those doubters was Alfred Henzler, who had declared at his hearing that he still wished to return to Germany to assist his ailing mother. Furthermore, when the Board quizzed Henzler about serving in the American military, he could not put aside the possibility of fighting against the men he had served with for two years in the German military. Still, he stressed his desire to return to the United States as soon as possible after the war.

Henzler was well aware that his answers had not pleased the Board. Consequently, he had little hope of a quick release from Ft. Lincoln.

Meanwhile, Henzler worked day and night organizing the "First Annual Ft. Lincoln Sportfest," which was to be a mini-Olympics, featuring boxing, gymnastics, track and field, soccer, fistball (similar to volleyball), tennis, and table tennis. Henzler often sat planning the Sportfest at his bunk desk long after Kurt had put away his writing for the night.

With the arrival of June, and the reappearance of the cheerful flowers in the garden behind T94, Kurt could not help but feel the promise and confidence of spring. Then on June 7, Kurt's long-awaited good news arrived as an official copy of the Hearing Board's recommendation, which had been forwarded to the Alien Enemy Control Unit. After setting forth the facts of the case of Kurt Heinrich Rudolf Peters, the report concluded, "There is nothing in the record to indicate that he would be a dangerous alien enemy, and the recommendation of parole is clearly justified."

What was in the record were the letters and testimonials on Kurt's behalf from all his supporters—principally Ft. Lincoln and INS personnel. Ironically, there was no mention of Henry Uterhart in the Board's citations. Yet, Kurt felt grateful for Uterhart's efforts, even though they had by then lost touch with each other.

Two days later Kurt was still in high spirits when he received the liberating order from Francis Biddle, attorney general of the United States. "Whereas," the order said, Kurt was being detained at Ft. Lincoln as a potentially dangerous enemy of the United States, but "whereas" an Alien Enemy Hearing Board had recommended his parole, "It is now ordered," Biddle wrote, that Kurt Peters be paroled!

Biddle's order had a catch. Kurt was to be released "to the custody of a reputable U.S. citizen." Immediately, Kurt wrote Bert Fraser in Montana, informing him of the good news and requesting that he serve as sponsor. Fraser gladly agreed and notified McCoy to send Kurt on his way. However, since Montana was beyond the St. Paul INS District, Kurt's release was delayed while a request was made to INS headquarters in Philadelphia to release Kurt to a sponsor outside the St. Paul District.

It was an arrangement which had the blessings of Fraser, McCoy, and Alonzo Fleming, the chief district parole officer in St. Paul. Yet, Fleming was not able to take any action in the matter until he had the approval of the central office.

On July 19, more than a month after Kurt had been ordered released, the central office wrote that the parole of Kurt Peters to another district "will not be considered at this time." Undismayed, Kurt went straight to McCoy's office for permission to write a letter to the editor of *The Bismarck Tribune*. His letter, which he asked them to print, summarized his situation and pointed out that he could be a free man again if someone in Bismarck would step forward and agree to be his sponsor.

Two days later, early on a Saturday afternoon, William S. Moeller, the business manager of *The Bismarck Tribune,* and Mrs. G. D. Mann, the publisher, appeared in McCoy's office at Ft. Lincoln and asked to meet Kurt. He was immediately summoned to the headquarters building where Moeller and Mrs. Mann grilled him for two hours.

It was explained to Moeller that bi-monthly reports on Kurt's behavior would have to be sent to the INS if Moeller agreed to sponsor Kurt. Moeller was willing, but only if Kurt would agree to work for the paper. They needed somebody immediately.

Kurt had no idea what they wanted him to do, but he accepted on the spot, promising to report to *The Bismarck Tribune* the following Monday morning. McCoy produced the required INS papers for Moeller to sign as Kurt's official sponsor. Signatures were affixed, handshakes exchanged, the last between McCoy and Kurt. "Any time you want to leave," McCoy smiled, "you're free to go."

Kurt was driven by INS patrol car into Bismarck, where he spent the afternoon of July 24, 1943, with his feet on the windowsill of his second floor room in the Annex Hotel. The door was shut and locked, and Kurt sat half asleep looking out the window, relishing the sensation of being alone and free for the first time in over two years. "Now if I want to go out and have a beer," he thought, "I can do it. Or if I want to go out and have supper, I can do that. Whatever I want to do...."

Back at Ft. Lincoln, the *Schlageter* posted Kurt Peters' picture on the bulletin board of the mess hall. *Verräter* was printed across Kurt's face. "Traitor!"

On Monday morning, Kurt Peters stood before the young, attractive receptionist at *The Bismarck Tribune* offices and explained that he was from the internment camp. The receptionist was Evelyn Klein, whose father had been among the hundreds of Bismarck citizens who had gone out to witness the arrival of the "Nazi" aliens in 1941. Recalling how her father had come home and characterized the Germans as just harmless boys, Evelyn Klein led the young, earnest-looking German back to the office of Mrs. Mann, publisher of the paper. There, it was explained to him that he would deliver bundled newspapers by truck to various drop sites around Bismarck.

Kurt had hardly settled into the routine of his new job when he received an anonymous message that he was to report at a specific hour to room 308 of the Patterson Hotel in Bismarck. Ignorant as to the purpose of the meeting, but vowing not to let any circumstance ruin his first days of freedom, Kurt reported as directed to the Patterson Hotel.

He was greeted by three men in room 308, two wearing civilian clothes, the third dressed in a military uniform. Without introducing himself, one of the men in civilian clothes began by explaining that they were recruiting German-speaking agents with shortwave radio experience to be parachuted into Berlin. "What we propose," the spokesman concluded, "is six months training, immediate citizenship, and ten thousand dollars."

He had until the next morning to decide, and he was instructed not to discuss the offer with anyone.

"And if I don't accept this?" Kurt asked.

"Ft. Lincoln will be it, then," came the reply.

The three men whose blunt proposal bewildered Kurt that afternoon were members of the OSS. The Berlin mission for which they were trying to recruit agents was part of an on-going Allied espionage effort that sought to penetrate the heart of the Third Reich. But however skillfull he was in German and shortwave radio, Kurt knew that the men could not have picked a less likely candidate for espionage than himself.

Kurt left the hotel room that afternoon and wandered the streets of Bismarck almost until dark, wondering who he could turn to for advice. Finally, he found himself in front of Mrs. Mann's house.

Before Mrs. Mann could even invite him inside, he plunged into an anxious description of his meeting with the three men that afternoon. She listened carefully, her eyes widening with each detail of secrecy and espionage. Finally, Kurt explained they had threatened to return him to Ft. Lincoln if he refused.

In search of advice, Mrs. Mann drove Kurt to the home of her friend General Heber L. Edwards, head of the North Dakota National Guard. After hearing Kurt's worried explanation that he had been threatened with a return to Ft. Lincoln, General Edwards recognized that Kurt might be attributing to the OSS the same far-reaching authority as the German SS, or even the Gestapo. The general went on to point out that such secret police tyranny wasn't possible in America.

At 8:00 a.m. the following morning, Kurt knocked on the door of room 308 of the Patterson Hotel. The three men invited him inside for coffee and a seat. Kurt declined politely and remained standing in the half-open door. Bluntly, he explained that his decision was no. "As much as I want to be a citizen," Kurt said, "it seems to me that I can't do it this way."

"All right," he was told, "then you'll have to face the consequences."

Kurt left immediately, thankful that he had bothered to see Mrs.
Mann and her friend General Edwards, to learn that he couldn't be
forced into joining the OSS. Still, he was angered by the men's clumsy
efforts to force him into accepting their offer. Kurt never heard from
them again. Ultimately, the agents for the project, code-named HAM-
MER, were recruited from the ranks of German labor exiles in England,
many of whom were communists.

Because Kurt had never been behind the wheel of a vehicle before,
he crashed the panel truck three times in the first few days of his job
with *The Bismarck Tribune*. But Mrs. Mann, who thought the accidents
were related to stress, called him in and told him to take some time off.
"I know what you are going through...your mother and father still in
Germany," she referred obliquely to the news of stepped-up Allied
bombing attacks against Germany that summer. "Why don't you go
home," Mrs. Mann went on, "and relax. Whatever happens, it's O.K. In
time, everything will be all right."

Despite Mrs. Mann's comforting words, Kurt went home still worried about the fate of his parents in Germany. The last week of July,
after Kurt had returned to delivering newspapers in America, 738 British bombers approached their targets over Hamburg, Germany, where
they dropped three-and-one-half pound thermite base stick bombs,
which fell through the rooftops and then exploded into flames. The air
in the streets, where people ran frantically seeking escape, turned
furnace hot and began to rise over Hamburg. Cool air drawn into the
vortex created forty-mile-an-hour winds a mile and a half from the
center of what had become a firestorm. Before the week-long attack was
over, 37,554 citizens of the city were scorched to death in the streets, or
helplessly sucked into buildings burning like crematories. A total of
18,418 females died. One of them was Frieda Peters, Kurt's mother.

In August Kurt was promoted to circulation manager of *The Bismarck Tribune*, which meant that he had time to talk to "Miss Klein," as
he called the attractive receptionist the first months of his freedom. By
the end of the summer, Kurt had taken an apartment on Mandan
Street, and spent the cool fall evenings walking the streets of the capital
with Evelyn Klein. On several occasions that fall, Kurt and Evelyn took
a cab out to Ft. Lincoln to see where he had spent two years and to visit
with Alfred Henzler. Henzler would eventually be paroled to do forest
service work in Montana with Bert Fraser as his sponsor.

Kurt had become more anxious than ever to obtain his citizenship and to serve the war effort in any way he could. In November, he registered with the Selective Service Board of Burleigh County, after having written the INS that he was "quite willing to serve in the U.S. military force, if such were possible."

Kurt was classified 1A on December 22, 1943, and informed that he could expect induction into the armed services momentarily. On March 22, 1944, he reported to Ft. Snelling, Minnesota, for his physical exam, after having written the INS to inform them that "after my acceptance into the armed forces of the U.S., I shall be under military jurisdiction."

Closer than ever to his citizenship, Kurt bid goodbye to Evelyn by asking if she would wait for him. "I've been a lonely man for too long," he told her. "I'm twenty-three years old. I know what I want, and you are it."

"My mind was made up long ago," she assured him.

Kurt was inducted into the Navy on April 24 and sent to Farrugut, Idaho, for boot camp. Technically, he was still an enemy alien, however, and on May 5, W. F. Kelly of the Border Patrol recommended to the attorney general that Kurt Heinrich Rudolf Peters be given an "unconditional release under alien enemy proceedings."

Attorney General Biddle's order unconditionally releasing Kurt was issued in June. Immediately, the Navy directed Kurt to appear with two witnesses before the Bonneville County District Judge, in Sandpoint, Idaho, in order to be sworn as a citizen of the United States.

Grabbing two sailors with whom he had made friends, Kurt went off as ordered to the small brick courthouse in Sandpoint. The courtroom was empty when Kurt and his two witnesses entered in their uniforms. The bailiff directed them to take a seat in the front, and Kurt sat in what he thought of as church-pew silence and went over in his mind all the aspects of the constitution and democracy he had spent so long teaching others.

Then he began to worry he would be asked dates, perhaps names of American presidents. He knew that he understood fully the *principles* of democracy. But what if they quizzed him on trivial particulars?

Finally the judge entered and took a seat at his bench.

Kurt and his two friends stood.

"Kurt Heinrich Rudolf Peters?" the judge's voice resounded in the empty room.

Kurt stepped toward the bench.

The judged leaned forward. "I am looking at you wearing that uniform," he said smiling suddenly. "It would be foolish to ask why you want to become a citizen." He took a pen and quickly scribbled his signature. "Here are your citizenship papers. Now go have a beer."

Die Wanderkameraden

CONFINEMENT BY HEARSAY AND THE NAZI-JEW CONFLICT IN CAMP

The Liaison Office, later called the Internal Security Office, just inside the main gate to the compound, winter 1941–42 This office was run by Chief Liaison Officer Will Robbins and his assistant, E J "Red" Selland (Courtesy of Red Selland.)

Patrol Inspector E J "Red" Selland, Assistant Liaison Officer at Ft Lincoln, in Border Patrol uniform, 1941–42 (Courtesy of Red Selland)

Left, the entrance to Ft Lincoln, with the internment compound and northwest surveillance tower in background, winter
1941–42, approximately when *Die Wanderkameraden* arrived
(Courtesy of Red Selland)

Unloading of Japanese
enemy-alien arrivals at Ft
Lincoln, early February
1942 Patrol Inspector
Clifford Peck with subma-
chine gun (Courtesy of
Will Robbins)

Brick barracks 31, which
housed *Die Wanderkameraden*.

Die Wanderkameraden

Monday, December 8, 1941, Eddie and Liesl Friedman spent the day in their San Francisco apartment listening to news reports of the war. That evening they dressed in overcoats and set out from their apartment on the corner of Pierce and Sacramento to deliver hors d'oeuvres and pastries to the residence of Baroness von Rescnizeck.

The Baroness was one of six hundred San Francisco customers to whom Eddie Friedman delivered home baked Viennese cookies and pastries, and she had once confessed to Eddie that because of her anti-Nazi sentiments, she would never return to Germany. Still, that evening it was expected that Fritz Wiedemann, the outspoken, pro-Nazi German Consul General in San Francisco, would be attending her party.

The pastries delivered as ordered, Eddie and Liesl walked in silence back to the apartment. Then, from the street, Liesl saw that a light had been left burning in their living room. They quarreled over who was responsible for the burning light, and still arguing, climbed the short stairs to their apartment. Eddie put his key in the lock, but the door swung open.

Liesl's voice froze in the middle of a sentence. Eddie drew back. Three tall, husky men were standing at the bookcase which Liesl had had specially made in Germany. Eddie thought they looked like thieves caught in the act of ransacking the apartment, and he demanded to know who they were. One of them stepped forward, flashed a document and a badge, and explained they were FBI agents.

Eddie wasn't sure he understood what the FBI was, except that it was a federal agency working somehow against criminals. Liesl, however, understood and protested sharply that even though Eddie was German, he was also Jewish. He considered his departure from Germany an escape.

"Mrs. Friedman," one of them answered, "many German Jews have left relatives over there. They are compelled now to work

50

for the Nazis or their relatives will be killed."

Angry now, Liesl explained that Eddie had no one else there. Eddie's brother had hanged himself in a concentration camp, and his sister had emigrated to Palestine. As for herself, she was not even Jewish.

Nevertheless, the agent ordered, "Mr. Friedman, you have to come with us."

"If that's what you want, I'll go," Eddie said.

A second agent moved closer to Eddie to handcuff him. But Eddie protested that he had never been handcuffed in his life, not even in Sachsenhausen, and he was not going to be handcuffed now.

Eddie Friedman was born to Jewish parents in Hamburg in 1892. After World War I, Eddie received his law degree and immediately served a three-year internship as a judge in Hamburg courts. Then in 1930, he went into private practice in Hamburg.

In 1934, he met and married Liesl Dollmann. After the marriage, Liesl and Eddie watched with apprehension as Hitler rose to power and slowly promulgated those political and social restraints which were designed to isolate and then eliminate the Jews. But because Eddie had never taken his Jewish heritage seriously, it wasn't until 1938, when Hitler excluded Jews from practicing law, that Liesl finally declared they ought to leave Germany.

With visa and exit permits secured and all their belongings stored for shipment to the United States, the Friedmans had only to wait for their scheduled sailing to America in December of 1938.

One morning, however, two Gestapo agents came to the apartment and asked for Dr. Friedman. Liesl could only stammer that perhaps he was in court.

When the two agents arrived at court, they explained politely that he was under arrest. Eddie looked puzzled. He knew both of the men, having met them many times in his legal work. As they escorted him out of the courthouse, they said, "Now, Doctor, you go ahead of us. We don't want to embarrass you."

Eddie Friedman was taken to Oranienberg-Sachsenhausen Concentration Camp just outside Berlin. His barracks was one long room, with approximately seventy-five people in it. It was cold, there were no beds or mattresses, and they slept on the floor, squashed against each other.

The next morning when they went outside, Eddie saw half a dozen bodies stacked up within the shadows of his barracks. He asked who they were and was told they were prisoners from his own barracks who had died during the night.

A week after Eddie arrived at Sachsenhausen, he was approached by a camp official and told he was "lucky" because he would be permitted to leave that afternoon. At first, Eddie thought it might be a cruel joke. It wasn't, however; Liesel had prevailed upon Eddie's lawyer friends in Hamburg to use their Nazi connections to secure his release. By late afternoon Eddie found himself standing at the main gate. Before he was let go, he was given a thick sandwich to carry with him, "so that the people outside won't think we let you hunger," they said.

Eddie and Liesl arrived in San Francisco on March 1, 1939. For four months they lived with Eddie's uncle in Marin County, across the Golden Gate Bridge from San Francisco. Finally they found an apartment over a garage on the corner of Pierce and Sacramento in San Francisco.

By this time Eddie was nearly fifty, and he discarded forever the idea of working as a lawyer in the United States. He knew he would have to go back to school, and then in all likelihood he'd be hired by a firm of attorneys, only to be low man, getting all the dirty work. Besides, a lawyer's tool was language, he complained to Liesl. "I like French...Italian...Spanish. I don't like English."

Then a Viennese couple who heard about Eddie called him to their apartment in the San Francisco Marina district and asked him if he wanted a job selling homemade cookies and pastries door-to-door.

"I'm an attorney," he said proudly. "I've never done any selling."

The Viennese couple encouraged Eddie to give it a try, then sent him out with a bagful of cookies and pastries.

When he returned to the apartment, he had a grave look on his face. The Viennese couple wondered anxiously, "So you didn't like it?"

"Yes," he protested. "I like it. But I don't have any more merchandise."

It was as the couple had expected. Eddie's story of flight from Nazi Germany was soon his calling card, even if after a while he tired of repeating it. He made five dollars a week selling door-to-door at residences in the Marina and to secretaries in the office buildings in downtown San Francisco. "I am Dr. Friedman," he would announce politely to the office receptionist in his heavy German accent. "Would you like to buy some cookies and pastries?"

One of the offices where Eddie called regularly was in the same downtown office building which housed Fritz Wiedemann, the controversial German Consul General in San Francisco. Wiedemann had been Hitler's military superior during World War I. It was Wiedemann who had recommended the young corporal for the Iron Cross. When Hitler came to power in Germany, he rewarded his former superior by making him his adjutant. Wiedemann apparently continued to believe he was Hitler's superior, and he argued vehemently in the early 1930s that the Third Reich should be seeking stronger alliances with the United States. The argument offended Hitler, and he sent Wiedemann off to be Consul General in San Francisco, where he was supposed to be cured of his notion that America was a world power. Meanwhile, Wiedemann remained an ardent Nazi, and in San Francisco his pro-German public comments soon earned him the label of America's number one Nazi. Even though Eddie delivered pastries in the same building where Wiedemann had his office, the two men never met.

The proceeds from Eddie's pastry delivery business were meager, so on Sundays, Eddie worked as an elevator operator in office buildings around San Francisco. The buildings were usually deserted, giving Eddie the opportunity to type letters to his German friends using a typewriter he brought with him to work and put on a stand in the elevator.

In September of 1940, Eddie and Liesl reported to the local post office to be registered and fingerprinted as aliens under the Alien Registration Act, signed by President Franklin Roosevelt in June of 1940. This mass registration eventually listed three-and-one-half million aliens.

It was preceded by a vigorous congressional debate in May of 1939. Focus of the debate was the so-called Hobbs Bill (HR 5643), under which subversives or immoral aliens who had been ordered deported could be "detained" by order of the Secretary of Labor until such time as their deportation could be effected by the INS. (At that time the INS was a branch of the Labor Department.) It smacked of imprisonment without due process, and during the heated congressional debate, Congresswoman Caroline O'Day of New York remarked, "I can imagine with what satisfaction Hitler will learn that his emissaries in this country have so influenced Congress that it is following his example in setting up concentration camps during peacetime" (*Congressional Record—House*, May 5, 1939).

Despite those who felt it permitted concentration camps in the United States, the bill passed the House by a vote of 289 to 61. Yet it failed to pass the Senate. On December 7 and 8, 1941, when Roosevelt signed the proclamations ordering the arrest and detention of "alien enemies deemed dangerous to the U.S. security," his authority to do so lay in an act of Congress dated July 6, 1798. That act (which now stands as Sec. 21, Title 50 of the *United States Code*) stipulates that upon declaration of a state of war, or the threat of invasion, enemy aliens "shall be liable to be apprehended, restrained, secured and removed."

On the afternoon of December 8, 1941, Attorney General Francis Biddle, who reported the incident in his book, *In Brief Authority,* brought the German and Italian arrest proclamations to the White House for the president to sign. Roosevelt wanted to know then how many Germans were in the country, and whether Biddle intended to intern all of them. Biddle hesitated at the idea of mass internment of Germans, but Roosevelt went on to explain, "I don't care so much about Italians. They are a lot of opera singers. But the Germans are different; they may be dangerous" (p.207).

Biddle left with his authorization for the issuance of arrest warrants. He telegrammed J. Edgar Hoover, saying the FBI was authorized and directed to arrest among others, Edgar Friedman, an enemy alien deemed dangerous to the public peace and safety of the United States. Hoover promptly teletyped the order on to N. J. L. Pieper, special agent-in-charge of the San Francisco FBI office. By 8:00 p.m. Eddie Friedman was in custody.

In the first three days after Pearl Harbor, the Group Presidential Warrant that Biddle forwarded to Hoover contained the names of nearly three thousand German, Japanese, and Italian aliens throughout the United States whom the Justice Department considered threats to the security of the country.

While federal agents were waiting in San Francisco for Eddie Friedman to return from his pastry deliveries, four policemen were knocking on the door of a new home out on Forty-ninth Street SW in Seattle, Washington. Inside, Wolfgang Johannes Thomas was poking the logs in his fireplace in an effort to dry out the plaster in the unfinished house, which looked out over Puget Sound. Thomas's wife and two small sons had gone to the nearby home of his father-in-law Carl Kroll, and Thomas now sat by himself in front of the warm fire, occasionally poking the logs as his mind wandered aimlessly over the circumstances of his life that had brought him there.

Wolfgang Thomas was born in 1904 in Hamburg, where his father managed the main office of a local bank. Because Wolfgang was a sickly child, the family moved to the country twenty-five miles outside Hamburg, hoping that Wolfgang's health would improve. However, the years following World War I were difficult, filled with hunger and bitter cold, and Wolfgang remained in frail health through his high school education and a year of apprenticeship as a general office boy for a steamship company in Hamburg. He soon came down with bleeding ulcers, and finally a kidney infection. Again he was advised by his doctor to leave the industrial city of Hamburg, and in 1925 he travelled to Los Angeles in search of sunshine and improved health. In California he took a job with another steamship company, writing out bills of lading and manifests.

Then Wolfgang's father got seriously ill in Hamburg, and Wolfgang returned to that city to take over and modernize his father's bank. However, his father's associates considered Wolfgang too young to know about banking matters and they disapproved of his efforts. It was not long, therefore, before Wolfgang left the banking business.

Cashing in on his experience in the shipping industry, Wolfgang went to work as an importer of palm leaves and artificial flowers. In July of 1933, he married Margareta Kroll. She was an American citizen of German parents, and her father had established a successful business exporting lily of the valley bulbs to the Seattle area. By the spring of 1939, it was clear that Margareta's American citizenship would prove difficult in the event of war, and Wolfgang left the import business in the hands of a partner and sailed to Seattle, Washington, with his wife and two small children.

In Seattle, Thomas and his family lived with Margareta's parents while Wolfgang and Margareta began to search for a home of their own. News came in August that Wolfgang's business partner was absconding with funds, and Wolfgang returned immediately to Germany to dissolve the business. Shortly after he arrived there, Britain declared war on Germany, and Wolfgang found that exit from Germany via the West was impossible because of the Atlantic Blockade.

Thomas went then to the same travel agent who had sold him tickets for his emigration to America almost a year earlier. Since at thirty-six Wolfgang was still young enough to do military service, the agent predicted that Army officials would never grant him an exit visa.

The only chance he had was to leave the jurisdiction of local Hamburg officials, who were all obedient Nazis and made no decisions on their own. If Wolfgang Thomas wanted an exit visa, he would have to go to Berlin and apply there.

After the agent booked Wolfgang on a ship leaving that week, Wolfgang went straight to *Wehrmacht* officials in Berlin. An officer studied Wolfgang's papers, which detailed the history of his poor health. "We have no objection," the officer said at last.

The next day Wolfgang headed east by train, spending seven days on the trans-Siberian express, which took him to the borders of Manchuria, thence to Peking and Pusan, where he caught a ferry to Japan. In Yokohama he boarded the *Tatuta Maru* to Honolulu and finally to San Francisco. There, he went straight to the immigration offices and made application for American citizenship, which he thought he would receive after a three-month wait. When they told him it would be a three-year wait, his disappointment was quickly replaced by the happy realization that he was safely back in the country that would one day be his new home, however long the wait.

Back in Seattle with his wife and children, Wolfgang went to work for an export firm, and he and Margareta resumed hunting for a home of their own. In the fall of 1940, a nearby lot on a cul-de-sac overlooking Puget Sound came up for auction because of delinquent taxes. Margareta attended the auction and purchased the lot for seven hundred dollars. Construction on the site was begun immediately, and in the summer of 1941, Wolfgang and Margareta and the two children moved into the still unfinished home.

At 6:00 p.m. on December 8, H. B. Fletcher, special agent-in-charge of the Seattle FBI, received orders from Washington that he was to arrest Wolfgang Thomas as a dangerous enemy alien. Fletcher phoned the Seattle police and assigned the actual task of arresting Thomas to them. However, the four uniformed officers who set out at approximately 7:00 p.m. to apprehend Thomas went first to his father-in-law Carl Kroll's house. There they were met by Margareta, who told them that she and Wolfgang now lived out on Forty-ninth Street. Unaware of their purpose, and with no reason to fear that Wolfgang was in trouble, she took the four officers to her new home.

Despite Margareta's presence, the two policemen who went to the door with her insisted on knocking. Wolfgang left the warm fire where he had been lost in thought for almost an hour, and opened the door. Then, while he and Margareta stood in the middle of the living room, the four policemen began a systematic search of the house, inspecting briefly and then seizing film, correspondence, and books. Wolfgang thought to ask to see their search warrant, but then decided against it, since he did not want them to think he had anything to hide.

The search completed, the officers escorted Wolfgang to their car. Two officers climbed in front immediately and started the engine. Margareta and Wolfgang embraced briefly on the curb, while the other two men stood nervously on either side of an open rear door to the car.

Margareta stepped away then as they guided Wolfgang into the rear seat. They explained to her only that he was being taken for questions. She could call the INS District Office in Seattle first thing in the morning, they suggested. Then they both slipped into the car and flanked Wolfgang. The driver backed the car around in the cul-de-sac and sped off down the street, Margareta watching as the taillights disappeared in the dark.

In San Francisco, FBI agents moved next against forty-five-year-old Dr. Arthur Sonnenberg. Born in Kiel in 1896, Sonnenberg had served with German light artillery and infantry in World War I. After his discharge, he attended the University of Kiel, where he continued medical studies he had begun before the war. In 1921 Sonnenberg received his medical degree and immediately took a post as assistant health officer for the city of Kiel. He was soon married to Elizabeth Beckmann, whom he called Lilly.

As a health official for Kiel, Dr. Sonnenberg's major responsibility was to examine the sixth and eighth grade school children for infiltration of tuberculosis. He found that because of primitive, postwar living conditions, nearly half of the children were infected. However, articles critical of the city's treatment program began to appear in the Kiel papers, and he was ordered to stay away from the infected children.

At about this time, Sonnenberg received news from his brother Otto, who had emigrated to the United States in 1912, that America could surely make use of his medical skills. Despite the fact that Kiel officials begged him to remain in Germany, Dr. Sonnenberg left for the United States with his wife and their infant son in 1923.

The Sonnenbergs came directly to San Francisco, where the doctor began to study for the State Boards. He supported his family by assisting another doctor in the tiny, northern California town of Weed.

Early in 1924, Sonnenberg returned to San Francisco, passed the State Boards, and set up his practice in the city, eventually opening up offices in the Flood Building on Market Street. He joined the staff at St. Joseph's, a Catholic hospital operated by the Franciscan Sisters, most of whom were German born. His family grew with a second son and a daughter; and his reputation grew as a skilled and dedicated physician who had special interests in surgery, gynecology, obstetrics, orthopedics, proctology, and anesthesia. Before long he had developed a huge, successful general practice with many patients from the German colony in San Francisco.

In September of 1938, Dr. Sonnenberg filed his declaration of intention to become a U.S. citizen. Required to wait three years before he could take his citizenship exam, he used what little spare time he had to study those aspects of American history and the constitution on which he still felt weak. Meanwhile, he continued to enjoy a distinguished reputation in the San Francisco German community, and he served now as a physician to the San Francisco German Consulate, treating the consular attachés including the German Consul General Fritz Wiedemann.

In January of 1940, the detained seamen from the scuttled liner *Columbus* arrived in San Francisco and were quartered at Angel Island. Private hospitals in San Francisco refused to treat the German seamen, many of whom were in need of medical attention and hospitalization. Finally, Dr. Sonnenberg made arrangements for a ward to be set aside in St. Joseph's Hospital. Well aware that the city was already aggravated enough by the unwelcome presence of the "Nazi" sailors, Dr. Sonnenberg instructed the seamen that there were to be no political disputes while in the hospital. Then he quietly went about the business of treating the men, up until they were transferred early in 1941 to Ft. Stanton, New Mexico, for internment.

Six o'clock the evening of December 8, 1941, just two weeks before he was to appear for his citizenship examination, Dr. Sonnenberg was in his office in the Flood Building seeing the last of a crush of patients who had filed through his office that day. Armed with a teletype arrest warrant which they had just received from Washington, three FBI agents entered the doctor's office and presented him the warrant as half a dozen patients watched.

Eager to avoid the spectacle of a public arrest, the doctor led the three men back to a small examination room, where they were joined by his office nurse. The five of them stood almost shoulder-to-shoulder in the tiny room.

Learning he indeed was under arrest, he directed his nurse to go back out to the waiting room and dismiss the remaining patients. The three FBI men took him to his apartment on Pacific Avenue. There Lilly demanded to know where they were taking her husband, but the three of them busied themselves investigating the clothing she had thrown together for the doctor. Then he was taken down the elevator and out to a waiting car.

Dr. Sonnenberg and Eddie Friedman were driven to FBI headquarters on Sutter Street in San Francisco, where they were fingerprinted and turned over to the INS. They were moved then to a temporary detention facility on Silver Avenue. No charges were read against them, and no explanation was given for their arrest, beyond the formal explanation read each alien as he arrived at the Silver Avenue facility that he was considered a potentially dangerous enemy alien.

At the temporary detention station, Eddie Friedman was relieved of his wallet with ten dollars, thirty-one cents in postage stamps, his watch, his driver's license, and a few wallet cards. He and Sonnenberg slept that night in a huge ward packed with beds arranged in orderly rows. German and Italian aliens occupied the outer row of beds, equipped with only mattresses. The Japanese, who cleaned the whole ward, occupied the middle beds. Most of the men were handcuffed, and unarmed INS guards stood at the entry to each ward, occasionally patrolling through the rooms.

Eddie and Dr. Sonnenberg remained at the Silver Avenue facility for a week. On the morning of December 17, the German aliens in the ward were greeted early by a booming voice, which advised them to get ready to leave San Francisco. They were headed for Bismarck, North Dakota, they were told. The men were taken in groups by police cars or busses across the Bay Bridge to Oakland. There, they were loaded into a passenger train with barred and blacked-out windows. Inside each car, a mounted machine gun was aimed at the aliens, who sat up or tried to sleep lying across the seats. In Portland the train stopped to pick up twenty-two aliens from the Northwest. Among them was Wolfgang Johannes Thomas. The convoy then totalled seven cars and 110 aliens.

Eddie Friedman could not sleep that first night as the train lugged up through the northern Rockies, moving past the darkened wooden railroad depots with dimly lit signs that marked their progress—Missoula...Billings...Miles City. Eddie sat up all night and hoped that the selection of Bismarck as their final destination somehow revealed a cultural sympathy which the government felt for these German aliens. Then again, he feared, what if Bismarck was Sachsenhausen all over again? What about Liesl? What if she never learned where he had been sent? Unfortunately, it would make no difference to her when she did know. If anything, she would only see in the German place-names a reprise of the anti-Semitic horrors he had escaped in Germany.

The train with Eddie Friedman, Arthur Sonnenberg, and Wolfgang Thomas arrived in extreme cold at Bismarck on Saturday afternoon, December 20, 1941. The men were loaded into army trucks, under the watchful eyes of Border Patrol guards carrying submachine guns, and driven to the camp. With the arrival of this first group of alien enemies arrested on presidential warrants, it meant there were now 410 aliens detained at Ft. Lincoln, 292 of them being German seamen taken from ships in U.S. ports.

Friedman, Sonnenberg, and Thomas quickly made friends and staked out a private corner for themselves in room 31C, one of the lower dormitory rooms of the brick barracks. They were joined by other older, highly educated men: Richard Birkefeld, an articulate businessman from Seattle; Edward Heims, like Eddie Friedman, a Jew and a lawyer; and a Ph.D from Los Angeles named Alfred Bretthauer. The little group of men soon began to call themselves the "democratic intelligentsia" of the camp. They enjoyed talking quietly late into the night in their corner of the barracks, isolated somewhat from the often abrasive and disagreeable German seamen.

Immediately after Eddie Friedman had settled himself in the barracks on December 22, he wrote out a Christmas telegram to Liesl. "Merry Christmas," he greeted her. "We remain united in the heart." Then, having sent the telegram on its way, he wrote her a letter which explained that he and Heims were the only Jews in camp. He begged Liesl to go to the highest officials necessary to gain his release.

The morning after Eddie was arrested, Liesl Friedman called the FBI to learn what had been done with him. She was told only to pack a suitcase with his warm clothes and send it to Ft. Lincoln, North Dakota. Having done this, she waited nervously for further instructions from the authorities. She smoked, fretted, and lost ten pounds. Convinced that the only thing she could do on Eddie's behalf was to suffer along with him, she sat alone on Christmas Eve in their darkened apartment.

Then the doorbell rang. It was a young Quaker man who had heard about Eddie, and he offered Liesl money, which she refused. But she asked the man to do whatever he could to get Eddie freed.

After Christmas, the letters began to pour in from Eddie, sometimes three or four in a day. In each letter, he urged her to write various authorities and request they release him. Write President Roosevelt, he implored her. Write Eleanor Roosevelt. Write, write, write! But in Liesl's mind it was all hopeless.

During the day at Ft. Lincoln, Eddie slept or walked the inside perimeter of the fence with Dr. Sonnenberg and Wolfgang Thomas, the three of them calling themselves *Die Wanderkameraden,* or hiking comrades. They talked about history, politics, the war, their families, classical music (Thomas complained that he couldn't get used to Mahler, and Stravinski was too wild), and their health. Dr. Sonnenberg advised Thomas, whose stomach was still sensitive, to eat in the hospital, where the food was less seasoned and salty and not apt to aggravate his ulcer.

Then one day as they walked in the cold, Eddie complained to Dr. Sonnenberg that he was suffering *Gitterkrankheit,* or "fence sickness." It was the same thing he felt in Sachsenhausen, he remembered. Wolfgang Thomas agreed. Each morning he woke up, looked at the fence, and thought, "Another damn day!"

Sonnenberg understood. But it was as if the two men wanted some fast-curing medicine. All he could offer was the belief; born perhaps of his important contacts in the San Francisco medical community, that they wouldn't be detained long.

Eddie could not share that hope. The joy of his escape from Germany was remote, lost. For him, getting out of Germany seemed only a fairy tale now, and that feeling of loss was laced with bitterness in the letters Eddie wrote to any official he thought might be able to get him released. To Edward Ennis, director of the Alien Enemy Control Unit, Eddie wrote on December 29 to complain that he still hadn't received a hearing before an Alien Enemy Hearing Board. Eddie explained then in detail his flight from Sachsenhausen, and the hope with which he had taken up a new life in America. He concluded by pointing out that he and Heims were the only Jews in camp, and, "It hurts our feelings to see rooms decorated with swastikas and pictures of that supergangster Adolph Hitler. Please, Mr. Ennis, do us a favor, to bring about our immediate release."

Having made his appeal to Ennis, on behalf of himself and Edward Heims, Eddie went on to appeal his case to Eleanor Roosevelt. Complaining that the reason for his arrest was still a mystery, he wrote that he had only been "selling cookies and pastries, homemade by other émigrés in San Francisco. As you are in a position to help people in distress more than anybody else in the country, I would like to ask if it would be possible to bring about an early release."

On January 6, 1942, I. P. McCoy, acting Officer in Charge of Ft. Lincoln, received a letter from Frank Kronenberg, a Chicago attorney. He asked to know the charges against Eddie Friedman, and what could be done to hasten his release. Although he said he was inquiring on behalf of Friedman's family and friends, neither Eddie nor Liesl ever learned who had contacted him. They speculated it might have been the mysterious Quaker or perhaps Mrs. Roosevelt.

McCoy answered that the question of Friedman's release was under the direct jurisdiction of the U.S. attorneys, who would soon be conducting hearings at the various detention camps. All correspondence, McCoy said, should be directed to P. W. Lanier, U.S. attorney in Fargo for the North Dakota District.

Soon the camp was buzzing with the news that the promised hearings would commence. The hearings, Attorney General Biddle and the Justice Department explained, were being held "not as a matter of right, but in order to permit aliens to present facts in their own behalf." Detainees could not be represented by a lawyer, a provision which Biddle later claimed in *In Brief Authority* "greatly expedited action, saved time . . . and put the procedure on a common sense basis" (p.208).

The aliens would be allowed only an *advisor*, who would not be permitted to object to questions or make any arguments concerning any evidence or otherwise act as an attorney.

Biddle assumed the job of appointing a three-man Alien Enemy Hearing Board from each judicial district. One member had to be an attorney and all had to be reputable citizens of the United States and residents of the judicial district. Interestingly, a government circular of January 7, 1942, claimed that Hearing Boards "would be" composed of prominent members of the alien's own community. It was not required by law, however, so the Hearing Board for Eddie had two residents of North Dakota.

Individual cases were presented to the Hearing Boards by the U.S. attorney for the judicial district. In his presentation to the Board, which was supposed to establish the alien's enemy status, the U.S. attorney relied on information developed by the FBI. Following that, witnesses were permitted to testify on behalf of the alien. Finally, the Hearing Board was to dismiss the subject, consider the evidence, and recommend to Biddle whether that person was to be released, paroled under supervision of the INS, or interned.

P. W. Lanier, highly respected U.S. attorney for the North Dakota District, was a tall man whose deep voice, some said, was a dead ringer for Lionel Barrymore's. At first, Lanier planned that the hearings would be held at Fargo, some two hundred miles east of Bismarck. However, Ike McCoy objected to trucking the aliens there, and Lanier then went ahead with plans to hold the hearings at Ft. Lincoln, on the first floor of the headquarters building.

On January 8, Heinz Georg Albers Fritsch, a German national who had been residing in Chile, arrived for internment at Ft. Lincoln. He talked of midnight apprehension in Chile, then extradition to the United States, a procedure that Biddle later (February 1944) called "unusual circumstances." Fritsch expressed confidence that his diplomatic connections would get him out in a matter of days. Eddie Friedman smiled at the man's seeming naivete. What had Dr. Sonnenberg's San Francisco connections gotten him? What had Eddie's letters to every political official he could think of produced? Nothing! So what strings could a man who didn't even live in the United States pull?

Yet, two days later, on January 10, Fritsch was released. The news infuriated Eddie. Immediately he sat down and dashed off an angry letter to Ennis, director of the Alien Enemy Control Unit.

According to Dr. Sonnenberg, the next day the Ft. Lincoln censor, a short, officious Swiss named Matthaus Gerspacher, appeared in 31C carrying Eddie's letter. "Next time, a little more moderate, Edgar," he warned and returned the letter.

By the end of January, all Eddie's efforts were directed toward the approaching hearings, and he wired Liesl that she should forward character references to Lanier in Fargo. These references would be permitted as documentary evidence during the hearing. Meanwhile, the hearings were commenced in order of the date of the detainee's arrest.

As soon as the proceedings were under way, rumors began to circulate throughout the camp concerning Lanier's grim, hostile manner with those who appeared for hearings. Yet Lanier himself felt that most of the Germans who had been detained had been dealt with unjustly. He privately confessed that the FBI agents who did the investigation work for the case files were young, over-zealous, self-important hotshots. He was instrumental in the firing of an FBI agent who had falsified a report used in an alien's detention.

On February 2, Wolfgang Thomas was the first *Wanderkameraden* to have his hearing before the Alien Enemy Hearing Board. Chairman of the Board was Horace Young of Fargo, a studious man who spoke several languages and prided himself on the fact that, although not Jewish, he could speak fluent Yiddish.

Thomas's wife Margareta travelled to Bismarck for the hearing, to lend what support she could to her husband's case. Thomas entered the hearing wearing a clean suit which Margareta had brought along with her. Lanier, who presented the evidence against Thomas, instructed Margareta and Wolfgang to be seated in front of a long table behind which sat Chairman Young, flanked by his two fellow Board members. FBI documents, along with Wolfgang's lengthy Alien Enemy Questionnaire, were laid on the table.

Lanier took a seat at the end of the table and began the questions that challenged Thomas to explain how he had been able to travel freely between the United States and Germany. Specifically, Lanier was curious about Thomas's trips to Germany in August of 1939, and his return to the United States in March of 1940.

Wolfgang explained the circumstances of his trip: the business problems, the declaration of war, and his eligibility for military service due to his age.

But Lanier was not satisfied. How was it, then, that he had been able to escape the draft? The questions were becoming more pointed, and Wolfgang could feel his stomach began to flutter.

Thomas explained his poor health and guessed that he had been permitted to leave because Germany was in high spirits at that time. Poland had fallen. The *Wehrmacht* was young and invincible. They didn't feel they needed middle-aged, sickly men in the army. However, because of the Atlantic Blockade, he had been forced to exit Germany via the East, on the trans-Siberian express.

It was clear now to Thomas that Lanier's major concern was how he had been allowed to get out of Germany during a declared war, and he braced himself for a tough cross-examination.

But Lanier suddenly switched his approach. Now he wanted to know how Thomas had managed to build his new home. What had it cost? Who had built it? How had he financed it? Thomas answered nervously, glancing at Margareta for verifying nods as he did.

Despite Thomas's explanation, Lanier charged that Thomas had in fact been paid enormous amounts of money to spy on shipping in the sound.

Thomas protested that since his arrival in the United States he had done everything to abide by the laws.

Again, however, Lanier switched abruptly to a new subject, Thomas's in-laws, who according to Lanier had strong Nazi loyalties and belonged to various pro-German organizations.

Thomas confessed that his father-in-law Carl Kroll had a history of pro-German beliefs. But what organizations Kroll belonged to was none of Wolfgang's business.

So, Lanier pried, Thomas had a good relationship with his in-laws? "All right, I guess," Thomas replied.

Abruptly, then, Thomas was told, "This hearing is over."

Startled by the sudden ending, the Thomases walked in silence to the visitors room of the headquarters building. There, they had an opportunity to discuss briefly their disappointment over the fact that everything at the hearing seemed already determined. "I'm going to Washington to raise hell!" Margareta vowed before she said goodbye to Wolfgang.

Wolfgang returned to his barracks too shaken to remember anything about the hearing, except the Board's concern over the details of his exit from Germany. To Wolfgang, that seemed their major concern. In fact, it wasn't. Among those documents which Lanier and the Board referred to were numerous FBI letters and "Security Reports," the subject of which was Carl Albert Kroll, Margareta's father.

A German by birth, Kroll had become a naturalized American citizen after his immigration in 1903 to the United States. By 1939 a series of confidential FBI reports quoting anonymous informants and hearsay evidence maintained that Kroll was "possibly" engaged in espionage because he had signalled boats anchored at Elliott Bay. Furthermore, the reports indicated, he had hosted meetings of Germans in his home.

Kroll's son-in-law first appeared in the FBI reports on Kroll in November of 1939, when an informant charged that he was an official employee of the German government. Then on May 27, 1940, the FBI in Washington received an anonymous letter postmarked in Brookline, Massachusetts. The informant wrote "I think it is my duty to call your attention to a man of military age, German, who came to the U.S. at the end of March, 1940, by way of Russia and Japan. I believe that he is connected with the German government." J. Edgar Hoover forwarded the tip to the Seattle FBI and directed them to continue investigating Thomas and his father-in-law. The subsequent investigation by the Seattle office established only that Kroll did *not* have a radio transmitter in his basement.

Shortly after receiving the Seattle report on Kroll and Thomas, J. Edgar Hoover contacted the Special Defense Unit of the Justice Department, which was charged with directing and coordinating all Justice Department activities relating to espionage, sabotage, and subversion.

With Hitler's invasion of Poland in the fall of 1939, the United States was already alert to the possibility of war with the Axis powers. In the spring of 1940, the Special Defense Unit had been created and charged with the responsibility of compiling lists of Axis aliens who had connections with their homelands. In the event of war, these lists would be used to determine which aliens were dangerous enough to warrant custodial detention. The Special Defense Unit was under the direction of L. M. C. Smith, heir to the Smith-Corona typewriter fortune. Under Smith's leadership, the SDU began compiling lists that classified aliens according to how dangerous they were considered. The most dangerous were categorized as "A" risks and recommended for immediate arrest in the event of war. Group "B" was considered somewhat less dangerous. Group "C" was believed to be the "least dangerous."

Hoover thought in March of 1941 that the activities of both Kroll and Thomas were suspicious enough to warrant recommending them as "A" risks to be "considered for custodial detention in the event of a national emergency." Along with the FBI dossiers on Kroll and Thomas which Hoover passed along to the Special Defense Unit, he promised that additional information would follow from time to time. Accordingly, the names of Kroll and Thomas were immediately added to the custodial detention lists kept by L. M. C. Smith.

By mid-1941, Hoover had read enough about Wolfgang Thomas "possibly (being) a German agent" that he instructed the Seattle office to conduct an independent investigation to learn the truth. He asked for immediate reports on the matter, and Seattle agents promptly began a surveillance of Thomas, finally interviewing him at his unfinished new home on Forty-ninth Street SW.

During the interview it was noted by the agent that there were

German books on the shelves, which did not appear to be propaganda, "but merely German books." Thomas was asked to explain how he had escaped German military service and immigrated to the United States. The reasons he gave included his age, bad kidneys, and an ulcer, which frequently hemorrhaged. Although he admitted feeling bitter because of the anti-German feelings that had kept him from getting a job in America, he remained "personally opposed to Hitler's form of government, because you could not feel free to say or do what you wished."

After the interview the Seattle FBI prepared a report for Hoover, dated September 22, 1941. It concluded with the comment, "Inasmuch as no information has been developed concerning espionage activity, this case is being closed." The same day, A. M. Cornelius, agent-in-charge of the Seattle office, "respectfully suggested" to Hoover that Thomas no longer be considered for custodial detention, since the Seattle office's investigation had failed to "reveal any evidentiary information which would warrant further consideration."

Hoover, however, did not accept the recommendation of his field office. Instead he sent the report to the SDU as evidence supporting detention. He wrote back that he had already recommended to the Special Defense Unit that Thomas be considered for detention. Because Thomas was an alien who had travelled to Germany, no action would be taken with respect to the Seattle office's recommendation. So it was Hoover himself who saw from Washington something subversive and dangerous in alien Wolfgang Thomas.

Meanwhile Lawrence Smith of the Special Defense Unit had responded on November 28 to Hoover's suspicions expressing extreme caution. Yes, he assured Hoover, Wolfgang Thomas was being "considered for possible detention" in the event of a presidential proclamation to that effect. But before taking any action, Smith wanted further investigation of Thomas, presumably to get answers which weren't apparent to him: Was Thomas engaged in subversive activities? Were any of Thomas's associates engaged in subversive activities? Was he working in a defense plant? Could he commit sabotage there? Was he an agent of the German government? Finally (perhaps because of official references to anonymous informants passing on hearsay information), Smith asked that Hoover include some statement as to the reliability and credibility of the informants providing the information.

If the Seattle office had been the sole judge, those were issues that had already been settled. In a report to Hoover of November 4, 1941, detailing further activities of Carl Kroll, the office reaffirmed its position that it considered the case of Wolfgang Thomas closed. Yet it was too late to stop the ball of suspicion which Hoover kept rolling, and on December 8, 1941, Attorney General Francis Biddle ordered the arrest and detention of Wolfgang Thomas.

While Wolfgang Thomas took up the regimen of daily walks at Ft. Lincoln, J. Edgar Hoover maintained that since Thomas had been turned over to the INS for detention, the matter of further investigation was out of his hands. The effect was to render nearly irreversible the innuendo, hearsay, and gossip that had led to Thomas's arrest.

Had Thomas known of Hoover's refusal to conduct further investigations, he would have been even more skeptical than he was after his hearing. Neither Dr. Sonnenberg nor Eddie Friedman knew those details, and they remained hopeful themselves that their own hearings would result in their release. This hope was bolstered by the news brought back to the barracks by the fourth *Wanderkameraden,* Richard Birkefeld, whose hearing had been an informal affair during which Lanier had seemed quite friendly.

Dr. Sonnenberg was next to go before the Hearing Board, accompanied by his wife and his brother Otto, who had come from San Francisco as witnesses. Again, as in Wolfgang Thomas's hearing, Lanier and the Board had Dr. Sonnenberg's FBI dossier spread out before them. That dossier began with a series of confidential reports to the San Francisco FBI. First came a statement to the effect that on May 28, 1940, a female informant had called the San Francisco FBI to report that Dr. Sonnenberg was "strongly pro-Nazi and favorable to Nazi leaders." The informant stated that she had it on hearsay that Dr. Sonnenberg had a brother in German intelligence and the doctor himself had served in the German army during the last war.

Then on June 4, 1940, the San Francisco FBI met with an informant who explained that he was "fairly well acquainted with some of the German colony in San Francisco." In the secrecy of the informant's office, the FBI learned that the man considered Dr. Sonnenberg to be the "most dangerous German in this area." Evidence of that danger, according to the informant, lay in the fact that Sonnenberg was on the staff of St. Joseph's Hospital, run by a German order of nuns who were "peasant girls" over whom it was possible for Dr. Sonnenberg to exercise considerable influence. On June 9, the San Francisco FBI office wrote up the informant's charges in a memo which went into Dr. Sonnenberg's file.

Less than a week later another informant reported that Dr. Sonnenberg was pro-Nazi. This information was followed two weeks later by an alert from the San Francisco Customs Office, advising that Sonnenberg was receiving German mail. However, translations of the letters revealed that they merely contained instructions concerning the disposition of German bonds the doctor had on bank deposit in that country.

On July 7, 1940, another informant's report was received by the San Francisco FBI. The informant confessed he had never seen the doctor in person, but related that it was "common rumor in San Fran-

cisco medical circles that Dr. Sonnenberg was pro-Nazi in
sympathy. . .and that two officers of the scuttled German liner *Colum-
bus* were living with him." A week later, it was further reported that Dr.
Sonnenberg was close to Fritz Wiedemann, the German Consul
General whose public, pro-Nazi comments continued to outrage the
San Francisco community (FBI, January 17, 1941).

By October of 1940 the San Francisco FBI had apparently heard
enough, and it recommended to the FBI headquarters that Dr. Arthur
Sonnenberg be considered for custodial detention in the event of a
national emergency. But more items were added to the file. At 6:30
p.m. on December 4, an informant with an office in the Flood Building, site of Sonnenberg's office, returned to his desk to file some ap-
pointments. Upon entering his office, he noticed a slip of blue paper on
the floor beneath an open window. Assuming the note had blown in
the window, he picked it up and read the following hand-printed message.

> We don't seem to be able to
> understand
> your sign language.
> Write a note for "Imp" and leave it
> in room 1083 with the nurse. Your's
> (sic) for a better signal.
>
> You do go farther with Signal.
> See you tomorrow.

Just what the curious note meant (other than the pun on what was then
a Signal Gas advertisement) or who wrote it was never established in
FBI reports subsequent to the one of January 17, 1941. But the note
was taken with enough seriousness to warrant further investigation of
Sonnenberg's mail by the Customs Office, which finally decided there
was "nothing of suspicious interest" to be found.

It was that series of informant rumors, hearsay reports, and cryptic
notes that prompted the FBI to conduct its first in-depth investigation
of the Sonnenbergs. The report, dated January 17, 1941, restated the
existing evidence, including the note that had blown in the window of
the Flood Building. (Still, no explanation was offered as to what the
note meant, or who had written it.) St. Joseph's Hospital was now
described by an informant as a breeding place for Nazi propaganda.
The nuns there, characterized as "not deep thinkers," received German
mail, and each nun had eight to ten outsiders to whom she passed on
propaganda.

There was, however, new evidence, gathered from a host of old and new informants. Most of the new information was as circumstantial and trivial as in previous reports, but there were three items which received lengthy and detailed descriptions.

The first was a narrative report from an informant who had attended a meeting in 1938 where San Francisco citizens had gathered to urge a boycott of Nazi goods. The meeting, at which the poet Louis Untermeyer delivered a speech critical of the German nation, had been interrupted by pro-Nazi hecklers. The informant had personally witnessed the police eject Dr. Sonnenberg from the meeting, after which the distraught and angry doctor was seen pacing outside the meeting "muttering to himself."

A second informant who often discussed the German situation with Dr. Sonnenberg reported that in his opinion, the doctor was pro-German (though not pro-Hitler). During these discussions with Dr. Sonnenberg, the informant argued that Germany and Britain would wear themselves out warring against each other, "and the U.S. would be the only power to win the war." It was a statement which incensed Dr. Sonnenberg, the informant claimed. Thereafter, the doctor had difficulty keeping his "emotions in check."

A third new piece of evidence was the report by an informant that Sonnenberg was so pro-German that he had had his two sons christened aboard the German ship *Karlsruhe,* when it had docked in San Francisco. (A christening aboard this ship had indeed taken place—of Sonnenberg's daughter.)

While the San Francisco FBI investigation continued, Hoover recommended in April to the Special Defense Unit that Sonnenberg be considered for custodial detention, noting further information would follow. Yet, three separate San Francisco field office investigations that spring failed to produce anything new on the doctor, who was still busily performing his medical duties. Typical of the insubstantial material which the reports accumulated was the news that the name and address of a suspicious Los Angeles associate of Dr. Sonnenberg was a dead end. There was no such street, the Los Angeles office reported, and the suspicious associate could not be located.

In September, Dr. Sonnenberg moved from 210 Vasquez Avenue, to a luxurious apartment at 3030 Pacific, overlooking the San Francisco waterfront and the bay. In October 1941, the San Francisco field office forwarded to Hoover a nine-page report. It was a restatement of previous information, which now by sheer force of repetition began to take on the appearance of substance. Yet the report also contained statements from Sonnenberg's medical colleagues who considered him a qualified, capable doctor who seemed "proud of his citizenship."

Since Dr. Sonnenberg still hadn't received his citizenship, perhaps evidence of his American pride was considered premature and unreliable. In any case, Sonnenberg busied himself for his citizenship exam, which he was scheduled to take on December 17, 1941. It would not take place. Instead, the *San Francisco Call Bulletin* reported on December 8, "Dr. Arthur Sonnenberg, widely known physician and surgeon here, was picked up and held today at the immigration station without official explanation. The doctor's incarceration came at the height of the roundup by FBI men of German, Japanese, and Italian aliens and others suspected of disloyalty to the United States."

After her husband's arrest and transfer to Ft. Lincoln, Lilly Sonnenberg quickly gathered recommendations from local physicians and acquaintances, which she sent to Ft. Lincoln in preparation for the hearing. Those references were included in the stack of documents which Lanier had with him at Sonnenberg's hearing. But there was a notable addition to the FBI dossier. It was a note from a patrol inspector at the camp, Frederick W. Harms, reporting that a "confidential informant" among the internees claimed Dr. Sonnenberg was a special friend of the San Francisco German Counsul General Fritz Wiedemann and wanted to establish a German government in the United States.

Lanier glanced at the note, while Sonnenberg, his wife, and brother Otto waited nervously for the first question.

"Now, Dr. Sonnenberg," Lanier finally began, "how could you entertain a subversive element like Mr. Wiedemann?"

Lanier's reference to the outspoken Wiedemann did not catch Sonnenberg by surprise. He and Otto had spent an hour before the hearing going over all the times he could recall having met socially with Wiedemann. Anticipating that those meetings might be a target of the Board's questions, he was prepared to explain that the Wiedemann dinner parties which he attended on several occasions were ceremonial, diplomatic events, with nothing conspiratorial or secretive about them. Dr. Sonnenberg explained that he considered the invitations he received to be polite acknowledgment of his respected position as a physician in the San Francisco German community.

"Mr. Wiedemann was always a gentlemen," Dr. Sonnenberg finished.

Lanier said, "Didn't you know what kind of man he was? It was in the papers?"

It was a reference to newspaper accounts of Wiedemann's activity in San Francisco. In May of 1941, when Wiedemann moved his consular offices to a brownstone mansion in Pacific Heights, at 2090 Jackson Street, outraged neighbors charged that the Nazi Wiedemann had a six-inch telescope installed, "to keep an eye on everything that goes on in the Golden gate" (*Time*). The telescope was so powerful, neighbors believed, that Wiedemann could see the gun batteries at Forts Barry, Baker, and Miley as if they were just across the street. In June, Wiedemann was arrested on charges of espionage. His principal accuser was Hungarian born Princess Stephanie Hohenlohe, who spent time with Wiedemann until deportation proceedings were instituted against her. The proceedings were cancelled, however, when she agreed to testify concerning Wiedemann's suspicious activities.

Confronted with the facts of his occasional associations with Wiedemann, Dr. Sonnenberg could feel his anger rising. Wiedemann's business was none of his. He had only been physician to the consulate.

"Dr. Sonnenberg," Lanier continued, "were you ever present with Mr. Wiedemann when the Nazi flag salute was given?"

Sonnenberg nodded. It was another question he and Otto had anticipated. He explained that he had been present at German Day ceremonies in San Francisco. The issue of which flag to show had been discussed beforehand, and all the elected San Francisco officials who were there as guests reluctantly agreed that the Nazi flag had to be shown, as a matter of courtesy, since the German ambassador was in attendance. Therefore, there had been a display of the Nazi flag.

Next, Lanier pressed Sonnenberg on why he had taken pains to have his son baptized aboard the ship the *Karlsruhe* when it was in San Francisco. Sonnenberg explained that it was his daughter who had been baptized, and it had been done at his wife's request. But Lanier continued to pursue his point. Wasn't the baptism aboard ship in lieu of baptism on German soil?

"That had nothing to do with it!" Sonnenberg raised his voice. "My daughter was baptized in the faith of my forefathers. She is an American citizen!"

But Lanier quickly continued by asking what language the doctor spoke at home. When Sonnenberg confessed that he spoke German, Lanier turned to the Board. "This man has lived here twenty-some years, and he still speaks the German language!"

"By God!" Sonnenberg swore. "I didn't know it was a crime to speak the language my mother taught me."

The hearing lasted fifteen minutes. When he returned to his barracks, Sonnenberg was quick to tell those who surrounded him, "At least I saved my self respect." Then he sat down on his bunk and began to shake.

Edward Heims, like Friedman a doctor of law, had escaped Germany with a good portion of the fortune which he had accumulated as a lawyer and a banker. Feeling that land ownership would be a good investment in America, and interested in farming, he bought a sizable farm near Inverness, California, and constructed sanitary milkbarns for dairy farming.

It was soon rumored, however, that Heims's ranch and milkbarns on the coast would be an excellent airstrip and camouflaged hangar for German and Japanese planes in the event of war. With his arrest and detention at Ft. Lincoln, Heims set up an office in the corner of barracks 31C, using his wealth to hire other detainees to act as typists and secretaries for the volumes of letters he sent out appealing his case. Despite the humiliation of detention, he remained a bossy, arrogant man who considered it beneath his dignity to bus his dishes in the mess hall.

It was Heims who went before the Hearing Board next, and it shocked Eddie Friedman to see this self-assured man stripped of all his confidence. Horace Young, chairman of the Board, had begun by explaining in Yiddish the purpose and format of the hearings. When Heims confessed he didn't understand Yiddish, Young seemed delighted for having exposed Heims as a bogus Jew.

Consequently, when it was Eddie Friedman's turn finally to present himself to the Hearing Board, he expected Young to challenge the fact that he was a Jew who also did not speak Yiddish. He prepared to defend himself by pointing out that very few German Jews understood it.

But Lanier began on another track. He asked Friedman to explain his relationship to a "Mr. Caracas," and the question caught Friedman off guard. Eddie denied knowing anyone by that name. Lanier's disbelief was obvious. Eddie struggled to recall who it could be he was referring to and he asked Lanier to repeat the name. Perhaps, since his own English was so poor, he wasn't understanding properly. Lanier repeated the name "Caracas" slowly and with irritation. Then it struck Eddie. He had a friend in Hamburg who was now in Caracas, Venezuela. That must be it! He was one of the people to whom he wrote while passing his time working as an elevator operator on weekends in San Francisco. Now he explained the connection while the Board and Lanier listened with embarrassment.

The Board pressed him to explain *why* he owned a typewriter. The implication was that he was using it for secret correspondence. Eddie explained carefully that it was only for his personal letters.

Then Eddie was asked if he knew anybody in Germany.

"No, they are all dead." Eddie saw a chance to work in his own story as a Jewish refugee. "My brother hanged himself in a concentra-

tion camp. My uncle died in a camp. They would not give him his
pills."

"You have no one else?"

"No."

"You have no friends?"

"Yes, I still have friends."

"That is what we are asking!" Lanier snapped.

"None of them are Nazis," Eddie said quietly.

Finally, the Board began to probe into Eddie's acquaintances in the
United States. Specifically, he was asked to explain his relationship with
the Baroness von Rescnizeck. It was clear to Eddie that the Baroness had
somehow aroused the suspicions of the authorities, and he took pains to
emphasize that other than on the occasion where she had expressed her
anti-Nazi sentiments, he had never spoken privately with her. He
merely delivered his pastries and left.

Lanier thanked Eddie politely for his testimony and dismissed
him. Eddie left aware that it was his relationship with the Baroness von
Rescnizeck that had aroused the most suspicion on the Board. "Obviously I have been watched making those deliveries," Eddie concluded
later in a letter to the National Refugee Service, "and become suspected
therefore to the FBI."

While *Die Wanderkameraden* waited anxiously to hear the recommendations of the Hearing Board, they napped, played cards, did their
laundry, attended lectures, wrote letters, or relived their hearings, trying to find some clue to the prospects of release. Dr. Sonnenberg kept
medical office hours in the hospital just outside the west end of the
compound. He had volunteered his services to the camp, and the offer
had been eagerly accepted by G. P. Lipp, the Bismarck physician who
was under contract to Ft. Lincoln but whose practice prevented him
from keeping regular office hours there. In his place, Dr. Ludwig
Borovicka, a medical officer off one of the Standard Oil tankers, treated
the detainees. But back in December, Dr. Lipp had complained that
Borovicka ordered "unnecessary X-ray plates, unnecessary special medi-
cines, and other therapeutic measures" for the Nazi sailors in camp.
Now, it was hoped, with Dr. Sonnenberg to balance off the coddling of
Dr. Borovicka, camp medical procedures would go more smoothly.

With the arrival of the first Japanese aliens at Ft. Lincoln in early
February, Doctors Sonnenberg, Borovicka, and Lipp were permitted
inside the Japanese compound to go from barracks to barracks, vac-
cinating everyone against smallpox. The Japanese accepted their shots
and their detention stoically, and Dr. Sonnenberg was able to learn only

that many of them were farmers from around coastal military installations and airfields. When Dr. Sonnenberg brought that report back to his friends, it was ironically the arrogant and contemptuous Heims who was the most sympathetic, finding in the Japanese situation something of the specific injustices of his own case.

The Germans in the camp saw the Japanese close up only during mealtimes. The mess hall had been divided into two wings with two kitchens and two separate mess lines, one of which served a diet more agreeable to the Japanese than the German wurst-and-potato staple. On their walks around the inside fence perimeter, *Die Wanderkameraden*, joined now by Heims, passed slowly along the double row of fence and stared through at the Japanese, who sometimes gathered along their side of the fence, fingers curled in the cyclone fence holes, and stared back.

It was during these walks that the first of several incidents occurred which would inflame Eddie Friedman's bitterness. He related them in a letter to A. S. Hudson on February 19, 1942. One morning, while passing along the fence near the brick barracks where a small group of the fanatical Nazi sailors—the *Schlageter*—regularly congregated, one of the Nazis pointed at *Die Wanderkameraden* and shouted at Eddie Friedman, "All Jews should be shot!"

Dr. Sonnenberg tried to pass over the incident by characterizing the *Schlageter* as fools. But then a few days later in the barracks that had been renovated to show movies, the same sailor refused to let Eddie sit on a crowded bench. "I do not want to have a Jew sitting next to me," he announced.

Finally one day, Dr. Sonnenberg recalled, after he, Eddie Friedman, and Heims had eaten together in the mess hall, Heims, as usual, refused to bus his tray after dinner. Walking back to 31C, they were caught up with by an angry mess steward. "Hey, you dirty kike!" He spun Heims around. "Bus your dishes!"

Dr. Sonnenberg separated the two men, then accompanied Heims back into the mess hall for protection. Eddie knew Heims was to blame, but he couldn't help noticing—and it rankled—that other men who refused or forgot to bus their dishes did not receive the same threats.

On February 13, 1942, Attorney General Francis Biddle issued an order of parole for Arthur Robert Sonnenberg. The order stipulated that Sonnenberg be paroled to the custody of a reputable U.S. citizen of San Francisco, and was conditional upon his reporting weekly to his sponsor and twice a month to the INS in San Francisco. That order was forwarded to Ft. Lincoln, and on February 18, A. S. Hudson wrote to

Dr. Sonnenberg inside the compound that "Authority has been received for your release." Sonnenberg promptly met with Hudson to sign an affidavit agreeing to the parole conditions. Then he wired his wife Lilly in San Francisco, "WILL BE PAROLED."

Next, he was given an official travel letter that, according to the Justice Department, was supposed to avoid "embarrassment to the alien enemy in his performance of the travel."

Finally, he said goodbye to *Die Wanderkameraden,* each of whom had cause to hope now that his own parole would come just as suddenly. By nightfall, Dr. Sonnenberg was gone.

The effect of Sonnenberg's parole on the remaining *Wanderkameraden,* especially Eddie Friedman, was short-lived. Their buoyant spirits gave way quickly to the relentless *Gitterkrankheit* — the fence sickness. Now it was worse than before. For Eddie Friedman, Dr. Sonnenberg's quiet, intelligent companionship had been a tonic which he didn't fully appreciate until Sonnenberg had left.

"My dear Wanderkameraden," Eddie wrote Dr. Sonnenberg on February 20. He thanked him for the "many aimless kilometers walked in the icy winter of North Dakota, 1941-42," and for helping *Die Wanderkameraden* "jointly to suffer through the Gitterkrankheit." Eddie signed the postcard, added the note, "Don't forget your fellow camp birds," and then he had all the other men in 31C sign it also.

With each day that passed bringing no news on his parole, Eddie Friedman began now to dwell again on the ironic senselessness of it. They were confining him with the very jackbooted Nazi element he had fled in Germany. In England, he knew, the Jewish refugees were separated from the so-called Aryan Germans. Why should he be forced to stay in a camp where inmates gave the Hitler salute to each other and swastikas decorated the rooms?

While Eddie Friedman fretted over his situation, Wolfgang Thomas and Richard Birkefeld volunteered to work as clerks in the Liaison Office just inside the east gate to the compound. Thomas immediately won the respect of Patrol Inspector Red Selland, second in command in the Liaison Office. Selland appreciated having Wolfgang handy for typing copies of the mounds of records and documents that piled up as new detainees arrived. Thomas's typewriter clattered all day long as he typed copy after copy, using the same piece of carbon paper until it was tattered and torn. But when Selland tried to point out that a fresh piece of carbon paper would make the dim copies readable, Thomas lectured him on the foolishness of being wasteful when there was a war going on.

It was not long before Selland offered to write a recommendation for parole on behalf of Thomas. Thomas accepted the offer graciously, but inside he was skeptical that a minor official like Selland, no matter how warmhearted he was, could stir the bureaucracy.

With Sonnenberg gone, and Thomas and Birkefeld working as clerks, it left only the irritating Heims to walk with, so Eddie Friedman gave up his compound hikes and concentrated on writing more and more letters in hopes of striking a responsive chord with somebody who could gain his release.

"I came here to be saved from Nazi persecution," he wrote the National Refugee Service on February 25, 1942, "and now, what fateful irony, this land of freedom just locked me together with the same people she gave me shelter against.... Of course, everybody here knows me being a Jewish refugee, who ought to be shot such a bad Kyke he is, as they are shouting very often at me here."

So Eddie slept or wrote letters through February and March, hardly paying attention to the news that A. S. Hudson had been replaced by Ike McCoy as new OIC of Ft. Lincoln. Eddie merely went on writing his letters of appeal to anybody he could think of.

Then one day Richard Birkefeld burst into the barracks and interrupted Eddie's letter writing. According to Birkefeld, who had been called out of his bed to go to the Liaison Office to take stenographic notes, a Japanese internee named Jinosuke Higashi had felt so dishonored and disgraced by detention that he had just committed suicide after his barracks comrades had given him a farewell party. News of Higashi's death spread quickly throughout the compound and was hailed by the Japanese as an honorable escape from a dishonorable situation.

The suicide was followed shortly by a week-long, violent blizzard with icy winds which kept many of the men inside. Despite the cold, many of the detainees turned out to witness the arrival of an additional seven hundred Japanese from Terminal Island, Los Angeles. Thinly clad and bareheaded, the Japanese arrivals "stepped gingerly in the brisk weather," *The Bismarck Tribune* reported (February 26, 1942). There were "cries of recognition and back-slapping as the new detainees met their Japanese friends" who had been brought to Ft. Lincoln weeks earlier. The idle German seamen braved the cold to gather along the fence alley and watch those greetings and celebrations, fascinated by allies who would kill themselves rather than accept the humiliation of detention by the enemy.

The days following the arrival of the new Japanese, the entire camp was a beehive of clerical activity. In the Liaison Office, Thomas and Birkefeld were kept busy daily typing out billeting lists and filing Alien Enemy Questionnaires that the Japanese filled out in their barracks.

Throughout this busy time, Wolfgang Thomas continued to worry about the final disposition of his own case. It had been almost two months since his hearing, and as each week passed with no news, and as others were paroled, he began to suspect that his case was encumbered with vague suspicions that could never be disproved. "We have nothing specific. It is only the potential," they had told him at his hearing. But what potential, he wondered. How could he clear himself of something so general? It all gave him the sinking feeling that he might be facing internment for the duration of the war because of some vague potential that had a momentum as relentless as the war itself.

In keeping with Wolfgang's worst fears, that vague potential *had* developed a momentum of its own. Despite J. Edgar Hoover's refusal in December to investigate Thomas further after the Special Defense Unit had asked for it, the Seattle office of the FBI continued to investigate a case it had already closed, submitting to Hoover on January 9, 1942, another report on Thomas.

The report was a rehash of previous rehashes. If anything, what was new in the report ought to have been to Wolfgang's credit: one informant stated that Thomas's sympathies were anti-Hitler, another reported that Thomas appeared elated to be able to leave Germany. The report was followed a few days later by a translation of the documents that had been seized when Thomas was arrested. An FBI memo of February 7 stated the translation revealed "nothing of importance in his diary, and letters which were strictly personal."

Meanwhile, as Thomas sweated out news of parole, Hoover either must have forgotten he had refused to investigate further, or changed his mind, for he forwarded the January Seattle report to the Special Defense Unit of the Justice Department. Ironically and sadly, the SDU felt the FBI evidence against Thomas was not satisfactory to substantiate the charge. Nevertheless it immediately classified Thomas in Group A, that group consisting of individuals who in the event of war were "considered to be the most dangerous."

With the arrival of April in North Dakota, and the first buds of spring, Wolfgang Thomas received the news that, whereas he was not a naturalized citizen and had therefore been apprehended as potentially dangerous, and whereas the Alien Enemy Hearing Board had heard his case, "Now therefore upon consideration of the evidence," Attorney General Francis Biddle wrote on March 25, "it is ordered that Wolfgang Thomas be interned."

It was weeks before Wolfgang could write to Margareta to tell her the news in a manner that would not break her spirit. Still, with resignation, she wrote McCoy and asked if she might be permitted to visit Ft. Lincoln twice a week with her children, who, she told Wolfgang, "should not lose contact with their father."

Meanwhile, with the news that Thomas had been ordered interned indefinitely, Eddie Friedman struggled harder than ever against the *Gitterkrankheit* which beset him. Then Heims was beaten up in the mess hall, and Eddie lost whatever semblance of patience he had been able to manufacture.

The incident involved a seaman named Otto Bernsdorf, who objected to having Jews sitting at his table in the mess hall. On the day of the attack, Bernsdorf demanded to know who had given Heims permission to sit there. Heims said that he had been seated there by the steward, but Bernsdorf stepped back and delivered a solid, roundhouse slap to the left side of Heims's face.

Bernsdorf fled the mess hall, while Heims retreated to his barracks. Bernsdorf received two weeks in solitary confinement in the guardhouse, but some of his shipmates and barracks comrades considered Heims the villain. Since he seldom came out of his barracks corner to face this ridicule, the seamen took out their anger on Eddie Friedman. "Jew...dirty Jew!" they hissed at him when he passed them in the detention area.

In February, before the Heims-Bernsdorf incident, Eddie Friedman had written a long, desperate letter to the National Refugee Service in New York, telling them about the anti-Semitic taunts he had been subjected to at Ft. Lincoln. "I refrained up till now from asking your help because I thought you might be bothered enough with other people's troubles. Now I am in such a jam that I have to ask for your kindly help." What he wanted, he wrote, was for the National Refugee Service to take up his case with Edward Ennis, director of the Alien Enemy Control Unit.

The National Refugee Service moved quickly to inform Ennis of Friedman's plight. Ennis then wrote W. F. Kelly in Philadelphia on March 23 and asked him to investigate Friedman's allegations that "detainees at the camp are making life difficult for him." Kelly in turn passed the order for an investigation on to McCoy at Ft. Lincoln.

It was four days later, at 5:50 p.m., March 28, that a coded radiogram was sent to Ft. Lincoln from the INS. The instructions were to parole Eddie Friedman. Eddie might have had cause to celebrate, at least until he discovered the conditions upon which his parole had been granted: he could not return to San Francisco, which was a restricted area for alien enemies; and he had to supply the INS with a list of sponsors from outside the prohibited area. Sadly, then, Eddie tele-grammed Liesl on March 30, "Paroled for unprohibited area." It was a message which wouldn't encourage her to hope for too much, since he felt it would be difficult if not impossible to find anybody outside San Francisco who would agree to sponsor him.

The next morning Eddie wrote a message to McCoy, officially spell-ing out the impossible conditions of his parole. Then he gave McCoy five prospective sponsors, all of whom lived in San Francisco.

McCoy forwarded Friedman's list of sponsors to INS headquarters in Philadelphia, noting that he had advised Dr. Friedman that his improper list of sponsors would delay his parole. On the same day, April 1, McCoy sent W. F. Kelly of the Border Patrol a one-page report of his investigation into the charges Friedman had made that he was the victim of anti-Semitism at Ft. Lincoln. In the report, McCoy wrote unsympathetically, "Mr. Friedman is one of about six Jewish members of this camp. . . . They have caused us considerable trouble playing up this persecution complex and, as a matter of fact, their entire troubles are brought on by themselves. It is admitted of course," McCoy con-cluded the report, "that Jews are in a very unfavorable light and are naturally unpopular with the German detainees at this camp."

Eddie's telegram to Liesl announcing his parole put her into just the state of expectancy which he had hoped to avoid. Her first act was to advise the Viennese couple, whose pastries she had continued to deliver in Eddie's absence, that she was temporarily unavailable for service because she had to clean and scrub in hurried preparation for Eddie's arrival. Then she sent Eddie road maps which she imagined he would need to plot his course back to San Francisco. These were immediately confiscated by the Ft. Lincoln censor.

Eddie followed his telegram to Liesl with a long letter that ex-plained he could be released provided they moved to an unrestricted area and were able to furnish sponsors. Liesl went immediately to the U.S. attorney in San Francisco, Frank Hennessey, and she explained to him that Eddie's parole conditions were impossible. Then using all the diplomacy she had developed in dealing with authorities in Germany, she asked graciously for Hennessey's advice. He assured her that if the Friedmans couldn't dig up a sponsor in the new community, the authorities would provide one in the person of a sheriff or a police officer, or, they would finally accept the sponsors Eddie had chosen in the San Francisco area. Hennessey suggested that if she wanted to do her best for Eddie in the meantime, she should go to see the San Francisco INS parole officer, identified only as Mr. Kuckein.

Liesl went straight to Kuckein's office, and the parole officer con-ceded that temporary parole in San Francisco was possible, but he advised her to write to McCoy, whose authority was final in the case.

On April 3, then, Liesl Friedman sat down and wrote a long letter to Mr. McCoy, pleading with him to "take this matter up with the INS headquarters in Philadelphia." Pointing out that the San Francisco authorities had already admitted that temporary parole in San Francisco was possible, she concluded, "Please, Mr. McCoy, do help us in this difficult situation. We really are willing to do everything that we are asked to do, but in this case it is beyond our ability to comply with the request made."

Liesl's letter to McCoy put the responsibility of Eddie's parole gently in McCoy's lap. But he wasn't ready yet to accept the authority which Liesl was pleading with him to exercise. His first reaction to her letter was to forward a copy of it to Kuckein in San Francisco, who had already heard Liesl's appeal face-to-face.

There the matter of Eddie's parole rested for two weeks until April 22, when McCoy finally wrote Philadelphia and reminded them that Eddie's parole order hadn't yet been sent to the San Francisco INS. "Perhaps you can expedite this case," he prodded his superiors, who must have been waiting for somebody else to decide if the Friedmans could stay in San Francisco.

In the same letter, McCoy objected to Philadelphia's suggestion that Jews in Ft. Lincoln could be segregated in order to eliminate the problems associated with Heims and Friedman. While assuring his bosses that detainees who mistreated Jews would be firmly disciplined, McCoy offered his opinion that segregating the Jews would "show a sign of weakness on our part, which would have an unsatisfactory effect on the camp as a whole." The note to his superiors concluded with McCoy's conviction that, "almost without exception, these instances of violence had been provoked by the Jewish detainees themselves."

McCoy's description of the problem must have convinced Philadelphia authorities that the ultimate separation of the likes of Heims and Friedman from the tormentors could only be achieved by parole. On April 24, almost a month after the Hearing Board had recommended parole, Eddie Friedman received the news that his parole to San Francisco had at last been approved. That night Eddie sent a night letter to Liesl, advising her, "Restrictions apparently lifted," inserting apparently because he wasn't sure what had happened. But he was certain now he was heading home, and he instructed Liesl to "Stop Moving Actions," in the event she was planning on relocating to some unrestricted area.

Late the next afternoon, Eddie was called for the last time to McCoy's office, where he received written authority for travel, specifying that he would leave for San Francisco that evening at 7:30 p.m. by Northern Pacific train. He signed his travel orders, shook hands with

McCoy, who wished him good luck, and returned to his barracks to get his suitcase.

Outside barracks 31C, he said goodbye to Wolfgang Thomas, who invited Eddie to come to Seattle some day and see his beautiful new home above Puget Sound. Washington was beautiful, Thomas declared; it wasn't all flat, like North Dakota.

Eddie walked to the east gate just as the sun set beyond the row of Dutch elms along the brick barracks. He was driven into Bismarck, where he boarded a train bound for Butte, Montana. During the five-hour layover in Butte, Eddie went to the platform agent and asked, "What is interesting in Butte?"

"Only the whorehouses," the agent smiled cynically.

To stretch his legs, Eddie took a walk through the city, past the row of wooden whorehouses which had fake, unpainted fronts like old ghost town buildings. Women old enough to be his grandmother, Eddie thought, hung out of the windows and stared at him as he gaped at them. He walked briskly back to the train depot, moved by the sight of those old hags, who were truly pathetic and doomed. He promised himself that he would not complain to Liesl about his detention. It was nothing, he assured himself. It's over. It was harder on Liesl than me...she could only stew and make a fuss.

Eddie arrived at the Ferry Building in San Francisco at 8:25 a.m., April 28. It was a warm, clear day, and Eddie decided to walk the nearly two miles to his apartment. But by the time he reached Pierce and Sacramento, his shoulder ached, his fingers were clawed from gripping the heavy suitcase, and he was short of breath.

Despite his aching legs, he climbed the steps to his apartment two at a time, opened the door quietly, and stepped into the hallway. "It's me," he called out. "Hello...I'm home."

After his parole from Ft. Lincoln on February 13, 1942, Dr. Arthur Sonnenberg returned to San Francisco to resume his medical practice. In May, the FBI officially considered its investigation of him closed. Yet the classification of "dangerous enemy alien" had been stuck on him, and curfew remained a condition of his parole. Sonnenberg immediately called the San Francisco Police Department and requested a police escort, which he volunteered to pay for, so that he could make night house calls. The offer was refused. The curfew stood. Shortly thereafter, an appendectomy was commenced at 7:00 p.m. At 7:45 p.m., the surgery still in progress, Dr. Sonnenberg excused himself and left a colleague to finish the operation. He arrived at home just in time to beat the 8:00 p.m. curfew.

Though released from custody, Sonnenberg's alien status brought him again before the authorities. On December 1, 1942, he faced an Individual Exclusion Hearing Board in San Francisco, to show cause why, as an alien enemy, he should not be removed from the Western Defense Command, which included California. At the hearing, his wife complained that he had already cleared himself before an Alien Enemy Hearing Board at Ft. Lincoln. "This is double jeopardy," she insisted.

Before the Exclusion Board, Sonnenberg repeated what he had earlier told the Hearing Board. His German connections in San Francisco, especially with Consul General Fritz Wiedemann, were strictly cultural. He had treated and entertained crew members of the *Columbus* while they were detained at Angel Island. He insisted that it was a ludicrous rumor that the nuns at St. Joseph's Hospital were pro-Nazi. He explained that he had not been thrown out of the 1938 boycott meeting, but rather had left on his own accord because the speaker had called the whole German country a nation of sadists. Finally, he stated that since 1936, he had "lost hope of any good being accomplished" in Germany, because of the violent persecution which had taken place. With respect to the war, Dr. Sonnenberg felt, "it is unfortunate there has to be a war to the finish, but there is no question about it.... I want to see the U.S. the victor."

Upon consideration of that testimony, the Exclusion Board surprisingly concluded that Dr. Sonnenberg was "not only pro-German but pro-Nazi." On January 27, 1943, the headquarters of the Western Defense Command ordered him exiled from San Francisco.

Armed with professional recommendations from the San Francisco medical community, Dr. Sonnenberg travelled to St. Louis in his 1938 Buick, and he began medical service there as a staff physician in a local hospital.

On June 25, 1943, the St. Louis field office submitted the last official FBI report on Dr. Sonnenberg. In this report, Sonnenberg's colleagues in St. Louis commented that he was cooperative, never talked about war politics, and was not involved in any acts of a subversive or undemocratic nature.

A month later on July 16, Attorney General Biddle issued a stinging memorandum to J. Edgar Hoover and the Special Defense Unit of the Justice Department, which brought an end to the system of detention lists and danger classifications that had been applied to Dr. Sonnenberg, Wolfgang Thomas, Eddie Friedman, and other enemy aliens. Biddle's memorandum directed the FBI and the SDU to cease keeping custodial detention lists on aliens, and to stop classifying people as to dangerousness. "It is now clear to me that this classification system is inherently unreliable," Biddle explained his actions. "The evidence used for the purpose of making these classifications was inadequate; the standards applied to the evidence for the purpose of making the classification were defective; and finally, the notion that it is possible to make a valid determination of how dangerous a person is...without reference to time, environment, and other relevant circumstances is impractical, unwise, and dangerous."

Four months later, on November 13, 1943, Biddle officially ordered Sonnenberg released from parole. In the spring of 1944, Sonnenberg and his wife Lilly returned to San Francisco, where he resumed his medical practice.

In 1949, Senator William Langer of North Dakota visited the Sonnenbergs in their Pacific Heights apartment. During the visit, Dr. Sonnenberg explained that he still had not been permitted to secure the U.S. citizenship he was two weeks away from receiving when he was arrested in 1941. Three days later, he was called and sworn as a citizen of the United States. After the ceremony, the officials apologized. "You have been under suspicion as being one of the most dangerous men on the West Coast. Of course, there was not a bit of truth to it, Doctor. It was just wartime hysteria."

Shortly after Eddie Friedman was released to go home, Edward Heims was paroled, and Richard Birkefeld was released to North Dakota, where he ran a country store. That left Wolfgang Thomas, who had been ordered interned, the last of *Die Wanderkameraden* at Ft. Lincoln. Not wanting to hike alone, he stopped walking the camp perimeter, and his ulcers worsened. He continued to do clerical work for Red Selland in the Liaison Office, and the two men became close friends. Thomas did the clerical work generated by the transfer of the Japanese at Ft. Lincoln to other camps for permanent internment. Germans, who like Thomas had been ordered interned, were also transferred out of Ft. Lincoln, still officially only a "detention station," to permanent internment facilities at Stringtown, Ohio, and elsewhere.

Red Selland and Will Robbins of the Liaison Office spoke so highly of Thomas's dedication and service that he was permitted to remain at Ft. Lincoln. He continued then to perform valuable clerical work in the Liaison Office, mainly preparing internee payrolls. Margareta Thomas moved to Bismarck that May with the two small Thomas children, to spend the summer months with Wolfgang, visiting him twice a week.

While the FBI continued its investigation of Carl Kroll, Thomas's father-in-law, Thomas wrote Attorney General Biddle pleading for a rehearing of his case. On September 1, 1942, a reconvened Alien Enemy Hearing Board, led by P. W. Lanier, met at Ft. Lincoln to reconsider paroling Wolfgang Thomas. Red Selland testified at the hearing on behalf of Thomas. Margareta attended the hearing, testifying at length concerning her father's character and patriotism. Then in private, all previous FBI reports on the case were reconsidered by the Board, and a Seattle FBI agent introduced the latest FBI report on Carl Kroll, whom the Justice Department was now attempting to strip of citizenship. After reviewing the case, the Board voted unanimously to continue the internment of Wolfgang Thomas.

Under treatment then at the Ft. Lincoln Hospital for bleeding gastric ulcers and chronic gall bladder disease, Thomas wrote immediately to Lanier, expressing his disappointment. "I have always lived a clean and honest life," he felt, "and so I consider the decision a disgrace to my family and myself, and punishment for something I have not done."

Despite Red Selland's and Mr. McCoy's efforts to keep Thomas at Ft. Lincoln for clerical work, he was transferred that fall to Stringtown, Ohio, and Margareta returned to Seattle with the children. Next to Stringtown, Thomas wrote Margareta December 4, "Bismarck was a paradise." For Wolfgang, Stringtown had a penitentiary atmosphere, with smashed windows, cockroaches, and worst of all, pro-Nazi radicals.

As a cure for the continuing ulcers and gall bladder problems, the doctors at Stringtown recommended removal of several of Wolfgang's teeth. Afterwards "my condition became worse," Thomas wrote in January of 1943 to the War Department, which operated Stringtown. Thomas also wrote to tell Mr. McCoy at Ft. Lincoln that after four months at Stringtown, he still couldn't get used to the camp. In the letter, he recalled that there had been a young seaman who had taught a course for detainees dealing with the American constitution and preparation for citizenship. Would McCoy send him copies of the books used in the course? (The seaman referred to was Kurt Peters.)

McCoy complied, and Thomas began reading and preparing for his American citizenship. Margareta, who had come to Ohio to be with Wolfgang again, went off to Washington, where she met with Edward Ennis of the Alien Enemy Control Unit, to argue for her husband's release. Ennis asked McCoy for his recommendation, and McCoy turned to Red Selland in the Liaison Office, where Thomas had worked for ten months.

Figuring that Will Robbins's authority might be more persuasive than his, Red Selland asked Robbins to write the recommendation for Wolfgang Thomas this time. Robbins wrote then that he was convinced Thomas was entirely trustworthy and a man of high moral character for whom all possible leniency should be shown.

While Thomas waited for a decision on his appeal, the commander of Stringtown recognized a mistake had been made. He wrote the Alien Enemy Control Unit that the German aliens who had been transferred from North Dakota didn't belong with the rabid Latin-American German radicals he had in his camp. As a result, 150 harmless "dangerous enemy aliens" were transferred back to Ft. Lincoln. Thomas was reunited with his old bosses and friends, Red Selland and Will Robbins. In the evenings, Thomas walked by himself along the interior fence perimeter of Ft. Lincoln, beneath the row of Dutch elms where *Die Wanderkameraden* had hiked more than a year and a half before. They were leafing out now in the warm North Dakota spring. Passing the houses where the ships' officers lived, Wolfgang admired their little gardens with beds of rich, wildly colored flowers. How long, he wondered, would it be before he could get back to his own garden?

On May 28, 1943, Attorney General Biddle ordered Wolfgang Thomas paroled. "Released!" Thomas telegrammed Margareta, "Send Grey Suit Immediately." He departed Ft. Lincoln for the last time on June 5. Two days later, he was back in his new home among his garden flowers. He had been interned for two-and-one-half years. Still, he confessed no bitterness in a letter to Ike McCoy, thanking him for all the consideration he had been given at Ft. Lincoln. "It is a wonderful feeling," he only wanted McCoy to know, "to be home with my family again."

Eddie Friedman returned to his apartment on the corner of Pierce and Sacramento in San Francisco, where he and Liesl lived for the next twenty-five years. In 1944 Eddie became a naturalized U.S. citizen. For a while during the war, he worked as a shipfitter, even though Liesl argued that he couldn't drive a nail. With a twinkle in her eye, she told her friends that the ships Eddie was building would never float.

After the war, Eddie capitalized on his experience selling pastries to secure work selling cosmetics door-to-door on the West Coast. He never returned to the practice of law. But for the thirty-nine years he sold cosmetics, he always fixed his deep, sad eyes on each new customer and introduced himself proudly, "I am Doctor Friedman."

The Railroaders

AN INTERNEE WORK PROGRAM AND AN ESCAPE

Above, the "Pumpernickel Parade," entering the Ft Lincoln compound through the main gate (the east gate), August 1941 This gate was the site of the near riot in 1943 over the return of Lothar Baas to camp (Courtesy of Will Robbins)

Poster which was put up October 3, 1943, by internees who objected to railroad work. Translation: "Railroaders: The *Schlageter* (Nazis) are watching you!"

Patrol Inspector Boyd Kimmins, who helped quell the near riot in 1943 (Courtesy of Boyd Kimmins)

Below, Northern Pacific Railroad internee track gang workers, 1943, Steele, North Dakota (Courtesy of Victor Petereit)

The Railroaders

Shortly after the arrest of the first enemy aliens in December of 1941, the Justice Department issued written instructions to the directors of all detention facilities spelling out the minimum standards of treatment to be accorded the detainees. Those standards were based upon provisions of the Geneva Convention relating to the treatment of POWs. In explaining its motive for extending the Geneva Convention to include civilians, the Justice Department voiced concern for U.S. nationals abroad. "Nothing must be done or permitted to be done...(which would provide) an excuse under the guise of retaliation for harsh treatment and cruel abuse of nationals of this country in the hands of our enemies," wrote an assistant to the attorney general, April 28, 1942.

One of the provisions of the Geneva Convention which proved the most difficult to apply to enemy aliens was the restriction concerning work. Several articles of the Convention stated that a prisoner could not be compelled to do work which would aid the war effort he had fought against.

Despite that restriction, the use of imprisoned men for railroad work was irresistible to both sides. On March 13, 1942, Senator Robert Reynolds of the Senate Committee on Military Affairs wondered "why we can't use those enemy aliens to help win the war against their respective countries....The Axis powers are making utilization of all the enslaved manpower over there in building railroads....Why can't we?" (Grodzins, 334).

Strangely enough, railroad work was an idea that appealed to some of the enemy aliens at Ft. Lincoln who were eager to prove their American loyalties. Others merely wanted the opportunity to pass the time of day doing meaningful work — beyond planting carrots in the compound gardens.

Accordingly, in late April of 1943, when the Justice Department finally agreed to hold parole hearings for the interned seamen at Ft.

Lincoln, sixty-two of these men were released into the custody of the Northern Pacific Railroad as track gang workers. Subsequent to their departure, some five hundred men signed up for a general work program in hopes of easing the boredom of confinement. The work of the track gang parolees proved so successful that in July of 1943, Ike McCoy received a call from the Northern Pacific asking for more men for right-of-way maintenance work. McCoy explained that he had another five hundred men interested in work, but they were all still considered dangerous enemy aliens who would need strict supervision and guarding if they were to work on the railroads.

Reassured by the railroads that the work would be away from the Canadian border, and outside of populated areas, McCoy wired the Central Office in Philadelphia on July 30, asking for approval. Philadelphia granted McCoy his request, with the important condition that the Northern Pacific Railroad hire and pay for additional civilian guards to supplement the patrol inspectors assigned to the track gang.

Inside the Ft. Lincoln compound, news that supervised track gang work was available bitterly divided the internees. Railroad work was clearly treasonous, argued the outspoken *Schlageter*. Immediately, the list of five hundred work volunteers diminished to just over a hundred men. In deference to the camp Nazis, this group suggested that they receive a ruling on the matter from the Swiss Legation, responsible for handling German affairs in the United States. Since the Swiss had already granted approval for forest work, the prospective *Eisenbahner*, or railroaders, were confident they would receive similar approval. However, such an approval did not appeal to the *Schlageter*, who felt the Swiss Legation had tainted itself by condoning forest work. The *Schlageter* would be appeased by no ruling short of a wire direct from Berlin.

Gerhard Sprenger, who had replaced the uncooperative Captain Fred Stengler as camp spokesman, immediately ordered the Swiss to wire Berlin for approval of railroad work. When word was received by cable that Berlin had no objections, only the most die-hard Nazis in camp continued to insist that the volunteers were traitors.

The workers elected internee Karl Klein as their spokesman, and on August 5 Klein sent a memo to Ike McCoy requesting a swift completion to the details of the railroad work program. After months of "depressing confinement," Klein wrote, they were looking forward to their first real opportunity for gainful work. Attached to Klein's memo were the names of 102 men who, "with a feeling of good will," had signed up for the work.

McCoy began checking the list carefully, verifying the character of each applicant with Will Robbins, Charlie Lovejoy, or other staff members who were familiar with the men. Then McCoy pulled the individual files for further indications of reliability. McCoy found that many of the men were complete strangers to his staff, since they had only recently been transferred back to INS custody from the Army. Before long, however, one of those strangers would become perhaps the most notorious internee in the five-year history of the camp. His name was Karl Heinz Alfred "Fred" Fengler.

Fred Fengler, born June 4, 1916, in Leipzig, Germany, entered the United States in 1933 as a young man in search of opportunity and employment. Sporting a pencil-line mustache, which made him a dead ringer for the actor Douglas Fairbanks, Jr., the dream went sour and Fengler soon found himself broke in Chicago. In an effort to steal a new car for transportation to California, he pulled a pistol on the salesman giving him a test drive and shot him in the arm and chest.

The salesman survived, but on February 16, 1934, Fengler was convicted and sentenced to from one to fourteen years in prison. Immediately, the conviction was forwarded to the INS, which in March of 1934 ordered that Fengler be deported upon his release from the Pontiac Correctional Center.

It was not until March 31, 1942, that Fengler was recommended for parole. The warden of the Pontiac facility noted that if Fengler were "permitted freedom at this time, (he) would very likely engage in activities of a subversive nature which would be detrimental to the welfare of this country." Furthermore, a prison psychiatrist's report stated that Fengler was "somewhat unstable in his reactions."

Consequently, when Fengler walked out of prison in the spring of 1942, he was promptly arrested by the INS and booked in the Cook County Jail. Since it was not possible to execute the deportation order outstanding against him, he was ordered interned as an enemy alien, and by the summer of 1942, he was behind bars again, this time at Camp McCoy, Wisconsin.

Fengler spent almost a year at Camp McCoy before the Army, in need of more room to imprison German POWs, decided to return enemy aliens to the custody of the Justice Department and the INS. It meant that in May of 1943, Fengler was transferred to Ft. Lincoln along with forty other German nationals from Camp McCoy.

During that May, over a thousand enemy aliens from various Army camps also arrived at Ft. Lincoln, where they were scheduled to sit out the war. For Fengler, imprisonment for almost a decade had made him closemouthed and withdrawn. At Ft. Lincoln, he kept to himself and made few friends. He particularly avoided the zealous *Schlageter,* whose pro-Nazi arguments he characterized as "hun-jabber."

Finally, Fred Fengler the ex-convict was among the 107 men at Ft. Lincoln who braved *Schlageter* intimidation and signed up to work on the railroads. After ten years behind bars, Fengler looked forward to the opportunity for work, open air, and a small measure of increased freedom under a relaxed surveillance. Perhaps there would even be an opportunity to visit the small prairie towns which dotted the bleak, North Dakota landscape.

On September 3, 1943, 107 *Eisenbahner,* including Fengler, assembled with their belongings at the main gate of the compound in preparation for their departure for railroad work. In charge of the contingent was Patrol Inspector William E. Danforth, handpicked by McCoy for the qualities of firmness and friendliness necessary under the extraordinary circumstances. Danforth's assistant was a guard named William Woods, whose years in police work appeared valuable. To complete the five-man surveillance crew, the Northern Pacific Railroad had hired three armed guards. While McCoy felt the latter three were either too old or uneducated to be of much use, he was satisfied they were the best men available under wartime employment conditions.

Jeered by a group of *Schlageter* as they departed, Fengler and the other *Eisenbahner* were taken into Bismarck and loaded into a twenty-four car work train equipped with sleeping, dining, kitchen, and office cars. The whole complement journeyed 165 miles east of Ft. Lincoln to a railroad siding just outside the little town of Buffalo, North Dakota.

As far as Patrol Inspector Danforth was concerned, everything went smoothly at Buffalo. It was only necessary at the start to replace two of the railroad company guards who were obviously bored with the supervision and therefore too lazy to be conscientious about enforcing the levels of security required. That security included only an internee count at 6:00 a.m. and then again at 11:00 p.m., when the men were to be in bed, lights out. The internees were permitted to go into Buffalo after work, as long as they signed out and in and kept clear of the bars. Watching the men while they were in town was one guard detailed to be on patrol somewhere around town at all times.

On Saturday, September 12, Ike McCoy and Assistant OIC Bill Cook travelled to Buffalo to inspect the work site. Danforth reported to McCoy that, barring a few instances of sickness and one or two fist fights, there were no problems of supervision. The men themselves, earning fifty cents an hour for the ten-hour workday, expressed to McCoy their satisfaction with the opportunity to work under relaxed surveillance. As for McCoy, he continued to worry about the competency of the railroad guards. Yet he kept this concern to himself. He returned to Ft. Lincoln and on September 16 wrote Willard F. Kelly (whose official title now was Assistant Commissioner for Alien Control) that before their departure, the railroad volunteers had had to put up with bitter criticism from the Nazi element in camp. "I mention this," McCoy explained, "only to show that the hundred men who are out there working...thereby prove their pro-American tendencies." The threat of escape was a dim possibility, McCoy wanted Kelly to know.

Sunday, September 13, saw McCoy in the midst of a tense, dramatic confrontation which reinforced his conviction that his worst difficulties lay with the *Schlageter* inside the Ft. Lincoln compound and not with the railroaders.

One of the men who went out on the railroad track gang was a young Americanized German from Chicago named Lothar Baas, who had made himself very unpopular. An internee priest in the same dormitory room of Baas's barracks had had a book of commissary stamps stolen, and Baas was caught trying to redeem the stamps for candy. For Baas, who often greeted *Schlageter* "Heil Hitlers" with "to hell with Hitler!" the railroad work had provided an escape from certain punishment at the hands of his barracks mates. Now, however, after two weeks of strenuous work on the track gang, he wanted no more and requested to be returned to Ft. Lincoln.

On the afternoon of Sunday, September 13, he came back to camp and was reassigned to his old barracks. Considered now a traitor as well as a thief by his former barracks mates, Baas was promptly thrown out of his quarters every time he entered. Finally Baas fled to the Liaison Office where Will Robbins directed guards Ed Pendray and Ray Scott to keep custody of Baas while Robbins himself went over to Baas's barracks. However, Robbins found the *Schlageter* adamant: if Baas wasn't reassigned by 5:00 p.m., there would be serious trouble!

Convinced the *Schlageter* meant business, Robbins went back to the Liaison Office and phoned McCoy, who had proposed and then organized the railroad work over the objections of some of the staff. One of those objections was that the railroad work would only be a lark to escape barracks friction. Once the railroaders discovered how strenuous the work was, some staff worried they'd be back in camp. To avoid just that, McCoy had laid down the restriction that if they returned, it would be to their old barracks.

Since the question of what to do with Baas was now in OIC McCoy's hands, he asked Robbins for the names of the barracks troublemakers. Seven men were designated, and McCoy asked to have them brought to the headquarters building outside the compound, where he himself would negotiate a settlement. However, en route to headquarters, the seven leaders were detoured under guard to the Control Center and locked up in the guardhouse.

By 7:00 p.m., the men hadn't returned to their barracks and news of McCoy's apparent double cross spread quickly through the compound. Within minutes, two hundred men had gathered at the main gate to protest McCoy's actions. Brandishing sticks and singing German songs, a group of the assembled protestors banged on the door of the Liaison Office.

Robbins quickly directed Pendray and Scott to hide Lothar Baas in the next room. Then Robbins opened the main door to the Liaison Office, and a crowd of angry men pressed inside to demand the release of their jailed comrades.

Convinced that McCoy had misled the first seven men, Robbins phoned McCoy at headquarters and urged him to come to the Liaison Office and negotiate with representatives from the growing crowd of protestors. McCoy refused; his mind was made up. The seven troublemakers responsible for ejecting Baas from his barracks would remain locked up. Furthermore, the protestors had better clear the compound streets immediately.

Meanwhile, Chief Surveillance Officer Charlie Lovejoy, on orders from McCoy, began assembling all available surveillance force personnel outside the main gate, six deep with angry internees. Among the guards was Boyd Kimmins, a self-confident, fearless patrol inspector who had once gone headlong into a barracks to rescue a Jewish internee who was being beaten by two dozen *Schlageter*. Now, stationed fifty feet outside the main gate, Kimmins stood with a loaded submachine gun over his shoulder and dared the shouting internees to climb the fence.

Lovejoy had taken the further precaution of stationing Clifford Peck, a tough, ex-heavyweight wrestler, in the east alley guard tower, where he trained a short-barreled gas gun on the gate. The weapon fired an eight-inch long impact-exploding tear gas canister, and Peck had been sent up into the tower with instructions to fire only if Lovejoy signalled by dropping a handkerchief. Nervously, then, Peck kept one eye on the crush of men at the main gate, the other on Lovejoy, who moved among his men, the incongruous, delicate handkerchief flapping in one hand as he encouraged his guards to stand their ground.

Yet it was Will Robbins inside the Liaison Office who was at the center of the rising tensions. Despite his earlier eagerness to let McCoy resolve the problem, he now found himself the mediator between a firm McCoy and a mob of internees. Made furious by McCoy's refusal to negotiate, yet determined to save face, the men now tried a new approach: they would exchange seven *other* men for the leaders McCoy had jailed.

Robbins phoned the offer to McCoy, but McCoy's answer was still a firm no!

There were shouts of disapproval over McCoy's stubbornness. But quiet was restored, and a compromise proposed. They would exchange fourteen men for the seven leaders.

Again Robbins nervously phoned over the terms; and again the answer came back. No! The jailed men had violated the terms of the Geneva Convention, McCoy insisted. They had threatened him and disturbed camp harmony. He would negotiate with no one. Furthermore, the curfew whistle would sound momentarily. When it did, he expected everybody off the compound streets.

Shouts of outrage filled the room. Along the fence, a crowd of nearly four hundred men had gathered to show their support for a protest begun by a handful of *Schlageter*. When word reached them of McCoy's refusal of both exchange offers, many of the men clutched the chain link fence as if preparing to scale it.

"Come on over!" Boyd Kimmins shouted. "Come on over!" Charlie Lovejoy froze and held up his handkerchief. In the east alley tower, Cliff Peck thought, "When he drops the handkerchief, lay that gas in there as fast as you can!"

It was then that the 10:00 p.m. curfew whistle sounded, an especially long, eerie blast which rolled out across the Missouri River bottomland. Slowly, unwillingly, in small groups, the men dispersed, their frustration and anger somewhat tempered by the realization that their futile show of force had at least put McCoy on edge.

The next day, the seven troublemakers were released and returned to the compound. Meanwhile, the *Eisenbahner* at Buffalo learned of the near riot which Baas's return to Ft. Lincoln had precipitated. Danforth was concerned and wrote McCoy on September 16 to say that if additional men were sent out as *Eisenbahner,* care would have to be taken to guarantee that the new volunteers were not coming out "just to wreck the camp." Consequently, on September 17, Danforth sent McCoy a list of ten Ft. Lincoln men the Buffalo railroaders felt would "fit in our group with little trouble."

Meanwhile, with war news now running consistently against the Third Reich, the bitter *Schlageter* grew more outspoken in their criticism of the "treasonous" *Eisenbahner*. Those men in camp who might have been toying with the idea of railroad work were cautioned against doing so by a barracks poster directed to *"Eisenbahner!"* The graphic poster, clearly inspired by Goya's famous "Execution of the 3rd of May," depicted a rifle-bearing firing squad taking dead aim at a blindfolded *Eisenbahner* roped to a blood-red cross. There was no doubt who the executioners were. "The *Schlageter* are watching you!" read the message scrawled in German across the poster.

Despite the friction in camp, out in Buffalo there appeared to be few disagreements among the men. Fred Fengler kept to himself and spent the hours after work and Sundays volunteering to do clerical work for Danforth. In the long run, Fengler hoped to earn himself a regular assignment as daytime clerk in the office car, where he could be free of the "goose chatter" of the rest of the men, whom he considered "German squareheads."

At first, Danforth was impressed with Fengler's typing skills, and he promised the often sullen but efficient Fengler the clerk's job. However, Danforth finally selected another man for the clerical work, after telling Fengler he didn't need any help.

Danforth's rejection stung Fengler deeply, and he spent the last weeks of September prowling the streets of Buffalo. Fengler's good looks quickly caught the eye of a young Buffalo café waitress named Joanne Weber, who gradually became a confidant with whom he could discuss his confinement restlessness and his anti-German sentiments. However, the developing affair was suddenly interrupted on October 6 when the entire work train was moved thirty-one miles east to the town of West Fargo.

Movement of the work crew to the vicinity of Fargo, a town of thirty thousand people, was in direct violation of the Northern Pacific Railroad's agreement that work would be done only in unpopulated areas. Meanwhile, Fengler found that the move separated him from the friendship of Joanne Weber just at a time when he needed consolation the most. A further aggravation to Fengler was a long, open-letter from Franz Hanke, an avowed Nazi at Ft. Lincoln, to the *Eisenbahner* at West Fargo. The letter dated October 12 chastised them for doing work essential to the American war effort. Since none of the railroaders needed the money, the motive for the work, Hanke maintained, was "nothing else than genuine American greed for money, on the part of irresponsible half-Germans."

Hanke's attack was final proof to Fengler and the railroaders that there could be no returning to Ft. Lincoln. On October 18, after just two weeks at West Fargo, the track gang moved again, this time fifteen miles back west to the town of Casselton. Fengler took advantage of the move to request permission to take a bus to Buffalo for a four-hour visit with Joanne Weber, after which he said he would join the work crew at its new site at a railroad siding three-quarters of a mile east of Casselton. Permission was granted. When Fengler arrived on schedule in Casselton as promised, neither Danforth nor his assistant, Bill Woods, had cause to doubt the wisdom of the extraordinary privileges they had granted the quiet, handsome internee.

Despite the liberties Fengler received, and despite the freedom all the men had to come and go in Casselton, most of the railroaders continued to chafe under the strain of even the relaxed confinement. Therefore, on October 22, Karl Klein, spokesman for the *Eisenbahner,* wrote a two-page letter to Edwin J. Clapp of the Alien Enemy Control Unit requesting parole rehearings for the track workers. Klein pointed out that the men were still considered "dangerous enemy aliens." But, he argued, "in view of the type of work we are doing, this suspicion should prove to be unjustified."

With Klein's letter in the mail, the entire work gang waited to hear the government's response to their appeal. Meanwhile, on October 29, Fengler was granted another extraordinary privilege, this time to leave the track gang in the afternoon to visit in Casselton with a young couple named Seidlinger, who had befriended him since his arrival in town. Fengler returned to visit with the couple that same evening, socializing with them one last time before they left the next day for Minneapolis, where the husband was scheduled to be inducted into the Army.

With the couple's departure on Saturday, and with no prospects for a speedy response to Klein's letter, Fengler was once again left with no one to whom he could unburden himself of his growing nervousness and frustration. Fengler spent Saturday night alone in his bunk car, convinced that if he remained on the railroad work gang much longer, he would crack the skull of one of the "jabbering Supermen" with whom he was confined. That would mean a return to Ft. Lincoln, and even worse circumstances.

Fengler was still awake and shaking when, near dawn, a light rain began to fall on the roof of the bunk car. Clearly, there would be no track work that day. The count would be made at 8:00 a.m. Not another would be made until 11:00 p.m. He could get a long way in fifteen hours! It was, he quickly decided, the right opportunity for escape.

At 8:00 a.m. Sunday, guard Charles W. Fowler made the count, advising the eight men in each car that because of the rain there would be no track work that day. Fowler reported to Danforth the correct count of 108 internees, including Fred Fengler, who shortly after the count signed out to go to church in Casselton.

After services in Casselton, Fengler had cake and coffee in a restaurant. Then, carrying a black hymnal and a Bible, he walked a mile south of Casselton to the intersection of Highway 10. There he used a filling station pay phone to try to summon a taxi from Fargo. Unable to do so, he went back out on the highway and attempted to hitchhike. The first few tries were unsuccessful. Finally at 11:30 a.m., he held up the Bible and hymnal, indicating he was bound for church. The next car stopped, and he climbed in and disappeared.

Patrol Inspector Danforth spent the Sunday afternoon and evening on duty in Casselton with internee Hugo Emil Troeksen, captain of the bunk car where Fred Fengler was quartered. It was not until 11:00 p.m. that Danforth and Troeksen began to walk back to the railroad siding, satisfied that the rest of the men had already returned. While the two men stumbled along the tracks in the pitch darkness, guards Charles W. Fowler and W. R. Voight began the count. Neither man performed the duty with any enthusiasm. Fowler, who had only a third grade education and could scarcely add, had already turned in his resignation to the Northern Pacific Railroad. The sixty-four-year-old Voight, shaky and frail, found the long walk from car to car tiring. Consequently, it was the younger Fowler who climbed up into each car and counted by flashlight, then called out the numbers to Voight. However, when they reached the guards' bunk car at the end of the train, neither man attempted to total the count.

At 11:15 p.m., Danforth and Troeksen reached the work train. Danforth said goodnight and entered the office car where he bunked. Troeksen continued on to his sleeping quarters and immediately noticed that Fred Fengler's bunk was empty. He returned quickly to the office car, pounded on the door, and informed Danforth of Fengler's absence. Both men then hurried along the siding back to Troeksen's car, where the six occupants were quizzed concerning Fengler's whereabouts. No one had seen Fengler at either the noon or evening meal.

Danforth went straight to the guards' car then and confronted Fowler and Voight. While neither one could verify what the total count was, Fowler maintained that he had noticed two empty bunks in Troeksen's car and assumed they were occupied by men who were up with Danforth sorting the mail, which arrived at approximately that time. Danforth angrily explained that one of the empty bunks belonged to Troeksen, the other to Fengler, who was missing.

Danforth woke up his assistant Bill Woods, who awakened the off-duty guard Edmund Whitmer. Woods and his three guards Voight, Fowler, and Whitmer, then conducted a thorough search of the entire train. When that effort turned up nothing, Danforth himself proceeded back into Casselton and made a hurried search of the few establishments in town which were still open. Finally, at 1:45 a.m., Danforth had to admit that Fengler was gone.

It was 2:15 a.m. Monday morning when the switchboard operator on duty at the Control Center at Ft. Lincoln received an urgent call from Casselton, North Dakota. Patrol Inspector Danforth was on the line, and he wanted to speak to Ike McCoy. The young, inexperienced operator informed Danforth that, as far as he knew, McCoy was away on business in Sand Lake, South Dakota. In that case, Danforth insisted, he wanted to be connected with Charlie Lovejoy.

Chief Surveillance Officer Charlie Lovejoy was sound asleep when the operator buzzed his extension. Well aware that McCoy had in fact returned from Sand Lake the previous evening, and was now probably sound asleep, Lovejoy listened without any particular alarm as Danforth explained that Fengler was missing. Lovejoy wrote the name down in a sleepy scribble. Next, he told Danforth to phone the North Dakota Highway Patrol, the Fargo Police, and all other police and sheriffs' offices in the immediate vicinity of the escape, with the idea of instituting a general area-wide search. At the same time, Lovejoy warned, Danforth was to avoid all publicity except what was necessary to facilitate a thorough manhunt. Then, figuring that it would take four hours to drive to Casselton, by which time it would be too late to assist in the search, Lovejoy hung up and returned to bed without phoning McCoy.

In Casselton, Danforth did as he was told, alerting a half dozen local police and sheriffs. Then he questioned car captain Troeksen, who guessed that the lonely Fengler had probably gone back to Buffalo to be with Joanne Weber. At 3:00 a.m., an officer of the North Dakota Highway Patrol arrived in Casselton. Danforth and Woods jumped into the officer's vehicle and drove quickly ten miles west to Buffalo to wake up and interview Joanne Weber and her family. The visit was not fruitful aside from Joanne's admission that she had frequently seen Fengler and talked with him by phone. Based on those conversations, she was not surprised that Fengler had decided to escape.

It was still dark when Danforth, Woods, and the highway patrolman headed back east on Highway 10, stopping at all open gas stations along the route. Just at sunrise, they reached the intersection of Highway 10 and the road to Casselton. The operator of the gas station there informed them that he had noticed a handsome man matching Fengler's description attempt to hitchhike east toward Fargo the previous day around 11:00 a.m. It was the first clue of Fengler's whereabouts, and in a matter of seconds Danforth was speeding east toward Fargo with Woods and the highway patrolman.

At 7:00 a.m. Monday morning, Charlie Lovejoy arose just in time to receive a second phone call from Danforth. He was headed toward Fargo, apparently in hot pursuit of Fengler. Lovejoy hung up and proceeded to dress slowly for duty, still unconvinced of any particular emer- gency.

It was 7:30 a.m. when Ike McCoy stopped by to inform Lovejoy that he would be busy most of Monday playing host to a visitor from the Central Office in Philadelphia. Lovejoy and McCoy talked for a few minutes, and then Lovejoy casually informed McCoy of the news: Danforth had had an escape from the track gang. McCoy looked shocked. However, he quickly recovered himself and began to grill Lovejoy on particulars. The escapee's name was Fred "Sengler," Lovejoy explained casually and incorrectly. As McCoy wrote the name down, Lovejoy went on to explain that during the night, Danforth had alerted all police authorities in the vicinity of the escape. Meanwhile, he felt there was little else they could do.

While Ike McCoy searched his files at Ft. Lincoln for information on the internee Fred "Sengler," Danforth, Woods, and the highway patrolman reached Fargo and informed the police there that the escapee had been last seen headed toward their city. The Fargo police were given a description of the German alien, then the three men began a race-horse reconnaissance of bus stations, railroad stations, and hotels for any signs of Fengler. But as noon approached, and with no solid leads, the three men were forced to admit they were at a dead end in Fargo. Hopes of finding Fengler anywhere were fading fast. Therefore, the three men turned their car west again and sped back toward Casselton, where they intended to interrogate Fengler's acquaintances once more in hopes of uncovering new clues.

Ike McCoy spent two hours Monday morning futilely searching the internees' files for Fred "Sengler" before the mistake was discovered and Fengler's file was located. However, the brief dossier on Fengler contained only his picture, the date he had entered the country, and his last address before internment — Box 55, Joliet, Illinois. Disappointed by the scant information in the file, and unaware that the escapee was an ex-convict and the post office box was in fact the address of the Illinois State Penitentiary, McCoy ordered copies of Fengler's picture made. Then he phoned the District INS Director in St. Paul to ask if a more complete file on Fengler was available.

While McCoy waited, the St. Paul authorities retrieved their file on Fengler. At this point McCoy learned for the first time that Fengler had spent eight years in the Illinois State Penitentiary for assault with intent to murder, and was considered psychologically unstable. McCoy listened carefully as the St. Paul official read from Fengler's prison file.

"If permitted freedom at this time," Fengler's prison warden had written, "(he) would very likely engage in activities of a subversive nature which would prove detrimental to the welfare of this country."

The revelation that Fengler appeared to be especially dangerous sent McCoy into a flurry of action. He requested that the St. Paul office ask WCCO, the most powerful radio station in the Midwest, to broadcast an escape alert. He then advised Lovejoy and Patrol Inspector Robert Devlin to make preparations for an immediate departure to Casselton and Fargo in order to take charge of the search. The two men left Ft. Lincoln at 11:30 a.m., clutching a stack of freshly developed pictures of internee Fengler. With their departure, McCoy phoned the Noyes, Minnesota, border station to request that they send men down to Fargo to assist Lovejoy in the search. He asked the Noyes station to be on the lookout for Fengler trying to escape into Canada.

Next, at 11:35 a.m., McCoy phoned his boss W. F. Kelly in Philadelphia to inform him of the escape. Confident that there was no dereliction of duty involved, McCoy explained to Kelly the measures he had undertaken to capture Fengler since being informed of the internee's disappearance.

Kelly was miffed that he hadn't been notified immediately of Fengler's escape. Furthermore he noted, the FBI had not been notified. The Central Office's repeated instructions were to alert the FBI twelve hours after an effective escape. Fengler had been gone now almost thirty hours. Why hadn't the FBI been called in, asked Kelly. He requested a detailed report as soon as possible.

It went unsaid, but it was perfectly clear what Kelly was driving at. In thirty hours, Karl Heinz Alfred Fengler could have gotten halfway across the country!

In fact, just thirty miles due north of Casselton in the tiny railroad stop of Luverne, North Dakota, a twenty-one-year-old waitress named Ethel Faust, on duty in Thompson's Café at 1:30 in the afternoon, noticed an extremely handsome man enter the establishment. What followed would later be recorded by McCoy in his log of the escape.

The man looked about thirty, Ethel thought. He was unshaved, and dressed in a workman's cap, dark trousers, and heavy-soled boots. Still, Ethel felt, because of his good looks he was very much unlike the railroad bums who often came into the café.

The man sat down at the counter and said he had had nothing to eat since Sunday. "I want food," he spoke with what Ethel Faust was sure was a German accent.

After ordering a sandwich, he explained that he worked on the railroad and had come into Luverne that morning on the local Great Northern No. 199 from Fargo.

In a few minutes, Ethel Faust brought him his sandwich. He stood up abruptly, and carrying a small clothing roll in one hand and the sandwich in the other, he thanked Faust and walked out without paying.

Ethel watched for a second, somewhat frightened by the sudden appearance and departure of the handsome but strange man who now walked toward the train stop. Then she went back to work.

Irritated by McCoy's failure to adequately explain the circumstances surrounding Fengler's escape, W. F. Kelly composed a memo on November 1 to INS Chief Earl Harrison, informing him of the Fengler escape. "From the facts available," Kelly wrote, "the escape would appear to place this Service in a bad light." Kelly's memo went on to fault McCoy for carelessness, loose surveillance, and failure to alert the FBI, after repeated instructions to do so in the event of an escape.

While Kelly was drafting his memo in Philadelphia, McCoy obeyed his superior's instructions by notifying the FBI in Sioux Falls, South Dakota, of the escape. Then at 2:00 p.m. McCoy called Casselton only to learn that Danforth and Woods had returned from Fargo with no leads. They were busy interviewing *Eisenbahner* and Casselton townspeople for any fresh leads.

McCoy advised Casselton that Lovejoy and Devlin were on their way to take charge of the search. They would be arriving momentarily. Then he hung up and took a few minutes to reflect on the situation. It was not the fault of McCoy's office that an incomplete file had accompanied Fengler to Ft. Lincoln. Had McCoy known of Fengler's criminal record, he surely would not have permitted the internee the freedom of railroad work. Since Lovejoy had been under the impression that McCoy was away on business, the delay in notifying the OIC had been understandable. Furthermore, McCoy could not recall any instructions to notify the FBI twelve hours after an escape. McCoy felt all that could be done was being done. Yet, Kelly had been irritated with him. Obviously the Central Office considered this a grave situation, and McCoy could only hope for a sudden development which would convince Philadelphia he was on top of the matter.

Within minutes McCoy received the break he was hoping for. It was a two-page typed letter from Fengler, postmarked the previous evening at 7:30 p.m. in Fargo. "This is a very difficult letter for me to write," Fengler began. "The grind is getting the better of me and I just have to get away." Then Fengler turned to the subject of railroad work, which he had volunteered for to get away from the rabid Nazis in camp. Yet even among the *Eisenbahner,* he found that their "political idiocy and goose-chatter of a language is exasperating." And all the silly talk of a Hitler victory was "just too much for a man's sanity."

Finally, to clear himself of any suspicions of espionage, Fengler insisted that he only wanted some "free air," and he promised McCoy that at war's end he would voluntarily leave the United States and notify the INS of his arrival in another country.

McCoy had Fengler's letter in hand when Danforth called at 3:45 p.m. to report that Lovejoy and Devlin still hadn't arrived at Casselton. Just what might be delaying the surveillance chief was of no interest to McCoy at that moment, however. Since he had just received Fengler's letter postmarked in Fargo the previous evening, the chances were that Fengler was still in Fargo. Lovejoy and Devlin, who could be expected to arrive any moment in Casselton, were to proceed immediately on to Fargo.

Because of radiator problems along the way, Lovejoy and Devlin did not reach Fargo until 9:00 p.m. The patrol inspectors who had come down from the Grand Forks border station to assist in the search had grown tired of waiting and returned home. Lovejoy phoned Ft. Lincoln to report his tardy arrival to McCoy; and then distributing pictures of Fengler as they went, he and Devlin began visiting the same hotels, bus depots, and train stations that Danforth had canvassed that morning. At 1:30 a.m., Lovejoy and Devlin returned to the Graver Hotel in Fargo and synchronized search efforts with the FBI. At 2:00 a.m., exhausted from a seventeen-hour day of radiator blowups and hectic searching, Lovejoy and Devlin went to bed.

Five hours later, at 7:00 a.m. Tuesday, November 2, both men were back on the streets, this time across the Red River in Moorhead, Minnesota. After flashing Fengler's picture around Moorhead, Lovejoy and Devlin still had no clues to his whereabouts, so they drove back to the Casselton railroad siding, to see if Danforth had uncovered any new leads. Danforth had learned from Fengler's Casselton acquaintances that Fengler had spent the day before his disappearance with the Seidlingers, both of whom had since gone to Minneapolis for the husband's induction into the Army. Furthermore, Danforth had discovered Fengler's friendship with a young woman living in Fargo named Wanda Flath, whose father-in-law owned a hotel-café in Buffalo.

It was 8:00 p.m. when Lovejoy made a quick phone call back to Ft. Lincoln to report to McCoy that he had the address of a Fargo woman who might be harboring the fugitive Fengler. For the second time in twenty-four hours, Lovejoy and Devlin roared off for Fargo.

McCoy spent Tuesday keeping careful track of the search efforts he had instituted from his office at Ft. Lincoln. He still had Danforth and Woods in Casselton in the event Fengler was holed up there, and he had Lovejoy and Devlin tracking down a promising lead in Fargo. Farther away, the Springfield, Illinois, FBI office was pursuing any possible connections Fengler might have made in Illinois during his residence and imprisonment there. While Fengler's letter revealed he was not a sabotage threat, he was still a lonely, perhaps even "unstable" enemy alien. McCoy was convinced that every precaution was being taken to have him swiftly apprehended.

Wednesday, November 3 dawned in Fargo as Lovejoy and Devlin discussed Karl Heinz Alfred Fengler with Wanda Flath. Flath had little to report on the escapee, and commented that it was really an acquaintance, Joanne Weber of Buffalo, with whom Fengler was very friendly. In fact, Weber had once stated she had wanted to go to Minneapolis to work, and Fengler had promised to meet her there.

It was not an encouraging lead. Fengler's association with Joanne Weber had already been established by Danforth, who had interviewed her on Monday in Buffalo. So she was obviously not in Minneapolis, hiding out with Fengler. Still, this was the second time that the trail seemed to lead to Minneapolis. The Seidlinger couple had in fact gone there just before Fengler's escape. Lovejoy decided at 8:55 a.m. to phone McCoy at Ft. Lincoln and pass on the information that the Seidlingers, who had befriended Fengler, were in Minneapolis. Lovejoy gave McCoy a description of Mary Ann Seidlinger and a possible address where she could be located.

The Fargo trail now ice cold, Lovejoy and Devlin checked in a final time Wednesday evening with the Fargo Police. They had nothing to report. The two patrol inspectors then drove on to Casselton for a last conference with Danforth and Woods at 7:30 p.m. Weary from near round-the-clock searching, the four men agreed that there was nothing more they could do. Danforth then phoned McCoy and reported they had exhausted all leads. Lovejoy and Devlin were heading back to Ft. Lincoln.

Lovejoy and Devlin returned to Bismarck in the early hours Thursday. However, a tired Lovejoy had hardly crawled into bed when he was rousted out by Immigrant Inspector Carl F. Brasek, an INS official sent from Chicago to investigate the escape. In response to Brasek's questions, recorded later in a report dated November 13, Lovejoy admitted that he had known McCoy was home the night Danforth had phoned Ft. Lincoln with news of the escape. But he hadn't promptly notified his superiors because Casselton was two hundred miles away. By the time anybody got there, it would have been too late to render any practical assistance. Besides, Lovejoy continued, he believed he saw a Central Office memo once which directed that all search efforts for escaped alien enemies be left to the FBI. He had not wanted to "infringe on FBI operations."

With Brasek's arrival at Ft. Lincoln, and his stern interrogation of both Lovejoy and McCoy, it was clear now that dereliction of duty might well be an issue in the Fengler escape. Consequently, at 10:30 a.m. Thursday morning, McCoy took the precaution of wiring Philadelphia to ask that the Central Office instruction about notifying the FBI, which Kelly had referred to, be forwarded by mail. Then, since Brasek was also charged with investigating circumstances at Casselton, he and Mc-Coy left for the escape site at noon.

No sooner were Brasek and McCoy on the road than they too developed car trouble, which necessitated abandoning their INS vehicle for repairs when they arrived in Casselton at 4:00 p.m. Danforth and Woods had no new developments to report to McCoy. Brasek therefore launched into a long interview of the two men, grilling them on the background circumstances of the escape from the site.

During the questioning, Danforth admitted that he had heard from other *Eisenbahner* that Fengler had a prison record. But sensing he was being blamed for Fengler's disappearance, Danforth protested that he had never been satisfied with either the intelligence or the agility of the guards the Northern Pacific had supplied him with. Brasek then interviewed guards Fowler and Voight, who had made the count the night of Fengler's disappearance and failed to tally the individual car totals. When Brasek confronted Fowler with a sheet of paper with a column of eighteen figures representing the individual car totals of the work train, the obviously uncomfortable man took several minutes to finally arrive at the correct figure. But, he shrugged, he had "hired out as a guard, and not as a bookkeeper."

Brasek's Casselton investigation finished, he and McCoy proceeded on to Fargo in a borrowed car. There his investigation was completed, and Thursday night in Fargo he caught a train back to St. Paul. McCoy phoned Ft. Lincoln to report no new developments in the case. Then he checked into a Fargo hotel for the night.

McCoy knew the District Office in St. Paul would make an assessment of the security measures involved with the railroad work program. Since the entire program had been his brainchild, if there was criticism of the plan, he'd take the brunt of it. Meanwhile, the escapee was still loose, and it remained mainly McCoy's responsibility to see that he was caught.

Friday morning in Fargo, McCoy reconnoitered the same checkpoints covered first by Danforth and then Lovejoy. It was not until 11:00 p.m. that McCoy had his first lead. The sheriff of Fargo reported a phone call from a young woman named Ethel Faust in the tiny railroad town of Luverne, North Dakota. She had heard the description of Fengler on the radio. A man answering his description had come off a Fargo train and been in Thompson's café in Luverne on Monday.

By 4:00 o'clock that afternoon, McCoy was headed north toward Luverne, his car trailing a funnel of dust as he raced along the gravel county roads. En route he had time to piece together what few solid clues they had on Fengler's disappearance. He had gone to church at 8:00 a.m. Sunday, then was seen at 11:00 the same morning hitchhiking toward Fargo. If the identification in Luverne was positive, obviously Fengler reached Fargo, mailed his letter from there Sunday night, then on Monday morning boarded a train west. McCoy guessed that he had jumped the train in Luverne to rendezvous with one of the female acquaintances he had made in the short time he had been a railroader. With his striking good looks, and the easy availability of lonely women in these out-of-the-way towns, it was possible that he was being sheltered by someone in Luverne at the very moment McCoy raced toward the little town.

McCoy reached Luverne at 5:00 p.m. and met Ethel Faust at Thompson's Café. He jotted what happened in his log. Immediately, McCoy presented her with pictures of Fengler. She was uncertain in her identification of the front view photo, but, yes, the profile picture, that "was like him." She explained that he came in at 1:30 on Monday afternoon, ordered a sandwich, left without paying, and went back down the street toward the train stop. She was sure he was headed west. Maybe, she guessed, he took the train on Tuesday.

McCoy thanked Ethel Faust for her alertness, then left the café and talked with three telegraphers at the train depot, none of whom had seen Fengler. At 7:00 p.m. McCoy headed back to Ft. Lincoln.

The Ft. Lincoln OIC was back in his office Saturday morning at 11:45 a.m., keenly aware that search efforts had gone far beyond his jurisdiction in North Dakota or even the Midwest. To facilitate the broader search for Fengler, Kelly sent McCoy an urgent radiogram at 2:45 p.m., directing him to furnish all Border Patrol Districts with notification of Fengler's escape together with a complete description and a photograph.

On McCoy's desk lay a copy of the instructions from Kelly, dated August 11, 1942, directing "immediate notification" of the FBI in the event of an escape. The instructions contained no reference to the so-called twelve-hour notification rule Kelly had insisted on. Still, failure to "immediately notify" the FBI may even have been worse, in Kelly's mind.

McCoy spent the rest of the afternoon composing an all-points bulletin, which by late that afternoon was affixed with the photograph of the escapee, looking remarkably similar to Douglas Fairbanks, Jr. The bulletin, dated November 6, 1943, alerted all Canadian and Mexican Border Patrol stations to be on the lookout.

The next day, Sunday, marked one week since Fengler's disappearance. It also presented McCoy the first opportunity he had had to put together the detailed report on the escape that Kelly had ordered him to submit. The account that resulted was also an analysis of the work program and its future. With few exceptions the project had been running smoothly. Despite the revelation that Fengler was a felon, McCoy doubted that he was a danger to internal security. McCoy conceded that the Northern Pacific Railroad guards were inadequate. However, they would be replaced with competent men. As an extra precaution, he intended to reinvestigate the individual files of all internees presently assigned to railroad work. Any "doubtful cases" would be returned to Ft. Lincoln promptly. Otherwise, McCoy contemplated no "drastic changes" in his policy of permitting men to work on the railroads.

The all-points bulletin issued to each Border Patrol station in the United States bore no fruit. Meanwhile, McCoy made good on his promise to reinvestigate *Eisenbahner* files, and as a result of that careful scrutiny, several of the track gang men were returned to Ft. Lincoln on November 10.

On November 15, Kelly sent McCoy a copy of the report Inspector Brasek had compiled as a result of his investigation of the Fengler escape. Relying solely upon Brasek's report, Kelly wanted to know how it was that Fengler, an obvious womanizer, had been permitted to go into nearby towns. Noting that Brasek's report faulted several aspects of the railroad work program, Kelly directed McCoy to, "Please give this office the benefit of your views as to the correctness of the conclusions drawn by Inspector Brasek."

In spite of the trouble over Fengler, Edward J. Ennis of the Alien Enemy Control Unit in Washington finally responded to earlier pleas by the railroaders for a rehearing of their cases. Acknowledging the verbal and physical abuse the *Eisenbahner* had taken from other internees, Ennis wrote track gang spokesman Karl Klein on November 17 that "there is merit in your proposal that rehearings of this group of internees be granted a preference over other German internees." Just as soon as a special board could be convened, Ennis promised, the rehearings would be conducted.

Notwithstanding Ennis's generosity, the grave repercussions of Fengler's apparently successful escape were beginning to be felt elsewhere in the Justice Department. J. Edgar Hoover fired off a memorandum on November 19, 1943, to INS Commissioner Harrison, pointing out that since Fengler's escape he had become aware of five particular *Eisenbahner* whose backgrounds were so pro-German that he considered them extremely dangerous to national security. One of them had even been a member of the Edward John Kerling spy ring that had tried to recruit Kurt Peters as a radioman.

It wasn't until November 22 that Ike McCoy had collected his thoughts enough to write Kelly with respect to the criticisms Brasek had levelled in his report. Tactfully reminding Kelly that it was inappropriate to treat internees like convicts, McCoy felt that the men should be permitted to visit adjoining towns under guard. But McCoy had hardly sent off his letter when he received a response by telephone from Philadelphia. Under no circumstances, Kelly instructed, were internees to be permitted to visit towns adjacent to the work projects. They were to be kept under constant guard, he stressed. Then, that correction still ringing in his ears, McCoy received on the twenty-fifth another stern notice from Kelly. Based on Hoover's intelligence, the five dangerous internees singled out by the FBI chief should be transferred back to Ft. Lincoln, unless McCoy could guarantee security was sufficient on the track gang to prevent them from committing an act of sabotage.

Hoover's concerns prompted him to assign two special agents to investigate the escape. McCoy briefed the two men at Ft. Lincoln, then sent them off to Casselton to consult with Danforth. However, just as soon as they were gone, McCoy let Kelly know that the Ft. Lincoln files on the five men Hoover had singled out revealed that only two might be security risks, and they would be returned to Ft. Lincoln immediately. Unless Kelly disagreed, the other three men would remain out on the track gang. Without contradicting Hoover specifically McCoy wrote November 29, "As far as any member of this crew committing an act of sabotage, that, of course, is possible but highly unlikely."

W. F. Kelly remained unconvinced by McCoy's assurances, and on December 17, when it was finally clear that Fengler had carried out the first successful escape in the enemy alien internment program, Kelly delivered a final critique of McCoy's role in the affair. Finding fault with the proprietary attitude McCoy seemed to have about "his" railroad work program, Kelly wrote, "We wonder if you are aware that this project was not by any means the first upon which...internees had been used successfully outside of a camp, and that the Fengler escape was in fact the first alien enemy escape we have had since the detention program started which can properly be charged to gross negligence." Fengler was a "person of criminal propensities" who had no family ties or honorable background, and he should not have been trusted, Kelly concluded.

Kelly's letter was a rejection of almost every confidence McCoy had in the railroad program. It was only a matter of time before what had seemed to McCoy a creative response to wartime manpower shortages, as well as a much-needed release valve for restless internees, was cut back, then finally eliminated. Meanwhile, McCoy could not help but lose confidence in his ability to administer even the ordinary affairs of the camp without looking over his shoulder to see if J. Edgar Hoover or someone else would ultimately second-guess him. Consequently, as 1943 drew to a close, and with Kelly's critique fresh in his mind, McCoy wrote his bosses that, "In the very near future this station plans on slaughtering its own cattle and hogs for camp consumption." An edgy McCoy now requested to be told if a report of the slaughtering must be made.

On February 22, 1944, nearly four months after Karl Heinz Alfred Fengler had escaped from the railroad track gang in Casselton, North Dakota, two New Orleans police officers on the streets of their city were randomly checking young men for draft cards. Spotting an obviously fit, draft-eligible passerby, the two officers confronted the man and politely asked to see his draft card. When he could not produce one, the officers asked him for any identification. When he could not produce identification either, apologizing for his failure with a suspicious accent, the officers arrested him. He was turned over promptly to the FBI, who within minutes determined that Karl Heinz Alfred Fengler had almost made it to Mexico.

Hermann Cordes (*left*) and Albert Gregeratzki, who reflected some of the characteristics of German cartoonist Wilhelm Busch's Max and Moritz (*below*) (Courtesy of Hermann Cordes and Albert Gregeratzki)

Max and Moritz

GERMAN LOYALISTS AND A TUNNEL TO FREEDOM

A patrol inspector investigates the interior of the Cordes-Gregeratzki tunnel, after it was discovered. (Courtesy of Will Robbins)

View from west-center surveillance tower of temporary barracks inside separate compound at Ft Lincoln Barracks T22, showing door to boiler room where Cordes and Gregeratzki worked, is first barracks in right foreground Their tunnel proceeded to the right from the boiler room, toward the south fence, which is not in the picture (Courtesy of Will Robbins)

Patrol Inspectors
Felix Rene (*left*) and
Earl Kocher (*right*)
Guard dogs Hooch
(*left*) and Waven
(*right*) (Courtesy of
Rita Rene)

Max and Moritz

Hermann Cordes was born in June of 1921, and from his boyhood on it was assumed that as the eldest of three children, he would one day take over his father's prosperous farm outside the little village of Sottrum in northern Germany. However, as he approached his eighteenth birthday in 1939, it was clear that the athletic, gregarious Cordes was not ready yet to settle down to the hard work and solitude of farming. Instead, he applied for a three-month visa to attend the New York World's Fair, at the invitation of an aunt and uncle who were grocers in Hoboken, New Jersey.

In New York City Cordes made friends with a group of ballroom dance instructors, and he was soon an expert dancer. When his three-month visa expired in July of 1939, he was too caught up in his new social life to consider returning to Germany. Instead, he applied for and received a three-month extension of his visa, fully intending to return at last to Germany on the *Hansa,* scheduled to sail from New York on September 4, 1939. But with Germany's attack that fall on Poland, and the subsequent Atlantic Blockade, Cordes found himself stranded in New York City. Five times between September of 1939 and the spring of 1942, he extended his visa to legalize his temporary residence in America, each time swearing before INS officials that he would abide by U.S. laws.

By the spring of 1942, Cordes's last extension had run out, and he was considered an illegal alien who had overstayed his visa. Confident that he would soon find a way back to Germany, Cordes registered for German military service at the German Consulate in New York, in accordance with the German Universal Military Service Law. At the same time, however, in obedience to U.S. laws, he was registered as an alien under the Alien Registration Act, and he reported to local draft board No.9 in Hoboken and registered for American Selective Service.

That spring, Cordes went to work for his uncle and aunt in their

Hoboken grocery store. Evenings were spent drinking beer with young German friends who, like himself, were now eager to return to Germany. On April 20, 1942, Cordes and a small group of friends enjoyed a vigorous workout in the old Union Hill Turnverein, a gymnastic society. After the workout, Cordes and his athletic friends went across town to the City Hall Tavern, a popular hangout for Germans and German Americans, and once the national headquarters for the German-American Bund, the pro-Nazi political organization. Among the regular guests that evening at the tavern were several former leaders of the Bund, including August Klapprott, eastern department leader of the Bund before its dissolution. Klapprott was now eastern trustee for the National Protective Trustees Committee, which had replaced the Bund.

Klapprott and his friends had gathered on the evening of April 20 to celebrate the birthday of Adolph Hitler. Unaware that the FBI had had the City Hall Tavern under surveillance the two previous nights, two dozen men and women were singing and celebrating when Cordes and his friends arrived to join the festivities. Across the street, eight FBI agents led by Special Agent Cecil Miller of the Newark Office and eight officers of the Union City Police Department observed from the shadows of the City Hall as Cordes and his group entered the tavern.

At 10:30 p.m., the FBI agents noted there appeared to be very few people at the bar of the tavern. After spotting a light in a back room known to be a meeting place for German groups, Miller and his sixteen-man force entered the tavern swiftly, blocked all exits, and broke into the back room (FBI, September 18, 1942).

Agents immediately began interrogating the surprised occupants of the room, who pretended not to know what the party was for. Then it was Cordes's turn to be interrogated by the agents, whose methods grew sterner as each subject refused to admit it was Hitler's birthday they had gathered to celebrate.

Cordes was asked for his visa, but since it had expired months ago, he admitted he didn't have one. Then, pressed to explain why he and his friends were gathered at the tavern, Cordes shrugged and said he didn't know about the others, but *he* had come to drink beer. Meanwhile, the rest of the celebrants insisted they were there to toast the return of August Klapprott to good health. Klapprott himself, suddenly feigning illness, requested to be excused to go home to go back to bed. Since agents knew the former Bund leader well; he was permitted to leave, while Special Agent Miller and his men arrested five patrons they identified as enemy aliens, among them Hermann Cordes.

Cordes and the four enemy aliens were taken across the street and booked that night in the Union City Jail. The next morning they were surrounded by reporters and photographers as they were moved from the jail to a van, and thence to Ellis Island for detention as enemy aliens.

Albert Gregeratzki was born in Hindenburg, Upper Silesia, on February 11, 1920. In school, Albert was quiet and shy, but showed a quick intelligence and an insatiable desire for stories about explorers and adventurers. Later, Albert attended business school in nearby Gleiwitz. However, when he got out of school, times were hard and apprentice positions were available for only those privileged few who had connections through their parents. Since Albert's father was only a painter, he could not find a job anywhere, and he worked temporarily at odd jobs to supplement the family's income.

When Albert turned nineteen, and as political tensions in Europe worsened, Albert bicycled west, seeking adventure and work. Relying upon his coolness, and his facility for innocent lies, Albert evaded several border arrests and eventually made his way to Nantes in northwest France, where he went to sea as a Polish sailor under the name of Woicieck Cyron. Consequently, Gregeratzki celebrated New Year's Eve aboard the *Morska Vola,* just prior to arriving in port in New York City on the third day of January, 1941. In port, Albert put on all the clothes he could wear without looking obvious, and he jumped ship.

Under his real name, Albert turned to the German Consulate for help. Consular officials secured him a place to stay in a German sailor's home for two weeks until he found a job as a cook's helper. Unwilling to return to the war scene in Germany, Gregeratzki applied to the German Consulate in New York for a passport to legalize his residence in America. However, before any papers could be processed, President Franklin Roosevelt ordered all German consulates in the United States closed by July of 1941.

That action left Albert Gregeratzki little more than a fugitive again, this time in America. Still, it had been almost three years since he had set out on his bicycle for adventure, using disguise and his wits to escape a dozen official efforts to arrest him. He was confident now that he could wait out the war in America, working as a cook's helper around New York City, changing jobs often enough to stay a step ahead of immigration authorities.

Almost a year later, on April 21, 1942, he was working as second cook at Concordia College in Bronxville, New York. There had not been even a hint that the authorities were suspicious of him. Two men entered the kitchen and stumbled through the pronunciation of his name. Despite his insistence that he was Woicieck Cyron, they claimed they knew him quite well. "We have been following you for months," they said, and flashed their FBI credentials.

Albert Gregeratzki and Hermann Cordes met for the first time on Ellis Island, April 22, 1942. In a dormitory room filled mostly with older German aliens, the two men just in their twenties spotted each other immediately and were quick friends. They were an interesting contrast. Gregeratzki, the taller of the two, had a recessed chin, sunken eyes, and a delicate face that suggested a withdrawn, perhaps even overly sensitive, poetic nature. The shorter, more muscular Cordes had sweptback hair and a defiant chin. It gave him a cocky, tough, athletic appearance that seemed at odds with Gregeratzki's sensitive features.

Still, Gregeratzki and Cordes remained together in the same dormitory room for three months at Ellis Island. Before long they thought of themselves as real life versions of Max and Moritz, two characters from the imagination of Wilhelm Busch, the German humorous cartoonist. Busch's Max and Moritz refused to listen to the advice of adults and ridiculed those who tried to advise them. Whatever differences there were between the two characters were forgotten in their battle against adults and authority. So it was with Cordes and Gregeratzki — one the privileged son of a well-to-do farmer, the other never having known anything but want and hard luck. Those differences were overshadowed by their mutual disrespect for the older internees, their common wit, and their love of pranks and adventure. Together they were unbeatable, determined to make the best of their circumstance.

On May 8, 1942, Hermann Cordes was granted a hearing before an Alien Enemy Hearing Board at Ellis Island to determine whether he would be paroled, deported, or interned for the duration. An arrogant Cordes explained to the Board the circumstances that had stranded him in the United States. It was not his fault, he insisted defiantly, that he was in New York illegally. He had obeyed all American laws. He had even registered as required for the American draft. Therefore he resented being treated like a criminal. All he wanted, he said, was the opportunity to return to Germany.

Albert Gregeratzki also went before the Alien Enemy Hearing Board and asked to be repatriated to Germany. Furthermore, when asked who he hoped would win the war, he answered that since he was German, he of course favored Germany.

Having left little doubt where their loyalties lay, in June of 1942, Gregeratzki and Cordes were transferred from Ellis Island to Ft. Mead, Maryland, for internment at the hands of the Army. Six months later they were transferred to Camp Forrest, Tennessee, for continued internment. Meanwhile, German prisoners of war captured in North Africa began to arrive at Camp Forrest in great numbers, creating a double compound, one for internees and the other for POWs. Men from the two compounds often gathered along the separating fence line and shouted greetings to each other, or they sang German songs together.

By May of 1943, Camp Forrest was filled with aliens and POWs. To make room for the arrival of more German prisoners from Africa, transfer of enemy aliens back to INS control was begun. On May 21, Hermann Cordes was sent by train to Ft. Lincoln, along with four hundred other German enemy aliens. Gregeratzki remained behind at Camp Forrest. After more than a year of companionship, the two men shook hands and said goodbye in the stuffy summer heat of their tent.

It was less than a week later, on May 25, that Gregeratzki was also sent off to Ft. Lincoln, where he was assigned to barracks T22, the same temporary wooden structure along the south fence line of the camp where Hermann Cordes had already settled in. Cordes briefed Gregeratzki on the ins and outs of the new camp, talking with an authority that suggested he'd been there a year instead of a week. So they were together again—Max and Moritz—each inspired by the truth that fate wanted them together to concoct whatever adventures they could.

With the transfer of enemy aliens like Cordes and Gregeratzki back to INS control, Ft. Lincoln's population swelled to 1,406 German internees. Meanwhile, Cordes and Gregeratzki remained in good spirits through their first summer. Soccer teams, started back in 1941 by the first seamen internees, were now organized into leagues with regular matches and play-offs. Albert and Hermann were teammates on a huge squad of men, each of whom wore a T-shirt stenciled with an ominous black-eagle silhouette.

Already busy enough with their soccer league, neither Cordes nor Gregeratzki had any interest in the program of railroad work that some of the men volunteered for, hopeful that they would be able to sneak into the small railroad towns and drink beer. Besides, the sale of beer in

a "casino" inside the compound was okayed on August 13 by Edward
Ennis of the Alien Enemy Control Unit; and work was going forward to
convert barracks T26 to a two hundred-man pub with Bavarian murals
and decor. What was the point, Cordes and Gregeratzki felt, of break-
ing their backs on railroad work for the opportunity to have an illicit
beer, when it would soon be available inside the compound?

In August, Attorney General Francis Biddle decided that rehearings should be granted to any enemy aliens whose cases warranted
review, or about whom additional facts were known. Biddle immediately created procedures by which the so-called Special Hearing
Boards were to convene at the various internment camps when enough
cases had been scheduled at each site for rehearings. There were divided
feelings among the men at Ft. Lincoln about the wisdom of taking part.
A few seamen internees eagerly petitioned the Special Hearing Board to
have their cases reheard. They felt the best hearing could be had at the
hands of fair-minded civilians rather than bored bureaucrats. But many
others shared the feelings of Otto Wagner, who wrote Will Robbins that
the hearings were a "spectacle" because of the "inexperienced and
sometimes prejudiced U.S. citizens" who sat on the Boards.

Cordes and Gregeratzki rejected the rehearings also and instead
plunged eagerly into a program of study at the Ft. Lincoln *Schule*.
Established in 1941 by seamen, the *Schule* had now taken over the
second floor of Building 61, the Internee Administrative Office. Classes
were conducted daily by qualified internees in subjects ranging from
boiler theory to philosophy. Cordes and Gregeratzki studied together in
algebra, physics, electronics, chemistry, French, Russian, and Spanish.
Convinced that being younger they were more alert than the other
men, they studied furiously in competition with each other, earning A's
consistently.

Cordes and Gregeratzki enjoyed most the instruction they received
from the bearded, snuff-chewing, seventy-year-old Professor Einzinger,
who taught their physics class by mixing philosophy with the material
world. "Everyone see to where he stands, and stand so not to fall," the
Professor admonished in German the men in his class. It was not just a
tough law of independence which Professor Einzinger had deduced
from the machinery of the universe; it was, Cordes and Gregeratzki
realized, Einzinger's personal maxim for surviving internment at Ft.
Lincoln. Stay away from the "pack dog" disposition which characterized
the *Schlageter* in camp. See to yourself first; prepare for your own
release.

It was a message which appealed to Cordes and Gregeratzki.
Neither man participated in the quarreling or the riot that ensued over

the *Eisenbahner*, those Germans who volunteered to work on American railroads. They were both too busy seeing to where they stood. Nor did they pay much attention to the Special Hearing Board, which arrived at the end of September and sat hearing cases until mid-October. They both felt they had told the government everything they intended to reveal about themselves. They weren't going to submit to what they felt were the criminal-like indignities of oath swearing and interrogation.

The only event that drew their attention from their studies was the escape that November of Karl Heinz Alfred Fengler. Neither had known Fengler, but they soon learned through the grapevine that the daring, handsome internee had simply walked away from a track gang. After two weeks of futile investigation by North Dakota authorities and FBI agents, it was obvious that Fengler had made good his escape.

The realization that it was possible to escape successfully from Ft. Lincoln was followed by the gradual understanding that the war was not going to be over soon. Therefore, as the cold, North Dakota winter set in, and as the two men began to tire of their strictly academic exercises, escape became the subject of animated discussion. For the athletic Cordes, the chance to begin work on an escape tunnel as soon as the ground thawed promised physical exercise and muscle toning, the likes of which he hadn't enjoyed since the Turnverein in New Jersey. Gregeratzki, the more imaginative of the two, took inspiration from the prospect of escape and adventure returning to his life. In fact, so great was their interest in the work and planning of a tunnel that neither looked much beyond it to the question of what they would do once they were out.

With the authoritative Cordes always the leader in their discussions about the tunnel, the two men pledged secrecy to each other that winter. It was to be *their* tunnel. No one else would be included. Meanwhile, the normally withdrawn Gregeratzki blossomed with energy and inventiveness as he devised detailed plans for lighting the tunnel, disposing of the dirt, and bracing the walls. Their plan was to gain access to the crawl space for plumbing beneath the barracks by way of a trapdoor in the boiler room at the north end. Since that room was occasionally used to make simple barracks furniture, they would use that pretense for being there. One of them would remain in the boiler room making appropriate noises while the other disappeared below.

While Cordes and Gregeratzki planned, OIC McCoy, still embarrassed by Fengler's successful flight, spent December reading up on escape prevention. From Canadian military officials, he received literature on what to look for. There were three principal types of escape — cutting the wire or climbing, tunneling, and a gate escape by ruse — the

Canadians warned, and "detection of tunneling is generally difficult." Still, through vigilance and intelligence, tunneling could be discovered. The Canadians advised looking for telltale signs of dirt and examining the barracks crawl space at least twice a month. Finally, one needed to keep in mind that it was not possible for would-be escapists to tunnel faster than a yard a day.

It hardly seemed necessary to take precautions against tunneling in the icy dead of winter. Besides, there were other matters which McCoy considered more pressing. On December 31, a group of *Schlageter* gathered without authorization inside building T92, normally used for skits and internee musical productions. Displaying a swastika over the stage, the group listened to several pro-Nazi speeches that characterized the news of bombings in Germany and defeat in Russia as momentary reversals on the way to a complete Nazi victory.

Rallies such as this were seen as leniencey toward Nazis by the news media (*Cosmopolitan*, 1944). Sensitive to the public criticism which news of such rallies created, McCoy promptly forbade political meetings, although it was not possible because of the size of the camp to stamp them out entirely.

In addition to troublesome political rallies, with the opening of the beer and wine casino on January 16, 1944, McCoy now had drunken quarreling to contend with. He responded by limiting the daily number of kegs delivered to the casino.

In February of 1944, a group of Bavarians who had been ski instructors in Idaho built a seven-meter-high wooden ski jump which sat on the soccer field inside the compound like a huge dinosaur skeleton. A heavy snowfall and intense cold brought a dozen expert skiers out of the barracks to try their skill on the makeshift contraption.

In T22 the younger men, including Cordes and Gregeratzki, watched the ski jumpers and quickly adopted antics of their own to dissipate their winter restlessness. Naked and roaring at the tops of their voices, they would take cold showers and rush outside, belly flop into a fresh snowbank, then sprint back into the barracks. Most of the older men in the barracks, inclined to modesty, looked upon these naked "snowbaths" as childish. No one was more outspoken in his disapproval than John C. Schultz, who lay on his bunk at the end of the barracks adjacent to the shower room and pronounced the snowbathers "children."

Born in Budapest and abandoned by his parents, Schultz had made his living in Europe as a thief before coming to the United States, where he was arrested for burglary in California. He was imprisoned in San Quentin, Folsom, and finally Sing Sing in New York before his arrest and internment as an enemy alien. Unclean in his personal habits, humorless, and often wide-eyed and incoherent when discussing his belief in political anarchy, Schultz was left alone in his corner, where he often sat for hours clipping political articles from newspapers. If it was necessary to address him, or, as occasionally happened, shout at him to get out of bed for the count, he jerked and twitched at the mere mention of his own name. Because he never showered at all (much less took snow baths), the younger men who received his scorn soon turned the rumor that he had only one testicle into an established fact. It gave his modesty a perverse origin.

Cordes and Gregeratzki made doubly certain they avoided the disagreeable Schultz. They felt he would betray their tunnel plans in a minute to McCoy if he could get them in trouble. McCoy, meanwhile, was kept busy through an intensely cold February trying to prevent the barracks-restless internees from fighting with each other. However, by the end of February, McCoy was relieved to learn that Fred Fengler had been caught during a random draft card check on a New Orleans street. As far as McCoy was concerned, it reestablished the fact that a successful escape from Ft. Lincoln wasn't possible.

Yet as the spring thaw began, McCoy continued to feel pressure from his superiors and the Congress to maintain a tough attitude with the men in his camp. In May of 1944, the House of Representatives considered and passed HR 4108, an act "relating to escape of prisoners of war and interned enemy aliens." Although it had never been made clear precisely how Fred Fengler had made his way from North Dakota to New Orleans, the presumption was that someone must have given him shelter, either innocently or deliberately. HR 4108 established a maximum ten thousand dollar fine or ten years imprisonment for anyone who assisted an escaped POW or enemy alien.

At the same time, the FBI was notifying the INS that it had received from one of its confidential sources identification of German nationals in the United States who had gone to the German Consulate between 1936 and 1941 and registered for German military service. The presumption was that these men were particularly dangerous. Among them, the FBI's list noted, was Hermann Cordes of Hoboken, New Jersey.

McCoy did not need the FBI to remind him of the special caliber of the men for whom he was responsible. In March 1944, as preparations were made to sign up men for forest service work in Montana, McCoy pointed out in a memo to his boss, W. F. Kelly, that only three hundred men had volunteered. Reminding Kelly that many of the less dangerous enemy aliens had been paroled, "one can readily see the caliber...of what we have left. I am beginning to feel that we were over-optimistic in thinking we can employ these people to much advantage outside the facility."

On a warm day the first week of May 1944, Albert Gregeratzki entered the boiler room of T22 unnoticed, while Hermann Cordes remained just outside the door hammering noisily on a makeshift desk he had begun working on weeks before in the Ft. Lincoln woodshop across the compound. Once inside the boiler room, Gregeratzki quickly lifted the trapdoor to the crawl space beneath the barracks, then slipped below, replacing the trapdoor over his head. He squatted for a moment in the three-foot-high crawl space, listening to Cordes's diversionary hammering outside as his eyes adjusted to what little light came in through the foundation air vents.

In a few minutes, Gregeratzki was able to make out that the foundation space beneath the boiler room and shower end of the barracks was approximately twenty-four feet square and separated from the sleeping section of the barracks by a concrete foundation wall. Gregeratzki crawled toward that partition wall, intending to inspect the ground adjacent to it for an appropriate tunnel head site. He was on all fours feeling his way along the wall when his hand struck a wooden surface, which echoed hollowly when he thumped on it with his fist. A few minutes of groping determined that the object was in fact a lid. Gregeratzki brushed loose dirt from the covering and slipped it aside. Then he struck a match to illuminate the discovery.

It was the opening to a small, neatly cut tunnel which went down at a slight angle beneath the concrete partition. Gregeratzki squeezed his head and trunk into the tight opening and struck another match, determining that the tunnel passed under the partition, then appeared to head south down the length of the barracks toward the fence. Sliding farther into the tunnel, he struck another match to see ahead. He had begun to squeeze himself through the tunnel's difficult curve, where it passed under the concrete cross partition, when he was suddenly seized with fear. The space was too tight to even turn around. What if it caved in? How would he get out? Cordes was making too much noise to even hear him!

Short of breath from fear and very little air, Gregeratzki backed out of the tunnel carefully, then sat beside the tunnel head and took deep breaths until he had shaken some of the terror which had gripped him. Once back outside in the fresh air, Albert explained his discovery to Cordes, who quickly went to investigate himself.

In a half hour, Cordes came out to report that he had negotiated what he described as a sink-trap curve where the tunnel went under the cross partition. He had come up on the other side in a long, narrow trench which ran halfway down the crawl space under the sleeping portion of the barracks.

Gregeratzki was still too shaken by his tunnel panic to discuss going back into it, but Cordes could not contain his excitement over what he felt was their luck. Somebody had already started their escape route for them. Since the tunnel was so small, and had obviously been abandoned for some time, Cordes guessed that it had been started by Japanese in the spring of 1942, when they had occupied the temporary barracks in the separate compound. With their removal in the summer of 1942 to permanent internment camps, the Japanese tunnelers had been forced to give up their efforts. Cordes and Gregeratzki were the beneficiaries.

It took considerable coaxing from Cordes before Gregeratzki made a second entrance into the tunnel. But Gregeratzki finally agreed, persuaded by Cordes's assurances that the tunnel came up to an open trench just beyond the sink trap. Still, Gregeratzki would not share in Cordes's excitement until it was agreed that their first order of business was to widen the tunnel head and the sink trap.

Both men checked out spades from the supply office, saying they wanted to begin spring gardening in a little plot beside the barracks. After half a day of theatrical garden digging, they slipped into the boiler room one at a time and loosened the screws attaching shovel and handle. At the supply office, they presented their shovels, which were checked off "returned." Then so no one would notice, they separated the two parts and clanked one shovel head and one handle on the implement pile. Cordes retained a shovel head under his jacket; Gregeratzki, a handle. Returning to the boiler room, they stashed the stolen shovel parts, confident that the supply guard would notice the returned parts but merely assume somebody's shovel had separated while working.

Gardening was not for them, they made it clear to the men in T22. The soil was too rocky and sandy. Instead, they returned to their carpentry, one man working outside the boiler room while the other set about widening the tunnel head and the sink trap. The original tunnel lid was replaced, then covered with three inches of loose dirt after each exit from the tunnel.

By mid-May Cordes and Gregeratzki had enlarged the tunnel head to permit easier passage for the taller, less limber Gregeratzki. The troublesome sink trap had been opened up, and the open trench on the other side of the cross partition had been deepened to allow either tunneler to move about in a nearly upright position. Finally, the trench had been extended to the south foundation wall of the barracks.

Digging in one-hour shifts during the noontime rest period, the two men covered for each other by working at their carpentry projects inside the boiler room, where the hammering reverberated throughout the barracks and muffled whatever sounds came from below. A series of three rapid hammer taps was the prearranged signal that digging should stop immediately to avoid discovery. But only once during that period were their efforts nearly compromised, and then not by a guard but by John C. Schultz.

It was noon, Gregeratzki's shift in the tunnel, and his shovel slipped and struck the floor with a thump beneath Schultz's bunk. Schultz leaped out of his bed, stood harkening over the floor like a bird, then went out the barracks and into the boiler room to investigate.

The minute Schultz stepped into the boiler room, Cordes gave frantic warning hammer taps, then turned his back on Schultz and resumed his carpentry while Schultz strained to hear where the mysterious thumps had come from. Finally, he left the boiler room and circled the barracks, trying to peer in through the foundation vents while Cordes watched from around the corners.

Cordes and Gregeratzki were sure that it was too dark beneath the barracks for Schultz to make out the trench by peering through the air vents. Besides, from the beginning they had mounded the loose dirt on each side of the trench, effectively shielding it from even a flashlight inspection through the vents. Short of a deliberate search of the crawl space for their buried tunnel lid, or some kind of accident, they were convinced their escape route was virtually undetectable.

So Schultz's prying was quickly forgotten and the two men began the underground tunnel which soon passed beneath the south foundation wall, then continued at a depth of three feet toward the compound fence some twenty yards away.

All that spring, Gregeratzki had made detailed plans in his head for carting the dirt out of the tunnel, reinforcing the ceiling, and running a light cord into the dark burrow. Since the boiler room was stacked with extra steel bed frames, Gregeratzki decided to utilize these as side props for the tunnel, supporting overhead bracing boards which they would scrounge however they could.

Because the trapdoor was too small to admit a steel bed frame, Gregeratzki had to enlarge it using a fine jigsaw blade. Once the steel frames were lowered beneath the barracks, the enlargement cut was stuffed with sawdust to make it unnoticeable.

Then they began to look around for crosswise bracing boards which wouldn't be missed, and found them in the boiler room itself. The wall studs between the boiler room and the shower room had facing boards on both sides. Since some boiler rooms in the row of temporary barracks had exposed studding, Cordes and Gergeratzki figured they could pry off the facing boards on the boiler room side of T22, and it wouldn't look unusual. Once they removed the boards, they sawed them into three-foot lengths and stashed them in the corner of the boiler room for use when needed.

Lighting the tunnel was Gregeratzki's job. Making use of the electrical knowledge he'd gained that spring in the Ft. Lincoln *Schule,* he pieced together scrounged barracks cord, then spliced into the wiring beneath T22. Two light bulb sockets spaced at twenty-yard intervals completed the rigging, and the tunnel became illuminated.

Finally, Cordes built a small dirt cart with wood wheels that he cut with the jigsaw in the internees' woodshop. The cart was fixed with tow ropes at each end to pull it back and forth in the tunnel. That meant it was necessary for both of them to work beneath the barracks. Less inclined to claustrophobia than Gregeratzki, Cordes did the digging on his knees at the lead point of the tunnel, filling the dirt cart and then jerking the rope. Gregeratzki drew the cart toward himself along ruts in the tunnel floor. This kept the cart centered in the tunnel avoiding the steel beds which propped the walls and supported the ceiling braces.

To keep from looking suspiciously dirty, both men stored extra clothing in the trench beneath the sleeping area. Each time they finished a stint beneath the barracks, they changed back into clean clothes, listened for a moment at the trapdoor, then came up quickly.

It was during one of these hasty exits that Cordes and Gregeratzki came squeezing up through the trapdoor, only to stare straight into the shocked face of Albert Kiffl, who slept in their barracks. Young, athletic, and capable of rambling for hours in idle conversation, Kiffl had watched Gregeratzki and Cordes entering and exiting the boiler room for weeks before he decided innocently to go in and prattle away with them as they worked. Kiffl guessed immediately what was going on. So despite his capacity for boring chatter, Cordes and Gregeratzki had no choice but to swear him to secrecy and include him in their plans. Besides, they rationalized, with both of them under the barracks, they could make use of Kiffl as a lookout who would continue the carpentry diversions and sound alarms with three hammer taps.

A hot spell in early June brought many of the internees out of their barracks stripped to the waist or clad only in athletic trunks. During the midday rest, they lay in the grassy shade of the elm trees along the north side of the compound. Cordes and Gregeratzki joined the group of loungers on several occasions, if only to be seen in order to avoid creating any suspicions.

These diversions were suddenly interrupted by the news of the Allied invasion of Normandy Beach on June 6, and the entire internee population, regardless of political convictions, was stricken with gloom. The *Schlageter* grew silent after arguing for so long that the Japanese-German might of 700 million would ultimately defeat the Allies. They listened morosely as American newscasts announced that the invasion forces intended to strike to the heart of Berlin and crush the Third Reich. Those who had already accepted as inevitable the collapse of Germany were distressed to think that loved ones were in the combat path of Allied forces.

By June 15, Cordes and Gregeratzki figured their tunnel had passed under the fence. In order to find out exactly where they were, Gregeratzki crawled to the end of the tunnel and ran a steel rod up through the roof. Cordes, doing calisthenics along the fence, was supposed to locate the rod and then whistle through two fingers, signalling Gregeratzki to withdraw it.

Watching the forty-yard wide grassy strip between the fence line and the surveillance road, Cordes spotted the steel rod sticking up about halfway out. On a number of occasions, Cordes and Gregeratzki had noticed farmers walking along the ditch just beyond the surveillance road with only their straw hats visible from just inside the compound. The near bank of that ditch would provide a concealed exit point for their tunnel. So, after almost six weeks of digging like blind moles, they were just twenty yards short of their goal.

The realization that they would shortly reach their objective brought Cordes and Gregeratzki face-to-face with the question they had so far avoided: where would they go once they got out? For Cordes, the answer was simple. He had no interest in aimless, wildcat roaming of the United States, inevitably to be caught and jailed again with perhaps more restrictions than he had at Ft. Lincoln. Despite the news of Allied victories in France, Cordes still wanted to return to Germany. Short of that, he only wanted the freedom to come and go as he pleased into Bismarck, where he could drink and find female companionship.

Gregeratzki, on the other hand, had decided to try to remain in the United States after the war. Despite his defiant attitude before the Alien Enemy Hearing Board, there was little back in Germany that appealed to him. Rather, the chance to slip out of Ft. Lincoln and go wherever he pleased in the sprawling United States excited him. Yet, Cordes was right. Where could they go where they wouldn't sooner or later be caught? Until a better idea came along, he would settle for sneaking into Bismarck to get a little taste of the American independence he would one day enjoy.

The inadvertent partner Kiffl wasn't interested in escaping at all. In fact he had already signed up for forest work in Montana. For him, tunnel digging was just something to keep him busy. So with Albert Kiffl taking regular turns at digging, the tunnelers were renewed with expectations that they would soon realize their goal. It was necessary, however, to angle the tunnel right for approximately ten feet, then straighten out again to skirt a light pole in their path. Their final destination remained the far side of the surveillance road and the deep ditch, where they could come out hidden in the shadows, unobserved at night from either the surveillance tower midway along the south fence or the tower at the southwest corner.

By Friday, June 30, 1944, the tunnel had reached the narrow surveillance road and was fifteen feet short of the ditch. Gregeratzki went to work in the boiler room making an exit lid, which would be sod covered and fit over the escape hole. As he hammered in the boiler room, and Cordes and Kiffl worked in the tunnel, their disagreeable barracks comrade John C. Schultz sat at the little writing desk beside his bunk next to the shower room, composing an awkward note to Officer in Charge McCoy:

> Sir:
> The two fellows Cordes and Gregeratzki have been fixing boards a certain size for weeks and weeks and no one knows where they go. There are still a lot of them in the back of barracks 22 where the gas heater is, although it is forbidden to file wood in there better investigate quick! I suspect on a stormy night some inmates will leave here.
>
> Yours very sincerely

Schultz put his unsigned note late that afternoon in the mailbox for internee correspondence on the outside door of the Liaison Office. Since Will Robbins and Red Selland had already gone to their family quarters for the weekend, the note remained unread until it was picked up by Robbins Monday morning when he reported to his office. In the meantime, Schultz had spent the weekend listening to more boiler room hammering, and he added a second urgent note:

> Sir:
> There are some strange things going on in the back of barracks 22 since weeks and weeks two fellows have been sawing and no one knows where the many boards go? There is still plenty left in there where the gas heater is.
>
> Yours very truly

Half suspicious that the anonymous letters might be pranks, Robbins read them to his assistant Selland. Joke or not, Selland felt the letters should be shown to McCoy, so Robbins walked the letters to the OIC's office. McCoy recalled the complicated, ingenious escape tunnel

of 1941, which had been discovered by luck, and he decided immediately to take the notes seriously. He summoned his assistant Bill Cook
to discuss the matter, along with Robbins and Ray Kocher, who was
temporarily in charge of the outside guard force in Charlie Lovejoy's
absence. The rest of the morning the four men debated what to do.
Finally, McCoy reminded them all of the embarrassment his predecessor
A. S. Hudson had suffered because of the earlier tunnel whose mystery
remained unsolved. This time the guilty parties would be trapped in
the tunnel if possible, McCoy vowed.

But time was of the essence, the others argued. They read again
the two notes. "Better investigate quick!" the anonymous writer urged.

McCoy recalled the Canadian document he'd received that winter,
which said that the fastest a tunnel could progress was a yard a day. The
tunnelers obviously didn't intend to come up in the grassy strip between the fence and the surveillance road, in plain view of the towers.
They had to be headed for the ditch beyond the road. That meant
between fifty to seventy yards of tunneling. North Dakota ground frost
would have delayed their start until late April or May. By now, the first
of July, they would be getting close to the ditch!

The meeting broke up with the agreement that Red Selland, in his
official capacity as fire chief, would make a routine inspection of all fire
hoses in the boiler rooms of the temporary barracks. Since the easygoing, friendly Selland was well liked by many internees, it was felt that
his nosing around would not arouse suspicions.

Selland entered the temporary barracks compound and began his
"routine" inspection in T10, then worked his way along the line of
fourteen barracks. Outside the boiler room of T22, Albert Gregeratzki
stood casual guard and followed Selland's movements. Satisfied that the
patrol inspector was on a routine check that would shortly bring him to
T22, Gregeratzki entered the boiler room quickly to deliver the warning
hammer taps, only to find that Cordes and Kiffl were already finished
digging for the day and were fitting the trapdoor in place. Gregeratzki
whispered that Selland was coming, and the three men arranged themselves around Cordes's still unfinished desk just as Selland entered the
boiler room.

The tunnelers greeted Selland with pleasant grunts, then turned
their attention back to the desk. Not familiar with any of the men,
Selland nodded and excused himself as he stepped around the desk to
make a conspicuous check of the coil of fire hose hanging at the far end
of the boiler room. Heading back toward the entrance, Selland shot a
glance at the maintenance trapdoor and saw the lifting ring was properly in place. Then he exited the boiler room and left the temporary
barracks compound.

Meanwhile, Will Robbins had begun a thorough check of his files in the Liaison Office to determine the roster of internees assigned to T22. In half an hour he had the names of twenty-three men. Then he began pulling their individual files, checking the handwriting on the anonymous notes against any samples of internee handwriting he could find in each file. At 1:00 p.m. he phoned McCoy to inform him that the anonymous notes had come from John C. Schultz. Furthermore, he reported, among the twenty-three men billeted in T22 were Albert Gregeratzki and Hermann Cordes, the persons referred to in the notes. Although Robbins had not had contact with either man, his files revealed both were young and in good health, making them excellent candidates for a tunnel project. But, Robbins told McCoy, Selland's investigation of the T22 boiler room revealed that the maintenance trapdoor appeared unmolested.

The next day McCoy directed Ft. Lincoln plumber C. L. Thompson to enter the temporary barracks compound and make another "routine" inspection, this time lifting the maintenance trapdoor in each boiler room in order to inspect the crawl space beneath.

It was 2:00 p.m. when Thompson reached T22. Their suspicions unaroused by Selland's visit the previous day, Cordes and Kiffl were in the tunnel, while Gregeratzki worked at sanding Cordes's desk outside the boiler room. Thompson's sudden approach with his kit of pipe wrenches and tools caught Gregeratzki by surprise, and he had no time to deliver the warning taps before Thompson was inside the boiler room. Hastening to the far end of the barracks, Gregeratzki delivered the warning taps on the foundation there. Deep inside the tunnel, Cordes froze. Kiffl, manning the dirt car, threw down the rope and cut the light switch Gregeratzki had improvised on the bell cord.

Thompson had just let himself down through the trapdoor and was crouched in the dark, fumbling for his flashlight, when Gregeratzki's frantic tapping reached him too. The hammer taps were too precise and measured, he knew from his own work, to be innocent. It was an alert. Quickly, he made a flashlight inspection of the crawl space, noting the tunnel opening with the lid pushed to the side. He started into the opening, then realized that he was risking a sudden confrontation with the tunnelers. At that point he withdrew and climbed back up through the trapdoor.

Once it was clear that Thompson had left, Cordes and Kiffl changed quickly out of their digging clothes and scrambled up out of the tunnel. The three men then discussed the plumber's appearance. They agreed that routine inspection or not, if the plumber had bothered to move around at all in the crawl space, he would have discovered the open tunnel. They decided to take turns observing the boiler room, to see who came and went. If the apparently routine inspections ceased, perhaps their tunnel had escaped detection.

In the meantime, Cordes felt, they had no choice but to abandon their project temporarily, even though they had only a few meters to go before they were out.

Despite Thompson's report that his own movements had surely been observed, McCoy continued to entertain the hope of catching the tunnelers in the act. At the same time, he intended to take every precaution to insure that no escape occurred.

First, McCoy directed Will Robbins to bring John C. Schultz to his office for interrogation. Schultz said he could add little to the suspicions he had already raised in his notes. The digging was being done during the day, he was positive. Cordes and Gregeratzki were definitely involved, possibly others. His eyes darting nervously between McCoy and Robbins, Schultz asked to remain anonymous. Certain younger men in the barracks had it in for him, he whined. He wanted no trouble.

After assuring his informant Schultz of secrecy, McCoy had an extra guard placed in the ditch of the surveillance road outside the ring of compound lights. Next, he instructed his post radio officer to solder a microphone to a piece of welding rod, which was to be installed after dark on the ground outside the fence directly south of T22. Wires would be run from this microphone to a listening device in the southwest tower. Then on July 4 McCoy sent a personal and confidential memo to W. F. Kelly, alerting his boss to the tunnel discovery. "We have fairly reliable information," McCoy wrote, "that two young internees, namely Albert Gregeratzki and Hermann Cordes are involved. There perhaps are others and we are going to try to watch the matter and endeavor to catch the persons involved (rather) than just go and prevent the escape and be unable to pin it on anyone."

By the afternoon of July 6, Cordes, Gregeratzki, and Kiffl decided that since two days had passed with no reappearance of officials for routine inspections of the barracks, their tunnel had luckily escaped detection. Still, they decided that a variation of their digging routine was necessary in order to avoid arousing suspicions. Besides, they were so close to the ditch they could not risk a daylight breakout. Thereafter all digging would be done at night, with every precaution being taken not to awaken their sleeping barracks mates.

That night, Cordes crawled to the head of the tunnel to dig, while Gregeratzki pulled the dirt box back and forth silently, ready to crawl forward with his completed wooden lid in the event of a breakout. Kiffl stood guard outside in the shadows of the boiler room eaves, alert for any approaching flashlights.

At the head of the tunnel, Cordes sat for a second, confident that he was far enough away from the barracks, and deep enough, that any sounds of his digging would be concealed. For a moment, he reflected back over the months of work. At first, the chance of an actual breakout had seemed remote; the whole affair had begun as a lark. But now, the next stroke of his shovel might break through to the ditch, and in expectation of that, he began to dig and poke energetically.

While Cordes dug, Patrol Inspector Boyd Kimmins relieved the guard in the southwest tower nearest T22. The newly installed monitoring device was explained, and Kimmins was instructed to be alert for any unusual noises picked up by the ground-staked microphone. Immediately, Kimmins thought he could make out scraping and then poking noises on the monitor. But it stopped before he determined what it was.

Realizing that what he had heard could well have been the sounds of pick and shovel, Kimmins later reported the suspicious noises to the senior patrol inspector in charge of his shift. But since the digging noises had stopped, it was decided there was no urgent need for action. In the morning, McCoy was informed, and he decided to put two men on duty outside the surveillance road in the event the tunnelers broke out.

The next morning a young employee of the maintenance department began to mow the high grass on the long strip running the length of the south fence. It was dull work, and by midmorning, he was in a half-stupor from the rising prairie heat and the drone of the mower. He stumbled along behind his machine, unaware that any special devices had been installed in his path. When he suddenly noticed the black wire running through the high grass, he jerked his mower to a halt. But it was too late. He had cut the wire cleanly.

Irritated by the accident, but unwilling to risk revealing his awareness of the tunnel by rewiring the microphone in broad daylight, Ike McCoy had to wait for the cover of darkness before making repairs. Impatient to know what was going on, he instructed Charlie Lovejoy, back in charge of surveillance, to conduct a routine midnight count, and to investigate the tunnel beneath the boiler room.

Just before midnight, Cordes, Gregeratzki, and Kiffl prepared to creep from their bunks for a second night in the tunnel. Cordes and Gregeratzki were just about to enter the boiler room, with Kiffl again watching outside in the dark, when they saw flashlights inside the temporary compound coming directly their way. They hurried to their bunks and, still dressed, were feigning sleep when Lovejoy's crew entered and made the count. Just as soon as they left, Cordes tiptoed to the shower room and peeked out the window. Observing the flashlights move down the row of barracks, Cordes was reassured that it had only been a routine count. He was about to return to his bunk when he heard the boiler room door creak open. One ear to the shower wall, he crouched and listened as Lovejoy and guard Raymond W. Glitschka entered the boiler room, lifted the trapdoor quietly, and lowered themselves into the crawl space.

All doubts removed from his mind, Cordes stood up and slipped back to his bunk. That was it, he whispered to Gregeratzki. The tunnel had been discovered. The guards were going down into it at that very moment.

In fact, Lovejoy and Glitschka had merely entered the boiler room crawl space to observe that the tunnel head was now concealed by dirt sprinkled over the wooden lid. Still hoping to keep their investigations secret, they withdrew without disturbing the lid and reported their discovery to Lovejoy, who was waiting in the Control Center. It was obvious, they all agreed, that the digging was still going on. Without delay McCoy sent Charlie Lovejoy and Ray Kocher, one of the dog trainers, to the grassy strip south of T22. Hidden by darkness they probed the ground in an attempt to locate the exact progress of the tunnel. Their efforts were futile, however, and they finally gave up just as the prairie sunrise threatened to expose their presence.

The next day was July 8. Coincidental with the abandonment of the tunnel, Albert Kiffl was ordered to depart by train for forest service work in Montana. The departure of the dull but garrulous Kiffl seemed to mark a sad finish to the tunnel project. Then, another coincidental event captured the attention of most of North Dakota, including the internees at Ft. Lincoln.

On July 10, two-year-old Naomi Sanders wandered away from her parents' farm home on a county road about thirteen miles northwest of Bismarck. At 2:45 in the afternoon, a general alarm was broadcast on Bismarck radio stations, and the search was directed by officials of the State Highway Patrol. A plea for help was made to Ike McCoy at Ft. Lincoln. If his police dogs could track down escaped Nazis, maybe they could find the little girl. McCoy immediately sent Charlie Lovejoy, Felix Rene, and the dog Hooch to the Sanders farm. After three hours of tracking, Hooch suddenly raised his head, sniffed at the north wind, and darted across three hundred yards of pasture, swerving only to avoid washes and brush patches. At the edge of the pasture, Hooch pulled his handlers down into a small, dry ravine, where he poked his head through a blanket of ragweed and laid his nose on a sleeping Naomi Sanders.

Of course the explanation behind Hooch's miraculous discovery was that all humans carry a scent as unique as a fingerprint. Turning his attention back to the tunnel at Ft. Lincoln, McCoy realized that in Hooch he had a sleuth who would identify the tunnelers as surely as if he caught them in the act of digging. All he had to do was find something in the tunnel that belonged to them, preferably clothing.

Convinced that further cat-and-mouse games were unnecessary, McCoy directed Lovejoy and two guards to enter the tunnel and confiscate what they could. They were also to measure the tunnel's length with string. Shortly after noon on Wednesday, July 12, Lovejoy and two guards went into the compound and headed straight for T22. While a group of curious internees gathered to watch, the three men entered the boiler room and lifted the trapdoor. With Lovejoy unrolling binder twine as he crawled, it was determined that the tunnel had reached a point eighty-five feet south of the barracks, just fifteen feet short of the ditch. In addition Lovejoy emerged from under the barracks grasping just the evidence McCoy needed: clothing discarded in the tunnel. He carried a blue chambray work shirt, an olive drab woolen shirt, a pair of overalls, and a pair of Navy sailor pants, monogrammed "T22:Cordes."

Fairly sure who his main suspects were, McCoy began laying specific plans for exposing others who were involved in the tunneling. Concealed microphones were installed in adjacent cells of the guardhouse, where Cordes and Gergeratzki were to be held. But they proved useless at first. The wires from the guardhouse to the Control Center passed between high tension lines and picked up a power hum in the monitor. Rewired successfully the next day, the microphones were secretly in place when on Monday, July 17, Cordes and Gregeratzki were brought separately to the guardhouse and interrogated by McCoy and Lovejoy.

Gregeratzki was escorted to the guardhouse first at 1:30 p.m. Manufacturing the look of innocence which he had perfected as he fled across Europe, he quietly denied knowing anything about a tunnel. When pressed to admit who his friends were in T22, he named everyone else in the barracks before admitting his friendship with Cordes. McCoy then produced Cordes's monogrammed sailor pants. But Gregeratzki had no explanation for why his friend's pants had been found under the barracks. Finally, he suggested that McCoy interrogate John Schultz, since he had been seen under the boiler room of T22.

Cordes was brought to the guardhouse at 3:00 p.m., and like Gregeratzki, denied knowledge of the tunnel. He also insisted that McCoy interrogate Schultz, who, he claimed, enjoyed crawling around under the barracks in search of stray cats.

Then McCoy produced Cordes's monogrammed pants and told him to put them on. Cordes did so, prompting McCoy to observe that they seemed to fit him perfectly; in particular, the dirt stains on the legs

matched exactly with Cordes's knees. Cordes protested that monogrammed or not, matched dirt stains or not, the pants weren't his! His
were still in his footlocker, and unlike the suspect ones, his had a
zipper. Confidently, he invited McCoy to check his footlocker.

Cordes and Gregeratzki were placed in adjacent guardhouse cells,
with the concealed microphones. Gregeratzki was suspicious immediately due to the grates in the ceiling. For an hour the two men
whispered to each other about what McCoy had been told. Cordes
described being confronted with his monogrammed sailor pants. But
that discovery would be no problem, he felt, since he had borrowed
replacement sailor pants just as soon as it was obvious their tunnel had
been discovered. He had no qualms about inviting McCoy to check his
locker. Gregeratzki explained how he had dissembled and stalled when
asked who his friends were in T22. Finally, they congratulated each
other for independently throwing suspicion onto Schultz.

Then, for the benefit of McCoy, Cordes raised his voice and began
to ridicule President Roosevelt. Shortly Gregeratzki joined in the sar-
casm, while in the Control Center, McCoy, Lovejoy, and the two guards
assigned to monitor the conversation stared at each other sheepishly. It
was obvious that their two prisoners were wise to them.

Aware that eavesdropping would not yield the information he
wanted, McCoy called two internees to his office the next afternoon.
Alvin Moeller, a carpenter who slept in T22, drew a diagram of the
sleeping arrangements; but he was quick to point out that where the
men slept had little to do with their friendships. He insisted that no
one in the barracks knew why Cordes and Gregeratzki were in the
guardhouse.

Still uncertain about possible accomplices, McCoy next summoned
John Schultz to his office for another interrogation. Since it had been
Schultz who first alerted McCoy to the tunnel, perhaps he could help
determine who else besides Cordes and Gregeratzki was involved. But
Schultz confirmed Moeller's testimony that no one else in T22 was
aware of what they were up to.

Because both Cordes and Gregeratzki had tried to throw suspicion
on Schultz, McCoy needed to check the reliability of his informant.

"Cordes says Kiffl saw you come out from under the barracks,"
McCoy confronted Schultz. "What were you doing under there?"

Schultz's eyes began to dart as he explained that he had hidden
certain "private possessions" from the prying eyes of other men in T22.

McCoy demanded to know what private possessions.

Schultz admitted that for a long time he had busied himself in Ft.
Lincoln by keeping news clippings of German military defeats. Since
the stories of disaster weren't popular with other men, he had to hide

them under the barracks. Despite his attempts at secrecy, Schultz claimed, Kiffl had spotted him there one day and told Gregeratzki and Cordes about it. The three men had whispered about the incident. Afterwards, Schultz finished, "they were all very bitter" towards him.

Since his eccentric informant's secretive behavior appeared as suspicious as his two suspects', McCoy decided not to waste any more time interviewing Schultz. Instead, he would attempt to link Cordes and Gregeratzki with all the confiscated clothing.

Starting with supply records on July 16, he determined that in fact Cordes and Gregeratzki had been issued the type and approximate size of the clothing found in the tunnel. Then, several times over the next three days, he employed the police dog Hooch. Cordes and Gregeratzki were brought from the guardhouse and told to walk a crisscross course over the pasture immediately west of the compound. Each time, Hooch was given the scent of one of the items of clothing found in the tunnel and commanded to trail. Whether it was Cordes's monogrammed trousers, or Gregeratzki's blue chambray work shirt, Hooch followed unerringly the path of the man who had worn it.

Despite the evidence accumulating against them, Cordes and Gregeratzki remained aloof and stoic. McCoy sent them back to share a single cell, on the chance that the closeness would encourage them to a careless, audible confession. But they spent the entire night whispering, or making loud satirical remarks obviously aimed at eavesdroppers. McCoy decided to attempt one last interrogation before, confession or not, he formally charged the two men with an escape attempt and sentenced them to the guardhouse.

Monday morning, July 24, McCoy ordered that T22 be sealed off and all occupants moved to other sleeping quarters. By Monday afternoon, when Cordes was marched from the guardhouse to McCoy's office for interrogation by McCoy and Lovejoy, the entire camp buzzed with the news of who was involved in the tunneling effort.

Cordes stood defiantly in front of McCoy's desk and began by firmly refusing to swear that the testimony he was about to give was the truth. He explained that he had signed so many things and been sworn so often since his arrest that none of it meant anything. He *always* told the truth, he insisted. Yet they kept him locked up!

McCoy ignored Cordes's bitterness and began asking questions. "When Lovejoy and I talked to you at the guardhouse concerning a tunnel under T22, you denied all knowledge of it. Is that right?"

Cordes insisted he still knew nothing of any tunnel, and as far as his pants were concerned, "It must be a frameup or something, is all I can say."

It was the second time that Cordes had denied that the pants found in the tunnel were his, even though the dirt stains on the knees matched his frame perfectly. So McCoy set out to prove that the pants found in Cordes's trunk were an obvious, ill-fitting replacement pair.

McCoy held up the pants and asked sarcastically how they fit.

"Well, they fit all right," Cordes answered. "A little long, that is all."

McCoy suddenly dropped the subject of the pants and asked Cordes to account for his wool shirt being in the tunnel.

Cordes insisted he didn't even have a wool shirt.

Now Charlie Lovejoy spoke up. "Did you get a wool shirt from anybody else?"

"No, sir!" Cordes faced Lovejoy. "I have no wool shirt at all."

"Did you ever get a pair of sailor pants from anybody else?"

"No, sir!"

"Well," McCoy resumed the grilling, "we have several statements and other evidence that the sailor pants and the wool shirt were yours."

"And I say they were not!" Cordes shot back.

"Well, I'm just telling you that for your own knowledge."

"They are not mine!" Cordes remained adamant.

"Then you deny all knowledge of any tunnel digging under T22?"

"Yes," Cordes nodded. "I deny everything."

While McCoy and Lovejoy discussed what they felt were Cordes's obvious lies, the suspect was returned to the guardhouse, where Gregeratzki was waiting his turn. Cordes's method of resistance had been a calculated defiance, which had begun with a refusal even to swear he would tell the truth. However, Gregeratzki had his own successful style of resistance, which began with raising his right arm and eagerly swearing to the truth. Then, for ten minutes, with a look of utter innocence, he insisted that he had never been issued clothing resembling the articles found in the tunnel.

"The pants that were found in the tunnel under T22 belong to Cordes," McCoy countered, "and there was a blue chambray shirt found there belonging to you. How do you account for that?"

Gregeratzki insisted, "A blue chambray shirt belonging to me can't be. It is impossible because I never was down there and I don't have a blue shirt and that is all."

McCoy reminded Gregeratzki that the police dog had tracked him across the pasture after sniffing the blue shirt found in the tunnel. "Do you suppose that was an accident?" McCoy wondered.

His voice filled with innocence, Gregeratzki explained, "All I can say is...if some dog picks up my trail or something, that means nothing to me, and you can take a hundred dogs and trails and that does not affect me."

Then McCoy turned to the subject of the whispered conversation in the guardhouse. "What do you and Cordes have to be so confidential about in conversations?"

"If I want to whisper to somebody, why can't I? Is it forbidden to whisper in your country?"

"No, it is not forbidden, but if you have nothing to hide, why is it necessary to whisper?"

Gregeratzki remained silent.

"Don't you recall whispering?" McCoy pressed Gregeratzki about the first night he had locked them in adjacent cells.

Gregeratzki conceded that he might have whispered to Cordes, but that certainly wasn't proof they were digging a tunnel. McCoy agreed it wasn't proof, but he still wanted to know if Gregeratzki remembered the conversation.

When Gergeratzki still couldn't recall, McCoy wondered, "Do you have trouble remembering things?"

"No."

"Do you remember then?"

"I don't remember every single detail of my life!"

"I'm not asking that. You have only been in the guardhouse for seven days, and if during that time you whispered for an hour, do you mean to tell me you wouldn't remember that?"

"We might have whispered," Gregeratzki admitted.

"Then it was certainly something of a confidential nature." McCoy pointed now to Charlie Lovejoy. "If Mr. Lovejoy and I stood out in the yard for an hour and whispered to each other, don't you think that would be rather peculiar?"

"It might be . . . it all depends on how people look at it."

Gregeratzki's cooperative innocence proved as unassailable as Cordes's defiance, and he too was returned to the guardhouse without having delivered a confession. Still, McCoy felt confident enough about his case against the two men to recommend to his Philadelphia superiors that Cordes and Gregeratzki remain in the guardhouse under solitary confinement for a period not to exceed thirty days. On July 28 while waiting for approval from Philadelphia, McCoy also notified Dr. Gerhard Sprenger and Captain Otto Trautman, spokesmen for the internees, that he was holding Cordes and Gregeratzki in the guardhouse "for their implication in the construction of a tunnel in the vicinity of T22."

Official confirmation of the fact that it was Cordes and Gregeratzki who had tried to tunnel to freedom made the two young men into overnight celebrities within the compound. The cooks' helpers charged with delivering meals regularly to the prisoners secretly took them extra rations and tidbits. Still, their solitary confinement kept the rest of the camp starved for the facts of their adventure. Was it true the tunnel had gone beyond the fence? Where were they headed after escape? Had the tunnel actually been started by the Japanese? What travel and identity documents had they managed to forge? Before long, camp scuttlebutt and rumor had turned Cordes and Gregeratzki into enterprising heroes who were every bit as ingenious as the fictional Max and Moritz they had sought to imitate.

"Could it be," the *Bismarck Echo* wondered, "that the two escapees had managed to secure rationcards" as well as other documents to use once they got out? Whatever, the camp paper concluded, the two escapees were still in custody, "and T22 is today an abandoned, desolate place. Lights, water, and heat are turned off. . . . The windows are barricaded, the spiders have taken over."

On August 5, W. F. Kelly warned INS officials in Idaho, who had custody of Albert Kiffl, to be especially watchful, since Kiffl was known to be close friends with two men who had tried to escape from Ft. Lincoln. Kelly also wrote McCoy at Ft. Lincoln that the confinement of Cordes and Gregeratzki for thirty days was approved. Since the two men had been first put in the guardhouse on July 17, McCoy notified Charlie Lovejoy that they were to remain locked up until the afternoon of August 16.

Determined not to take the Cordes-Gregeratzki escape attempt lightly, McCoy instituted a system of regular checks of the barracks crawl spaces. The guards who made the first investigation reported on August 6 "two shovels made from cans under T19, and there is lumber under all buildings." It confirmed McCoy's suspicions that the Cordes-Gregeratzki escape attempt was not an isolated event.

His caution influenced the outcome of another matter. For two months McCoy had been negotiating with internee representatives over the privilege of hikes in the vicinity of the facility. In mid-July, shortly after he learned of the tunnel, McCoy wrote to W. F. Kelly and explained that however much the hikes would improve internee morale, the sight of Germans strolling about the fields would present public relations problems with farmers out harvesting their crops. However, McCoy deferred to Kelly, preferring to take no further action in the matter until he heard from his boss. Kelly wrote back on August 17 doubting that many "loyal Americans will object (to the hikes) if they understand such action is taken because the German government is willing to reciprocate with American POWs." Still, Kelly concluded,

"Whether you embark upon the program. . . will be left up to you." In the end, McCoy prohibited the hikes.

Denied the privilege of hikes outside the compound, there was more talk than ever among the internees of *Stacheldraht-Koller* — prison phobia — particularly among those men who had been behind the barbed wire fences since 1941. It was common knowledge that several men, stricken with the phobia and overcome with depression, had tried to commit suicide. It was in recognition of the dangers of such a sickness that the camp authorities permitted Albert Gregeratzki and Hermann Cordes to exercise daily in the open air for half an hour.

Cordes suffered most from the isolation. Despite the exercise, after two weeks in solitary confinement, he began slowly to lose his nerve. At first, he had kept his mind off the oppressive closeness of the small cell by working crossword puzzles or sleeping. However, with only a half hour's exercise each day to stretch his usually active muscles, he began to feel the first effects of *Stacheldraht-Koller.* Each day after guards abruptly threw open his cell door for his exercise period, Cordes went out quickly and paced in the restricted exercise area like a restless animal.

Since it was Albert Gregeratzki who had panicked in the cramped space of the tunnel, it should have been he who was stricken with *Stacheldraht-Koller.* Yet, Albert remained calm and confident during his confinement, passing the time of day planning how he would take up as a free man in America once he was released from internment. Ironically, it was the normally deferential Gregeratzki who now propped up his friend and kept Cordes's mind off suicide by reminding him that the authorities couldn't confine them for longer than thirty days.

Cordes and Gregeratzki were released as scheduled from solitary confinement on August 16, 1944, at 1:00 p.m. For Hermann Cordes, the restricted world of the compound was now like absolute freedom, and he stood outside the guardhouse breathing deeply as if to cleanse himself once and for all of the prison phobia. Two guards walked them from the guardhouse to the main gate, where they were admitted back into the compound and greeted as heroes.

In September, Cordes was given a preliminary hearing at Ft. Lincoln to determine if he should be deported to Germany. Cordes refused to make a statement, contending, "I am going to be deported anyway, and I don't see any use in making a statement." In his complete hearing on December 5, he expressed German loyalties that had not wavered: he was not willing to bear arms for the United States, and he wanted Germany to win the war. Shortly after the hearing, the presiding officer recommended that Cordes be sent back to Germany as soon as war conditions permitted. Although Cordes immediately filed an exception to the recommendation, it was not to avoid deportation. He merely wished to establish that "it was through no fault of my own that I am here now. I would have gone back to Germany long ago if I could have."

Meanwhile, despite his hope that he would be permitted to remain in the United States, Albert Gregeratzki was also ordered deported. Since the Russians now occupied Gregeratzki's birthplace in Upper Silesia, he objected strenuously to being returned to eastern Europe, where he would carry the stigma of having been interned in America with Nazis. It would mean almost certain execution.

McCoy acknowledged Gregeratzki's dilemma. In a memo from McCoy to Kelly, July 5, 1945, he explained that internees like Gregeratzki considered repatriation to Russian areas inconceivable.

On July 14, 1945, after the German surrender, President Harry Truman ordered the deportation of all enemy aliens who had been interned in the United States, and who were deemed by the attorney general to be dangerous. The sharpest protest against the mass deportations came from an organization called the Citizens' Protective League. First organized early in 1936 to protect the rights of naturalized American citizens, the CPL had taken up as a test case the fate of nine hundred alien enemies awaiting deportation at Ellis Island. In that case the CPL was not authorized to speak for those at Ft. Lincoln awaiting deportation. Still, in a long letter to Attorney General Tom Clark, dated July 25, Chairman Kurt Mertins of the CPL could well have been speaking for Gregeratzki when he pointed out that "even if the deporation (of the German nationals) might not mean a sentence of death in Siberia, it would surely result in their being seized and put in concentration camps." Mertins complained further that the Justice Department had not been able to "unearth a single case of violent action against the United Sates by any of these 900 interned German nationals." The entire alien enemy program, he charged, was "based on such essentially weak grounds that it was found necessary to go back to 1798. . . to dig up a statute" as constitutional authority for the program of internment and then deportation.

Mertins and the CPL did send a letter to Ft. Lincoln internees directing them to resist deportation proceedings. Gregeratzki subsequently wrote the attorney general that since he was from Silesia, he no longer had a country to go home to.

On October 10, while Gregeratzki awaited a decision on his appeal, Hermann Cordes left Ft. Lincoln. For three and a half years, the two men had pooled their talents for cleverness and deception, and reinforced each other during their internment. Yet, now they seemed headed in utterly different directions, no longer the Max and Moritz characters they had become.

They shook hands and clapped each other boldly on the shoulder. Then Cordes strode off proudly down the main street of the compound.

Back in Germany and marked with a record of American internment, Hermann Cordes was promptly jailed with SA and SS officials in a Bremen prison. A month later he was transferred to Hohe Asperg, a maximum security prison for Third Reich Nazis. By March of 1946, he had lost thirty-five pounds. Not long after he was released and reunited with his aging parents in Sottrum, where he took over the hard work of single-handedly running the family farm. His only brother had been killed on the Russian front.

Despite many official appeals, Albert Gregeratzki was finally deported, and he too was jailed in Bremen upon arriving in Germany. Once released, he discovered that only his mother had survived the war, but she remained in Russian-controlled territory. Returning to be with her, he knew, would mean being jailed as a Nazi again. His efforts to secure immigration papers to America were not successful. Occupation forces still considered him a dangerous enemy alien.

For months Gregeratzki prowled the rubble of the Third Reich, seeking food and a job. Neither his cleverness nor the disarming look of honesty he'd used to escape Europe before the war were helpful now. Little food and few jobs were available. Finally, in desperation he headed for Sottrum and the Cordes farm. The drudgery of farming had never appealed to his adventurous spirit. Yet, it was clear that farmers, at least, weren't starving.

It was a warm day in early spring when Max and Moritz were reunited in Sottrum. Gregeratzki was almost apologetic in asking his old friend if he had any work for him. But of course there was work, Cordes grinned. Spring plowing. Digging!

Internee barracks, Tule Lake Segregation Center,
Newell, California (Courtesy of William Tsukida)

Hiro

JAPANESE-AMERICAN RELOCATION AND THE END OF INTERNMENT

Outside view of Ft Lincoln German casino
(Courtesy of Will Robbins)

Members of militant
internee organiza-
tions at Tule Lake
Segregation Center,
1944 *Second row,
third from right,*
Hiro Tanaka (Cour-
tesy of William
Tsukida)

Inside view of Ft
Lincoln German
casino (Courtesy of
Will Robbins)

Hiro

It was an especially joyous celebration, that Christmas of 1944, for the staff at Ft. Lincoln. Ike and Bernice McCoy held an open house the afternoon of Christmas day, decorating their home in a Mexican theme, which would appeal to all the patrol inspectors at Ft. Lincoln who longed to return to the warmer climates of southern border duty. It was a dream that didn't seem that remote. And, by January of 1945, Hitler's desperate counterattack in the Ardennes had been thwarted. Again the Allies were on the march toward Berlin, and the end of the war seemed near. Meanwhile, it had been six months of calm since the Cordes-Gregeratzki escape attempt. Other than a few minor barracks quarrels, there were no disagreements among the men. To guards and prisoners alike, then, it seemed the end of the enemy alien internment program was imminent.

In fact, the end was nowhere in sight, particularly for Ft. Lincoln.

On February 3, 1945, Edward Ennis wrote W. F. Kelly in Philadelphia on a pressing matter. With the Japanese attack on Pearl Harbor in 1941, 110,000 "persons of Japanese ancestry" had been removed from their homes and resettled onto so-called relocation centers in the interior. Now, Ennis's problem was five hundred bitter, pro-Japanese evacuees in the War Relocation Authority's huge camp at Tule Lake, California. The troublesome evacuees were mainly young Japanese Americans who had renounced their American citizenship after being confined. They thereby became alien enemies. While awaiting repatriation to Japan, their pro-Japanese demonstrations inside the settlement were proving a matter of public embarrassment and delaying the release of loyal Japanese Americans back into the community. In order to stop the agitation at Tule Lake and get on with the release of the loyal Japanese Americans, Ennis proposed that the five hundred troublemakers be removed from Tule Lake immediately.

Since several hundred agitators had already been sent to the INS internment camp at Santa Fe, New Mexico, Ennis's idea was not all that controversial. However, stuffing these additional five hundred men into Santa Fe "could create a real custodial problem," Ennis warned. Besides, Ennis noted, "As news of treatment of American citizens in the Philippines comes back next month, it will be just as well not to have all the Japanese concentrated in New Mexico, which had its National Guard caught in Bataan." If not New Mexico, where then? "It is strongly recommended," Ennis concluded, "that this group of 500 Japanese be transferred to Bismarck, North Dakota for internment."

Kelly directed his assistant N. D. Collaer to phone Ft. Lincoln and inquire whether five hundred Japanese could be handled. It was a quiet Saturday at Ft. Lincoln when Collaer's inquiry dropped like a bombshell. Five hundred additional men! A shocked McCoy checked his latest population figures. The next day, 231 German repatriates were scheduled to depart for Ellis Island and Germany. Their departure would bring the camp population to just over seven hundred men, less than half the number of prisoners confined during the camp's peak in early 1942. Reluctantly, McCoy had to agree he had room.

On Monday, February 5, Kelly wired McCoy confirming the telephone agreement concerning the five hundred Japanese. In addition, thirty-five Italians would be coming along. Sensing difficulties, McCoy called in Dr. Gerhard Sprenger, the German internee spokesman, and broke the news of Germans, Japanese, and Italians in the same camp. Dr. Sprenger was polite but firm: the Japanese were acceptable, but Italians were *verboten*. The next day Dr. Sprenger himself fired off a blunt telegram to Kelly, protesting that assimilation of Italians into camp life with Germans was impossible.

Dr. Sprenger's objections prompted Kelly finally to cancel the transfer of Italians to Ft. Lincoln. But in the meantime, the number of Tule Lake troublemakers destined for transfer had been increased to 650. Since Monday, preparations had been underway for a special train of 10 coaches, 2 diners, 3 sleeping cars, and 2 baggage cars to transport the 650 Japanese from Tule Lake. Fifty-two armed INS patrol inspectors would accompany the Japanese as guards. Also aboard would be Senior Patrol Inspector Red Selland from Ft. Lincoln, whom Ike McCoy had detailed to ride along and put together preliminary personal histories on each internee.

Finally, on Friday the ninth, Kelly wrote McCoy in an effort to prepare the Ft. Lincoln OIC for the new arrivals. "It is considered very important to prevent the continuation by members of this group of the acts which were considered subversive," he cautioned. It was particularly important, Kelly warned, that the Japanese not be permitted to write letters to Tule Lake designed to stir up more trouble and further delay the release of loyal evacuees.

On Saturday morning, February 10, the 650 Japanese renunciants at Tule Lake received notification that the attorney general had ordered them apprehended as alien enemies and transferred to a Department of Justice internment camp. They were to report at 5:00 a.m. the next day to the Internal Security Building. When it became known that 650 men had been arrested for removal to an internment camp, a huge crowd gathered just outside the administrative gate of Tule Lake to give the men a bugle-and-banzai send-off. Once the men had been trucked to a railroad siding in Newell, California, and loaded into a train car with blackened windows, Inspector Selland went through the train car by car and explained to the quiet, somber men that they would arrive in Bismarck, North Dakota, on Wednesday. Selland asked that each car elect a representative fluent in English to assist him in putting together a personal information form on each man. Finally, he explained that the INS was perfectly aware they had been a troublesome group at Tule Lake. Yet, he expected them to cooperate and he wanted no problems.

For the next three days, as the long train moved north to Portland, then steadily east, stopping sometimes for hours on a siding to let a scheduled freight train pass, the men sat quietly or slept in their seats. For Red Selland, who moved carefully through each car compiling brief personal histories on each man, the group's quiet behavior belied the reputation for unruliness which had preceded them. Despite the difficulty that some of them had with English, Selland found each man polite and cooperative, even eager to be as much help as he could, and none more so than a five-foot, four-inch, 130-pound evacuee with broken English named Hironori Tanaka.

Hironori Tanaka's father Sakuhei Tanaka had immigrated to the United States from Japan in the early 1900s, only to find that the New Land was much less promising than he had been led to believe. The number of Japanese residents on the West Coast, who competed with natives for jobs as cheap agricultural laborers, had so antagonized San Francisco that the School Board created separate schools for the Japanese children. Despite President Teddy Roosevelt's intervention on behalf of the Japanese, friction between West Coast whites and Japanese remained, and by 1911 the Immigration and Naturalization Service ordered that Japanese nationals could not file for citizenship. Two years later, the Alien Land Law prevented Japanese citizens from owning land in California. Finally, Congress passed the Immigration Act of 1924, which effectively blocked further Japanese immigration to the United States.

By 1926, Sakuhei Tanaka was dead from agricultural stoop labor and drink, leaving behind his wife, and five children who were citizens by birth of the country which had so disappointed their father. Hironori Tanaka was three when his father died, and already his mother's pet. Even Hironori's twin brother Kuninori, the quieter of the two, did not command as much attention from his mother. Still, widowed and unable to support her children by her own agricultural labor, Shiki Tanaka sent her five children including Hironori back to Japan in 1926 to be educated in Japanese schools and temporarily cared for by her relatives until she could afford to bring them back.

Separated from his brothers and sisters, Hironori was reared by an aunt and uncle in Kumamoto. Hironori's early education involved intense study in Japanese language, culture, and history. Meanwhile, in America, Shiki Tanaka found housework around Courtland, California (near Sacramento), and comforted herself with the knowledge that at least her children were *Kibei*—American born but Japanese educated. Then in 1937, Shiki finally sent for her eldest child, Yoneo, who had finished his Japanese education and now returned to the United States to live with his mother on Sutter Street in San Francisco, where she had found less strenuous work as a domestic cook in a San Francisco household.

Hironori Tanaka at sixteen returned to the United States on June 15, 1939. Yoneo, twins Hironori and Kuninori, and their sister Shizuko (their other sister remained in Japan), stuck together in San Francisco. At Commerce High, Hironori received a smattering of English and American history, which did little to ease his reintroduction to American life. The family was not fluent enough in English to feel comfortable even in the Japanese American community. By 1940, the only significant effect of Hironori's American education was a nickname hung on him by his classmates, who couldn't pronounce his full name. They ignored the Japanese traditions against name cutting and dubbed him "Hiro."

Shortly after the Japanese attack on Pearl Harbor in December 1941, the government began to formulate plans to clear the West Coast of 120,000 persons of Japanese ancestry, through a policy of "resettlement." The Tanaka family returned to the familiar area of Courtland, California, where Shiki found work again as a housemaid and cook, and young Hiro, now eighteen, registered for the draft, at which time he swore unqualified allegiance to the United States.

On February 19, 1942, President Franklin Roosevelt signed Executive Order 9066, which eventually created Relocation Centers under the jurisdiction of the War Relocation Authority headed by Dillon Myer. Consequently, on March 29, 1942, the Tanaka family was taken by train to the Turlock Assembly Center, where they were settled into horse-stall quarters at the Turlock Racetrack, which the Army had hastily hosed down and whitewashed in order to temporarily accommodate nearly four thousand evacuees.

Hiro found work in Turlock Assembly Center as an assistant truck driver, delivering vegetables to the Assembly Center's mess hall for eight dollars a month. Then on July 28, after four months at Turlock, the Tanakas were transferred to more permanent facilities now readied at the Gila River Relocation Center, in Arizona. Except for Yoneo, who had married and had separate quarters, the Tanaka family occupied half a Quonset hut, one of rows and rows of similar huts that housed thousands of evacuees at Gila River. Hiro worked forty-eight hours a week in the camp as a dish washer, earning four dollars a week through July, August, and September of 1942. It gave him pocket money to buy a few things he wanted in the camp commissary — cigarettes, soap, candy. Then, in December of 1942, Hiro Tanaka received notification from his draft board in Sacramento that he had been classified as 4C, meaning that even though he was an American citizen, he was considered ineligible for military service because he was an "enemy alien."

On January 16, 1943, Bill Tanaka was born to Yoneo and Kiyoko Tanaka in the Gila River Relocation Center. The birth of the first grandchild was an event which excited Shiki, but it only temporarily took her mind off the possibility that she might soon be separated from her own family. Daily rumors swept through the Gila River Relocation Center to the effect that *Issei* (first generation) like Shiki Tanaka would be soon repatriated to Japan, leaving behind them *Nisei* (second generation) children who were American citizens. Faced with this likelihood, Yoneo Tanaka argued that he and the rest of the Tanaka children should also request repatriation, in order to hold the family together. They would all then be returned to Japan, where they were still considered Japanese citizens.

It was an argument that Hiro could only half agree with. Yes, he wanted to stay with his mother. For years she had treated him as her pet. With that had come a special sense of responsibility for her which Hiro realized his brothers and sisters didn't carry. Yet he also remained convinced that America was the proper place for him. Even though Yoneo and Kuni took out repatriation papers at Gila River, Hiro stalled and tried to avoid the issue, hoping that some other solution would present itself. Finally it was Shiki herself who took out the repatriation papers for her son Hiro and insisted that he submit them. Consequently, in April of 1943, Hiro handed in his request for repatriation to Japan, quietly harboring in his mind the hope that nothing would ever come of it.

Just as Hiro Tanaka was divided by two conflicting loyalties, the larger Japanese community was split in two. Those *Nisei* seeking desperately to display their American loyalties had protested vigorously against the 4C draft classification that prevented them from enlisting and serving the war effort. Still, other *Nisei* resisted the idea of military service and argued for repatriation to Japan, in exchange for American citizens held there. A limited exchange took place June 1, 1942.

Two solutions to the problem of mixed loyalties surfaced toward the end of the year. General John L. DeWitt, in charge of the Army's Western Defense Command, suggested on December 30, 1942, a swift, midnight troop movement into the camp, in order to separate loyal from disloyal evacuees. Dillon Meyer had rejected DeWitt's plan, but expressed himself in favor of the idea which had been developed in the meantime for an all-*Nisei* military unit.

The idea of a Japanese American fighting unit was the creation of Assistant Secretary of War John J. McCloy, Secretary of War Henry Stimson, and Chief of Staff George C. Marshall. Finally FDR himself applauded the concept in February of 1943. The next step was to develop a questionnaire which would determine Japanese American loyalty with respect to Army service, or perhaps defense work. What was called a "Statement of U.S. Citizen of Japanese Ancestry" was soon distributed to the evacuees. On it were two questions the authorities considered critical to their determination of loyalty for military or defense duty: "Are you willing to serve in the armed forces of the United States on combat duty, wherever ordered?" "Will you swear unqualified allegiance to the United States of America and faithfully defend the United States from any or all attacks by foreign or domestic forces, and forswear any form of allegiance or obedience to the Japanese emperor or any other foreign government, power, or organization?"

Despite his previous draft registration, relocation bitterness and the prejudicial nature of the questionnaire (German Americans and

Italian Americans were not required to forswear their allegiances) prompted Hiro Tanaka to answer "no" to both questions. Thousands of others like Hiro also became "no-no's" out of bitterness and the feeling that they would merely become military cannon fodder for the American government. Furthermore, others who felt repatriation to Japan was inevitable feared punishment at the hands of Japanese authorities once it was learned they had agreed to American military duty.

Unable to determine the extent to which these "no-no" answers were mere resentment over evacuation, or outright disloyalty, the government was startled to discover that over five thousand residents in the camps rejected the idea of military service. Consequently, the plan offered earlier by DeWitt of segregating the loyal from the disloyal received new consideration by WRA officials who were growing increasingly edgy over disagreements in camp between the two factions of evacuees.

In an effort to ease the growing tensions, Dillon Myer proposed to Secretary Stimson that the WRA institute a resettlement program that would permit the loyal evacuees to settle outside the camps in areas not considered military zones. Myer's proposal would have achieved the desired separation of loyal from disloyal evacuees, without creating a separate camp for the so-called agitators. Despite the merits of Myer's idea, in May Stimson blamed the WRA administration for whatever problems existed in the camps. He insisted that the unruly be sent to a segregation camp first, then resettlement could proceed out of the remaining camps. On May 31, 1943, Myer called all his project directors to Washington to discuss how to handle camp dissidents. Myer's own project directors were unanimous in recommending to him that a separate camp be designated as a segregation camp, and he reluctantly agreed.

During the summer of 1943, while Myer and his staff set about determining which camp to designate as a segregation camp, the WRA project directors began identifying the specific troublemakers in their respective Relocation Centers. In that effort, suspicion fell immediately upon the *Kibei,* whose Japanese education, it was felt, had undermined their American citizenship.

Official distrust of the *Kibei* had begun in 1942. At that time Lt. Commander K. D. Ringle of Naval Intelligence wrote that the most potentially dangerous element among Japanese Americans were those young men who had gone back to Japan for an education. Ringle concluded that they may have been sent deliberately back to the United States as agents (Myer, 69). Consequently, in July of 1942, Japanese Americans but not *Kibei* were granted work privileges outside the camps. Then, when Milton Eisenhower resigned as the first Director of the WRA, he wrote FDR that, based on his experience, ninety percent of the *Nisei* were loyal. But many *Kibei* felt strongly attached to Japan (Hosokawa, 347). Eisenhower proposed the program of repatriation which was ultimately adopted. Those repatriation requests became another mark by which project directors could identify the potential segregants.

By virtue of his *Kibei* status and his request for repatriation, Hiro was identified by Gila River authorities as a potential segregant. In July of 1943, Tule Lake Relocation Center, set against the silhouette of Castle Rock Mountains in the lava deserts of northeastern California, was selected as the WRA segregation camp. Eager to make it clear that the segregants had chosen their lot, WRA authorities gave repatriates opportunity to reaffirm their intentions.

On July 28, Hiro again requested repatriation, this time without his mother's prompting. In broken English, Hiro answered questions before a WRA official who filled in the form for him. A problem in communication was obvious. Hiro's grade school, Rafael Grammar School, became "Ralph Ewell Grammar School" on the form.

Next, the government began to assemble the formal dossiers which would identify pro-Japanese segregants. Hiro's clearly placed him in this category. In his case, the Japanese American section of the Provost Marshal General's office issued a report on September 1 which banned Hiro from employment in any defense facility. He was, the report warned, Japanese educated, a dual citizen, a Buddhist, proficient in the Japanese language, and not a member of the Boy Scouts, the YMCA, or any national fraternity or club. Furthermore, he was not willing to serve in U.S. armed forces or swear allegiance to the United States, forswearing any form of allegiance to Japan.

Following that report, the WRA in Washington directed L. H. Bennett, Project Director at Gila River, to further investigate Hironori Tanaka. Bennett could establish nothing beyond what was already known.

Through September of 1943, thirty-three trainloads of evacuees, numbering fifteen thousand persons, were shuttled in or out of the Tule Lake Segregation Center. But almost from the very first arrivals at Tule Lake, the government found that the segregation camp was a ticking bomb. Those original Tule Lake evacuees who wished to remain there to avoid the inconvenience of moving away were permitted to stay. Furthermore, thousands of loyal Japanese Americans who would not otherwise have been segregated went to Tule Lake simply to accompany family members. The result was a more dramatic division of loyalties within the Tule Lake community than had existed at any other camp.

The Tanaka family arrived at Tule Lake on October 13, 1943. Row-dyism, precipitated by the new large group of pro-Japanese segregants at Tule Lake, was not uncommon. Immediately, *Kibei* segregants pressured Hiro and his brothers to join their large group advocating Japanization not only for themselves, but for those *Nisei* who had never been to Japan and did not speak Japanese. Yoneo and Kuni Tanaka eagerly joined the group as leaders. In the meantime, the program of rigid Japanese acculturation held little interest for Hiro. He could not help feeling sorry for those completely Americanized *Nisei* who were badgered and threatened with beatings until they joined the program. Despite Hiro's reservations, the influence of his own brothers, particularly Yoneo, and the growing power of the group itself left him no choice ultimately but to follow along with quiet reserve.

Then on October 15, an event occurred at Tule Lake which divided the entire camp's loyalties even further. A truck carrying evacuees out to the fields for crop harvesting overturned, and a young worker was killed. Agitators in the camp seized the incident as an example of WRA callousness, and the internee's funeral on October 23, attended by nearly two thousand evacuees, became a public affair during which the most outspoken agitators aired their grievances and spread their pro-Japanese arguments.

After the funeral, farm workers refused to return to work until a list of demands had been met. Instead of responding to the demands, Tule Lake authorities brought in evacuees from other Relocation Centers to harvest thousands of pounds of potatoes and barley in danger of spoiling in the fields. Many of the strike organizers were young men whose bid for leadership at other camps had been rejected, and whose strong, pro-Japanese position had not found much support. However, by the time the Tule Lake administration sat down to negotiate evacuee grievances on October 26, a growing number of bitter segregants waited on the outcome.

Several of the demands of the segregant spokesmen were quickly met. But what proved to be the most difficult demand was a proposal that a resegregation program be instituted at Tule Lake. The purpose was to weed out those *Nisei* who were eager to prove their American loyalty by signing up for the all-*Nisei* Regimental Combat Team which was being organized. The pro-Japanese internees in camp wanted no part of combat duty; furthermore, they resented having to live side by side in the same camp with those who did.

Ironically, WRA Director Dillon Myer was on the West Coast addressing the San Francisco Press Club on October 31, as the tension rose at Tule Lake. Having assured the press that the Relocation Centers were running smoothly, Myer went off to Tule Lake on November 1 for a brief inspection of the biggest camp. (The population then was almost eighteen thousand evacuees.) He had no sooner arrived than he found himself in a three-hour negotiation session in the Administrative Building, with seventeen members of a so-called Evacuation Committee. By 1:00 p.m., a crowd of four thousand evacuees waited outside the Administrative Building, while inside Dillon Myer insisted he would not negotiate "demands." Furthermore, it was unclear who the Evacuee Committee leaders he was meeting with represented. Although they claimed to represent various wards and blocks of the camp, residents did not know how or when these people had been chosen.

Meanwhile, Caucasian staff personnel at Tule Lake were rounded up, directed to the Administrative Building, and told to stay inside. They listened as the most forceful spokesman warned Myer that unless he got a proper response to the demands, he could not predict what would happen. It was not a threat, the spokesman explained, but a fact.

The trapped personnel looked out the windows at the gathering crowd. At the same time, word came that a small group of angry evacuees had just stormed the camp hospital, dragged out the chief medical officer, and beaten him up.

A phone call was promptly made from the Administrative Building to the Military Police garrison stationed across the road. Tanks were started up and positioned from outside the fence to face the crowd. MPs were alerted to be ready to come inside the compound with troops.

Despite Myer's firmness, the spokesmen went on pressing him with their demands. Mainly, the leaders wanted a resegregation of evacuees so that Tule Lake was a true segregation camp with only persons who wished to return to Japan. But more importantly, they urged that a plan be adopted by which *Nisei* could renounce their American citizenship and be assured of return to Japan.

At 4:00 p.m., Myer emerged from the meeting to announce that he would study the recommendations of the Committee. Shortly, the crowd dispersed and a crisis seemed avoided. Myer returned to Washington, hopeful that Tule Lake would settle down.

Yet, West Coast newspapers quickly learned of the demonstration at Tule Lake and reported that Myer had been held captive by fanatical militant "Japs." Events of the next two days contributed to the rumors and hysterics. On November 3, strengthened in their leadership roles as a result of the negotiations with Myer, the Evacuee Committee organized and held a pro-Japanese ceremony to commemorate the birthday of the Emperor Meiji, grandfather of the then current Japanese emperor. On November 4, 150 evacuee men, some armed with clubs, entered the administrative area intent on stopping trucks they mistakenly thought were taking food to the evacuees from other centers who had been brought to Tule Lake to harvest the crops. After threatening Project Director Ray Best, the evacuees severely beat a security guard. It was obvious that relationships between the Tule Lake administration and the evacuees had broken down completely. On the recommendation of Project Director Best, who realized he could no longer control the agitators, Tule Lake Segregation Camp was turned over temporarily to the Army.

The leaders of what was called the "Tule Lake riot" of November 1 to 4, 1943, were locked up in the Army's stockade until August of 1944. Hiro Tanaka watched these developments with a growing sense of confusion. Most of the demands of the Evacuee Committee seemed fair to him. It now seemed especially unfair that the leaders of the protest had been jailed across the road in the Army stockade where the tanks sat in a menacing row, their guns trained on the Center.

Yet, the new leadership which took the place of the jailed men seemed to Hiro to be mostly hotheads, whose main concern was to return to Japan. His own brothers Yoneo and Kuni quickly identified with this new group, and Hiro again felt the pressure to do likewise. While the previous leadership had been concerned with relocation center conditions as well as professing their Japanese loyalties, the new leadership accepted relocation center conditions stoically and focused on the removal from Tule Lake of all those evacuees who were not wholeheartedly loyal to Japan. Consequently, Hiro found himself being drawn closer and closer into a larger group of men whose every effort was directed toward being returned to Japan.

By the spring of 1944, a petition had been circulated at Tule Lake demanding expulsion of pro-American elements in camp. The sponsors of the petition were soon organized into a group calling itself the Resegregation Group. Unable to receive a satisfactory response from the WRA on the resegregation issue, the Resegregation Group drafted a long petition to Attorney General Francis Biddle with the names of more than 6,500 Tule Lake evacuees who wanted to be returned to Japan at the earliest possible moment. Until the ultimate repatriation could be achieved, the petitioners wished to be resegregated so that Japanese with the same thoughts and ideals could prepare for their return to Japan.

Hiro Tanaka followed these developments closely and waited apprehensively for a repatriation that seemed a step closer. Then the government began moves of its own to achieve the same end.

As a result of the widespread publicity given to the Tule Lake disorders of November, it occurred to Edward Ennis soon after that the Alien Enemy Control Unit could take custody of the pro-Japanese troublemakers desiring repatriation and intern them in INS internment camps. With the removal of the disloyal evacuees from the WRA camps, in particular Tule Lake, the government could then declare that the Relocation Centers were filled with completely loyal people who could be released to live outside critical military areas if they chose. Ennis discussed his idea with his assistant John Burling, and they both agreed it would restore some constitutionality to a relocation program Ennis had objected to from the start.

There were two significant catches. First, almost all the pro-Japanese involved were American citizens. To put them in INS internment camps, they had to be aliens. It would be necessary, therefore, to give these potential repatriates an opportunity to renounce their American citizenship. Here was the second catch. A specific provision of the existing Nationality Act provided that an American citizen could only renounce citizenship by applying to a consul abroad. One could not relinquish citizenship while in the United States.

The solution was obvious. The provisions of the Nationality Act prohibiting renunciation while in America would have to be repealed. Ennis then took his proposal for moving the violently pro-Japanese into Alien Enemy Internment Camps to Attorney General Francis Biddle. It was approved immediately. Congressional hearings were soon held on the issue of amending the Nationality Act. Appearing before Congress in support of the amendment, Francis Biddle predicted that perhaps from three hundred to one thousand renunciations would be the outcome. Sensing a solution to the nagging constitutional issues underlying the relocation program, Congress amended the Nationality Act as requested by the Department of Justice, and on July 1, 1944, FDR signed PL 405, making it possible for Japanese Americans to renounce their citizenship.

News of passage of the denaturalization bill now focused the attention of the Resegregation Group on renunciation. By August, these resegregants were confident enough about their aims to change their name to *Sokuji Kikoku Hoshi Dan,* meaning "Organization to Return Immediately to the Homeland." Then on the evening of August 12, the *Hoshi Dan* (as it was called) sponsored a meeting of nearly five hundred men at the Tule Lake high school auditorium. The purpose was to expand the organization by creating a separate young men's group. Called the *Sokoku Kenkyu Seinen-dan* (Young Men's Group for the Study of the Mother Country), the *Sokoku's* expressed aim was to prepare the young members for Japanese life after expatriation.

Hiro Tanaka joined the *Sokoku* at the urging of his brothers, but he quietly avoided a commitment on the requirement of renouncing his American citizenship. Meanwhile, he participated in the group's Japanese language study and cultural ceremonies.

However, on October 26 the issue of renunciation loomed large as the government announced that procedures had been set up. Potential renunciants would first apply to the attorney general on prescribed forms. Application would be followed by an individual hearing at Tule Lake. After the hearing, the applicant would file a formal renunciation of citizenship, which would be approved or disapproved by the attorney general, who would notify the applicant of his decision.

With renunciation procedures clearly spelled out by the government, the cultural aims of the *Sokoku* became less important than glorifying and training for the Japanese war effort. To that end, the organization changed its name to *Hokoku Seinen-dan* (Young Men's Organization to Serve Our Mother Country), and took on a distinctly militaristic tone.

First, regular outdoor *taiso* (exercises) at dawn became more than just calisthenics. Gradually, they were changed to marching, then close-order drill, finally goose-stepping while shouting "Wash-sho! Wash-sho!" (hut! hut!) to the accompaniment of bugles. Each man was soon required to wear a headband and a grey sweatshirt emblazoned with the rising sun. Shaved heads—the so-called *bo-zu* haircuts—were compulsory. Finally, on the eighth of each month (Pearl Harbor occurred on December 8 in Japan), prayers for a Japanese victory were offered facing east in an outdoor ceremony. To purify the mind and body before attending the ceremony, block representatives were instructed to take a cold shower at 5:00 a.m. Other members willing to join were requested to do likewise.

For Hiro Tanaka, it was all he could do to stagger out of his barracks at dawn and participate in the *taiso*. "What foolishness!" he told himself each morning. "But if I have to go, I have to go." Meanwhile, a cold shower remained unthinkable! Several times that month Hiro sat down to draft letters of resignation from the *Hokoku*. However, his older brother Yoneo immediately warned him that if he resigned he "would get hurt and it would make mother sorry."

As the *Hokoku* stepped up its efforts to recruit more renunciants, Hiro found himself under increasing pressure, if not to take ice-cold showers, at least to commit himself on renunciation. Ward VII, where Hiro lived with his mother, proved to be the stronghold at Tule Lake for the *Hokoku* activities. Those evacuees who hadn't joined soon did so in response to the pressure. Meanwhile, *Hokoku* members like Hiro, who hadn't announced their intentions to renounce, were directed to stop sitting on the fence. When the government forwarded only a handful of the renunciation application forms it had promised, the *Hokoku* leadership mimeographed extras and hawked them like street vendors.

Despite these measures, the Justice Department had received only 107 applications for renunciation by mid-December. Obviously, the high-pressure tactics and family coercion weren't having the desired effect. In fact there were many in the *Hokoku* who complained privately that they had been misled concerning the true aims of the organization. Relocation anger was one thing, but returning to Japan to fight as soldiers was quite another. Only the most militant *Hokoku* leaders were seriously considering it.

The *Hokoku* leadership reacted to the lukewarm response by doubling its efforts. Again, rumors were carefully sown which declared that nonrenunciants would be separated from families and never permitted to return to Japan. News was spread of Japanese naval victories. There were night beatings of outspoken and loyal *Nisei*. Specific attackers were never named, although there was little doubt who was behind the strong-arm tactics.

In early December, John Burling of the Alien Enemy Control Unit and several Justice Department attorneys arrived at Tule Lake to hold the promised renunciation hearings. *Hokoku* leaders, among them Yoneo and Kuni Tanaka, were the first to submit their requests. They were questioned to determine that their motives for renunciation were genuine. Later, Burling wrote to W. F. Kelly that the interviewees "repeatedly asserted their belief that the Japanese Emperor was a god and their desire to sacrifice anything for him. When making these statements they would jump to their feet and stand at rigid attention."

Burling left Tule Lake in December, carrying recommendations for the denaturalization of 117 men, including Yoneo and Kuni Tanaka. In addition, he made it clear to these men that if they persisted in coercive repatriation activities, they would be sent off to Justice Department internment camps. Since segregation of the men was the motive behind the denaturalization proceedings in the first place, Burling's warning was more than just a threat; it was a preview of things to come.

The procedure for eventual resegregation which Secretary Stimson had demanded of Dillon Myer was now set in motion. Therefore, Myer felt he could begin the long overdue release of loyal evacuees from WRA camps. Since it was feared that the Supreme Court would momentarily declare the whole relocation program unconstitutional, Myer was eager to begin turning evacuees loose. On December 17, 1944, shortly after Burling left Tule Lake with his recommendations for denaturalization, WRA authorities made a dramatic announcement that the United States government was about to rescind the mass exclusion orders of 1942. Whatever the intended effect of the announcement, at Tule Lake it created chaos.

Evacuees who had resigned themselves to remaining in Tule Lake for the duration of the war were suddenly told that resettlement was imminent. But to where? Radio and newspaper reports indicated that West Coast antagonism for Japanese Americans was still running high. There were reports of violence and outright rejection of resettlement by certain communities determined to "keep the Japs out." As a team of Army officers arrived at Tule Lake to begin interviewing evacuees to determine their loyalty for resettlement, the *Hokoku* took advantage of the confusion and anxiety to step up their advocacy of renunciation. It was the only way to avoid family breakup or being forced to resettle in some hostile community. Consequently, in December 1,106 renunciation requests were sent to the Justice Department, most of them from Tule Lake.

In Washington it was obvious to Edward Ennis that his renunciation idea was not the constitutional salvation he had imagined, and he proposed to Francis Biddle that the plan be scrapped. However, Biddle and his assistant Herbert Wechsler insisted that as a legal matter they could not put the law Congress had passed on the shelf. Anyone who wanted to renounce had to be given the opportunity to do so. Meanwhile, it was decided to try to halt the renunciation stampede by assuring evacuees they could remain at Tule Lake until January 1 of 1946. Finally secret plans were laid to remove from Tule Lake those *Hokoku* leaders thought to be behind the renunciation requests.

At 5:00 a.m. on December 27, 1944, forty-one armed Border Patrol inspectors from the INS swept into the various wards and barracks of Tule Lake and arrested seventy men, sixty-four of them *Hokoku* leaders. The men were taken from the barracks independently and marched to the main gate of the compound, where they were formed into columns of ten men each. Word of the arrests spread rapidly among the camp population, and by noon a large crowd of *Hokoku* members, along with drummers and buglers, had gathered at the departure gate in a blizzard to give the heroic leaders a farewell of banzais and patriotic songs.

Yoneo and Kuni Tanaka were among the seventy men taken into custody. Their destination was the INS internment camp for dangerous enemy aliens at Santa Fe, New Mexico. The removal of these leaders was an action the Justice Department hoped would defeat the renunciation movement. Instead, the opposite occurred and created another flurry of renunciation requests from fence sitters who were now convinced that renunciation was both heroic and the way to avoid resettlement.

Faced with a deluge of applications for renunciation, the Justice Department moved to do what it could to save the day. On January 11, 1945, John Burling returned to Tule Lake with a team of Justice Department lawyers bent on holding hearings in private, where each applicant could state his views free of the influence of the *Hokoku* organizers. The hearing officers were to do whatever they could to discourage the potential renunciants.

It was mid-January when Hiro Tanaka finally stood before a hearing officer at Tule Lake and declared his intention to renounce his American citizenship. With the departure of Yoneo and Kuni for Santa Fe, he felt sole reponsibility for his mother, who, he expected, would be returned to Japan eventually. Notwithstanding his determination to stay with her, Hiro was convinced that his *Kibei* status also meant eventual repatriation for him. It was clear to him that if he was deported to Japan without complying with the expatriation procedure, he would be treated as an enemy by the Japanese government.

Pressed by the hearing officer to explain his decision to renounce, Hiro offered the explanation that, "they asked us those questions, if we would fight for our country, the U.S. We said no, no. . . . Because a lot of us were citizens. We were against it, being uprooted. Why not some other races? Only Japanese. We are fighting Germany, Italy, Japan. But orientals are picked and interned. The country where I am born and am a citizen of, they uproot me. So I figure maybe I can go back to Japan."

The hearing officer explained to Hiro that repatriation was one thing, but renouncing his citizenship was another. Having renounced his citizenship, he could never return to America, he was finally told. Hiro left the hearing shocked by the hearing officer's last remark. He had convinced himself that renunciation of his citizenship wasn't all that final. Yet, the officer's surprise announcement gave renunciation the irreversibility of death.

Relocation anger, *Hokoku* pressure, and fear of resettlement into a hostile community produced nearly five thousand renunciations by the end of January 1945. Furthermore, these so-called disloyals felt a new bitterness over the manner in which the first *Hokoku* leaders had been jerked from their midst at dawn and trucked off to Santa Fe.

For Yoneo Tanaka, his arrest had meant separation from his wife, child, and new baby born in October who remained at Tule Lake. These forced family separations prompted newly elected *Hokoku* leaders at

Tule Lake to complain that the predawn arrest of the former leaders was an intolerable incident.

On January 10, the Justice Department, under John Burling's signature, responded to the complaint in a five-page letter posted on mess halls throughout Tule Lake. Before answering specifically why the seventy men had been arrested, Burling's long letter condemned the *Hokoku* organization for disloyalty because of their "semi-military drilling and Japanese patriotic exercises to the sound of bugles." Burling went on to charge that only "children or half-crazed people could suppose that the American government can look with friendship or approval on organizations openly engaged in acts designed to show loyalty to the enemy." Referring to the all-*Nisei* 442 Regimental Combat Team, already receiving battle commendations in Italy, Burling told the *Hokoku* members they were a "disgrace and shame to their brother Japanese Americans who have proved with their blood that they understand what it means to be loyal to the country of one's birth."

Burling's letter speculated what might finally happen to the renunciants. "Throughout the entire war, the U.S. government has been anxious to exchange Japanese nationals desiring to return to Japan for American citizens in the orient. Japan has agreed to only two exchanges, and (none) since October 1943.... In the second place, it is not at all clear yet what the condition of the exchange will be, or even if there will be one. Ordinarily, men of military age are not exchanged."

Burling concluded by stating that the *Hokoku* leaders had been arrested as alien enemies under Section 21, Title 50 of the *United States Code*. Their internment at Santa Fe was deemed in the national interest by the attorney general because of their subversive activities.

Despite the stern warning in Burling's letter against continued disloyalty at Tule Lake, the newly elected *Hokoku* leaders paid no attention, convinced that removal to Japan as an enemy alien remained a remote possibility worth risking in order to express their relocation anger. But, in a continuing effort to stamp out the troublesome *Hokoku*, the government moved in on January 26 and sent a second group of 171 men to Santa Fe, including many of the newly elected leaders.

The *Hokoku* organization responded to this latest round of arrests by stubbornly stepping up the fervor of its demonstrations, held within early morning earshot of the fenced administration compound. Thousands of militant *Hokoku* recruits gathered on Sunday morning January 28, to the shrill accompaniment of bugles, goose-stepping in defiance of any attempt to eliminate them. Immediately, Tule Lake authorities broke into the *Hokoku* headquarters and confiscated the membership lists. It was time, the government had decided, to pack every last *Hokoku* member off to an internment camp. By February 11, Hironori Tanaka found himself with 650 men on a train heading for an internment camp somewhere in North Dakota, two thousand miles away from his mother and Tule Lake.

Bismarck, North Dakota, was in the grip of a five-day cold spell with subzero temperatures when the train arrived at 8:00 a.m. on Wednesday, February 14. Army trucks promptly transferred the new arrivals to Ft. Lincoln, where they were assembled in the gymnasium just outside the compound. Packed together and squatting on their haunches, they were greeted by a huge sign "Welcome Japanese People."

Then they were welcomed briefly in English by Officer in Charge Ike McCoy. McCoy's main concern, he said, was their correspondence back to Tule Lake. They could write about matters of mutual personal interest, but they could *not*, he emphasized, make any reference to the conditions in the camp. For those who understood him, he seemed to be trying to censor any complaining about the difficult and Spartan conditions of their new camp.

Next, a German internee named Dr. Jung, who explained that he had once taught at the Imperial High School in Sapporo, spoke to them in Japanese and offered the services of the German casino, canteen, and theater. Then he went on: "It is certainly a pleasure to bid you a hearty welcome.... It was our intention to greet you with a band, but it was too cold.... We know why you were segregated and sent here. We are proud of you for being loyal to Japan."

Hironori Tanaka situated himself in a dormitory room in barracks 32, along with a dozen other *Kibei* who refused to take *Hokoku* militarism seriously. He and his barracks comrades quickly set about writing enthusiastic letters to family at Tule Lake, describing their new home. They had seen enough of Ft. Lincoln to learn that it was a huge improvement over Tule Lake. The barracks were warm. Each dormitory room had its own shower. The Germans were hospitable, sharing their canteen, casino, and theater. There was an indoor swimming pool, a skating rink, and the food was excellent. The letters were returned a few days later with instructions from the Ft. Lincoln censors reminding the writers that they were to refrain from any references to camp conditions.

Within a few days of their arrival at Ft. Lincoln, the Japanese were organized with much of the same efficiency that had existed at Tule Lake. Elected spokesmen met with McCoy and explained the grievances they felt they had suffered at the hands of the WRA. At Ft. Lincoln, they felt their needs would be simple. Highest priority, they maintained, was the immediate transfer to Ft. Lincoln of Japanese doctors, dentists, and a Buddhist priest.

While not appearing to be sympathetic with their WRA grievances, McCoy saw no objection to the need for doctors or the Buddhist priest, and he made an immediate request for them to Philadelphia. Noting that his new internees were nothing like those Japanese "interned at this facility in the early part of 1942," McCoy wrote Kelly on February 21 that the 650 Japanese were mostly boys who had been more than cooperative. Still, he promised to keep a "close watch" on them.

McCoy got his first chance to carefully observe the new arrivals the next morning at dawn when the sound of "Wash-sho! Wash-sho!" drifted to his quarters from the compound. It was the sound of the first morning's *taiso* by the new arrivals, who shouted from the porches of their barracks as they exercised in unison.

After a hasty conference with his Surveillance Chief Charlie Lovejoy, McCoy decided to let the exercise proceed. However, in a matter of a few days, the German internees protested that the sunrise calisthenics disturbed their sleep, and the renunciants were told to hold their exercises in small groups inside their barracks, where it was warmer anyway.

Beyond that restriction, McCoy found little need to interfere with the behavior of the Japanese. On March 2, 1945, McCoy wrote Kelly that "nothing of importance has occurred other than the usual run of developments from day to day." After explaining to Kelly about the exercises, and a morning ceremony in the barracks in which they "pay some sort of individual homage to the emperor or someone," McCoy explained that "it is apparently a matter of their religion and I believe it would be going rather far to try to prevent it." Furthermore, McCoy noted, when each Japanese received his tray in the mess hall, "after being seated he bows his head for a moment of silent prayer or blessing." As if in anticipation of objection from the Central Office, McCoy went on to say that "if they desire to pray silently there is little we or anyone else can do about it and I think it foolhardy to try to interfere."

By mid-March Japanese textbooks arrived at Ft. Lincoln and the *Hokoku* leaders started a school for the study of Japanese language, culture, and traditions. Conceding that textbooks for the Japanese school might be propagandistic, McCoy had convinced the Central Office that "young, active people (need) some outlet for their energies." Moreover, McCoy felt the study was "understandable, inasmuch as they had each asked for repatriation.... If they expect to return to Japan, it's only natural that they should endeavor to master various Japanese subjects."

Yet, for Hiro Tanaka the five hours of daily classes each *Hokoku* member was expected to attend were monotonous. Ironically, as March brought warmer weather to North Dakota, Hiro and the reluctant *Kibei* remained in their dormitory room, participating in the outdoor *taiso* only as often as was necessary to keep *Hokoku* favor. For exercise they swam with the Germans in the afternoon. However, even that proved uncomfortable when the Germans, who swam naked without embarrassment, began to chide the Japanese for their reserve.

Evenings were spent playing mah-jongg or writing letters to family back at Tule Lake. Fearing that his mother would suffer punishment at the hands of Tule Lake *Hokoku* if he confessed his indifference to their ideals, Hiro's letters spoke of his continued dedication to the program of Japanization and military training now in effect at Ft. Lincoln. In response to letters from his mother encouraging him to remain true to his resolve to return to Japan with her, Hiro wrote to reassure her that he would one way or another stay with her.

Meanwhile at Ft. Lincoln the truth was that Hiro was separating himself even further from *Hokoku* aims. For one thing, more and more of the young *Kibei* with whom Hiro associated felt that the *Hokoku* strictures against alcohol were foolish, and they began to frequent the colorfully decorated German casino to drink wine or beer. Soon the Japanese and Germans found themselves socializing regularly in the evenings in the German casino, discussing the war news, exchanging personal stories, and sharing the bitterness of internment.

Despite efforts to censor letters, coded or secret references to camp life continued to pass between Japanese in the Justice Department internment camps. So on March 9, Ike McCoy phoned Kelly in Philadelphia to warn that the Japanese at Ft. Lincoln were complaining that Santa Fe internees were permitted to do many things prohibited at Ft. Lincoln. Kelly then directed McCoy to meet with OIC Ivan Williams at Santa Fe and work out the inconsistencies.

With McCoy gone, Bill Cook assumed command of Ft. Lincoln. Just twenty-seven years old, Cook was articulate and diplomatic. His first undertaking during McCoy's trip to Santa Fe was to write Kelly in Philadelphia March 15 and tactfully beg off enforcing Central Office regulations for monitoring conversations between Japanese internees and their visitors. Such censorship could be achieved only through the constant eavesdropping of a Japanese-speaking supervisor, Cook noted. Since the Japanese-speaking Ft. Lincoln censor was already swamped reading and censoring letters, Cook concluded, "We do not believe there is any way to permit visiting and prevent the transmittal of the information which we desire to suppress." Still, the censor's office continued to suppress written messages from Tule Lake which encouraged the Ft. Lincoln internees to keep the *Hokoku* faith.

On March 20, Bill Cook forwarded to Philadelphia seventeen letters from Japanese internees, addressed to the attorney general. Since the renunciation stampede at Tule Lake in January and February, the Justice Department had not yet had time to process and deliver the promised notices of denaturalization to many of the Japanese. Each letter that Cook forwarded requested to know when the renunciant could register as an alien.

On the twenty-second, the Central Office wrote back snidely that "you may inform the aliens in reply thereto that they will be registered at such time as meets the convenience of this office." Furthermore, they weren't to pester the attorney general any more about it.

It was a reply which angered the most ardent *Hokoku*. Quickly, a petition was signed by 632 renunciants and directed to Attorney General Biddle, requesting a clarification of their status.

Half afraid to learn that his renunciation had been approved, Hiro Tanaka signed the petition directed to Biddle. Meanwhile, some of the Japanese began to express privately in their letters a change of heart, which the Ft. Lincoln censors considered noteworthy and therefore recorded. One *Kibei* wrote of the *Hokoku* leaders, "I cannot agree with their beliefs and principles." Another wrote, "How absurd they are to continue their worship and exercise." Still a third confessed he was beset with "various doubts...whether (renunciation) was the true path I should have followed." Several wished they could return to Tule Lake to be with families.

That sense of regret began to haunt Hiro Tanaka and other *Kibei*, and to escape from it, Hiro began sleeping more or playing mah-jongg all day long. He spent the evenings drinking in the German casino until just before the 10:00 p.m. curfew whistle. Then, even the drinking as an escape became difficult when Ike McCoy, who had returned to Ft. Lincoln on March 23, ordered the casino to ration the amount of beer and wine sold.

On April 11, Assistant Attorney General Wechsler finally clarified the status of the 632 Japanese petitioners from Ft. Lincoln. They were to be considered alien enemies. "The signers of the petition are advised," Wechsler wrote, "that all persons who renounced their citizenship and who were removed from the Tule Lake Center for internment in Department of Justice internment camps are considered by this Department to be alien enemies.... The Attorney General has approved the renunciation of citizenship of each person." Within days, Hiro Tanaka received official notification that his "renunciation of U.S. nationality has been approved by the Attorney General. Accordingly, you are no longer a citizen of the United States of America."

As the American government proceeded that spring to denaturalize most of the Japanese at Ft. Lincoln, rabid internees inside the compound became even more dedicated to the Axis cause. In April, the *Hokoku* leaders raised a fuss over whether they would be allowed to send a birthday telegram to the Emperor. Then, as May approached, an ardent anti-Nazi internee named Paul Hillman was badly beaten one night after he was rumored to have said that it would serve Germany right if her women were raped by American Negro soldiers advancing on Berlin.

Since several of the men implicated in the beating and hospitalization of Hillman were drunk, Ike McCoy decided to curtail drinking privileges since "the beer casino was perhaps indirectly responsible." Furthermore, he explained in a letter to Kelly May 8, "with the war news what it has been...feelings are at a fever stage.... For that reason, as a precautionary measure in anticipation of the collapse of Germany, I (am discontinuing) the sale of beer and wine."

Finally, on May 8, the *Schlageter* at Ft. Lincoln held a memorial service in the theater, to mourn Hitler's death. Over two hundred men showed up to listen to speeches, to sing the German national anthem, and to stand at attention just at dusk while a trumpeter from the Ft. Lincoln orchestra sounded a solemn taps.

For Hiro and many of his *Kibei* friends, news of the German surrender and Japanese defeats merely confirmed what they suspected, that *Hokoku* stories of Axis victories were the fabrications of die-hard fanatics. Yet, with the transfer of one hundred more devoted renunciants from Tule Lake to Ft. Lincoln in July, Ike McCoy worried that the pro-Japanese convictions of some of his first group of internees would be revitalized. "I do not consider these boys bad," he wrote Philadelphia on July 5, 1945, "but I do believe they have been handled very badly. It is quite easy to see...that they were at the formative age when they were subjected to (relocation and) were thrown among the rabid Nipponese."

McCoy had already written to Philadelphia July 3 that since "an idle mind was the devil's workshop," he had again offered the Japanese internees a chance to busy themselves with work outside the compound. In the past, *Hokoku* leaders had rejected such an idea. But now, McCoy noted, he had Japanese cutting grass, trimming trees, harvesting corn, gardening, and baking in the bakery.

Hiro Tanaka was one of three Japanese who went to work in the German bakery outside the enclosure, where they produced daily rations of pumpernickel rye for the German mess, and white bread for the Japanese. It was, he found, an activity demanding enough to take his mind off the confusion of his denaturalization.

At the same time, several of his *Kibei* roommates confessed that they had had private conferences with Mr. McCoy to express regret over having joined the *Hokoku*. Their main purpose, they told McCoy, had been to effect a speedy return to Japan, and they had not expected to be separated from their families. Now, they wanted to see if McCoy could help them be reunited. In reporting this turn of events to Philadelphia, McCoy wrote Kelly July 3, "I gave each (renunciant) quite a talking to.... I told them as far as I was concerned, there had been no change in their attitude, that they were still going around with their shaved heads."

Once McCoy let it be known that a changed attitude might help to avoid expatriation, many more Japanese renunciants gave up *taiso* and began to let their hair grow. Furthermore, when the *Hokoku* leaders at Ft. Lincoln decided to hold a memorial service for the Japanese war dead, it was quickly cancelled when it became apparent that the political overtones of such a meeting might hasten the deportation of whoever attended.

As a larger and larger group of Japanese at Ft. Lincoln sought to avoid any action which would contribute to their deportation, the Justice Department continued to move the renunciants closer to Japan. On July 14, 1945, as one of his first executive duties, President Harry Truman signed Presidential Proclamation 2655, declaring that "all dangerous alien enemies...who adhered to enemy governments ...shall be subject to removal from the U.S." By August of 1945, shortly after VJ Day, the INS announced that transportation to all European and some Far Eastern countries was now available to "permit the removal thereto of aliens against whom orders of deportation have been issued."

With the Axis collapse, the Justice Department was faced with the task of releasing, paroling, or deporting the last enemy aliens in its custody, and then closing its internment camps. In recognition of what it considered to be a commendable job of running the Ft. Lincoln facility, the INS rewarded Ike McCoy with a promotion to supervisor of the Border Patrol facility at Noyes, Minnesota. With McCoy's departure from Ft. Lincoln, Assistant OIC Bill Cook was elevated to Acting OIC, and given the responsibility of supervising the shutdown of Ft. Lincoln.

In the meantime, fear that deportation sailings would shortly be commenced had brought a deluge of appeals and threatened lawsuits from both German and Japanese internees determined not to return to vanquished, war torn countries. The Citizens' Protective League protested to Attorney General Tom Clark that mass deportation was an action born of hatred and racial persecution.

It was back at Tule Lake, however, that the greatest struggle to avoid deportation was shaping up. On October 8, the Justice Department announced that all renunciants would be repatriated to Japan on or after November 15, 1945. Thousands of renunciants at Tule Lake, faced with the very family separation they thought renunciation would prevent, now came forward to protest that their renunciation had not been freely given. Others explained that they had renounced out of fear of punishment by fanatical *Hokoku*. A thousand renuciants joined to form a "Tule Lake Defense Committee" (TLDC) to fight the threatened deportation. Yet, efforts to recruit legal help were fruitless. Soon, the government began to register, fingerprint, and photograph the potential deportees. Despite the flurry of activities to halt deportation, it seemed inevitable.

It was into this atmosphere of fatalism and desperation that a San Francisco attorney named Wayne Collins stepped. He was no stranger to the government's relocation program for Japanese Americans. In June of 1942, as counsel for the Northern California American Civil Liberties Union, he had argued before the District Court of Northern California, in *Korematsu* v. *The United States,* that the government had no authority to detain and intern loyal American citizens. Then, the Tule Lake disturbance of November 1 to 4, 1943, resulted in the jailing of several participants. In August 1944, Collins called the WRA office in San Francisco and threatened legal action if the prisoners weren't immediately released from the Tule Lake stockade. WRA officials immediately released the prisoners and closed the stockade. Less than a year later, however, the stockade was reopened and a number of residents were held without charges. It was while pressing that matter at Tule Lake that Collins suddenly found himself besieged by parents of renunciants about to be deported.

Collins's first move was to draft a long letter to Attorney General Tom Clark on November 1, 1945. In the nineteen-page protest, Collins objected to the Justice Department's theory that the renunciants had possessed dual citizenship. Renunciation did not automatically make them enemy alien Japanese. If anything, Collins argued, the renunciants were now stateless. Then Collins presented for the first time what would be a litany of criticism against the entire renunciation program. Those who had renounced, he claimed, were victims of coercion, fraud, duress, and menace by the government and organized gangs at Tule Lake. Collins wrote that, "These renunciants whom I represent have submitted to gross indignities and suffered greater loss of rights and liberties than any other group of persons during the entire history of the nation."

Collins hastily collected the names of over nine hundred Japanese at Tule Lake, who wanted to cancel their renunciations, and he appended the names to his letter. If the attorney general didn't act promptly, Collins threatened, he could expect legal action immediately to cancel renunciation, to prevent deportation, and to obtain release of those interned.

Collins delivered on his promise twelve days later on November 13, 1945, and filed suit in the District Court for the District of Northern California. Collins's action (*Abo* v. *Clark*) sought to declare that his clients were American citizens. The 987 named plaintiffs, beginning with Tadayasu Abo, were the same Japanese who had appealed to the attorney general on November 1 for cancellation of their renunciations.

Collins's twenty-three-page complaint listed several causes for his action. Principally, he insisted the renunciations were illegal and unconstitutional because the hearings afforded each renunciant at Tule Lake were only "pseudo" hearings with no opportunity for counsel or witnesses. Moreover, the congressional amendment to the Nationality Act, permitting renunciation, was unconstitutional. Then Collins asked rhetorically: How could the renunciants legally be deported as aliens of a wartime enemy, when the United States was now at peace with the world?

Collins's other major cause of action was an elaboration upon the duress and coercion themes he had raised in his November letter. He explained that Japanese parents, led by government action to fear deportation as aliens, had pressured their American children to renounce in order to keep families together. Furthermore, Collins maintained, the government permitted his clients to be subjected to "organized terrorist groups and gangs. . .who were fanatically pro-Japanese." Citing assaults and blacklisting by pro-Japanese goon squads in the relocation centers, Collins wrote that "many loyal and innocent internees were driven into becoming nominal but inactive members of (the *Hokoku*) to save themselves from danger, physical violence and probable loss of life." The government knew of these group activities and did nothing to suppress them. The result was a wave of terror at Tule Lake, which led to the renunciations.

Although not yet a plaintiff in the Collins suit, Hiro Tanaka could not have been a better example of what Collins was talking about. It was Hiro's mother, fearing deportation herself, who had originally taken out a repatriation application for him. It was Hiro's brothers who had urged him to join the *Hokoku* to avoid physical violence. In time, Hiro had become just that nominal member of the *Hokoku* that Collins was trying to save from deportation.

Eager to avoid charges that its deportation program was arbitrary and illegal, the Justice Department tried to make it clear to Japanese renunciants in internment camps that they could make a formal request to have their original renunciations revoked. At Ft. Lincoln, however, some Japanese like Hiro Tanaka who rejected *Hokoku* militarism continued to feel that renunciation was necessary to keep families together. Others felt it had been the proper response to a country which had rejected them.

With the first deep snows of November at Ft. Lincoln, it was announced that the first of several repatriation sailings would occur on November 25, 1945. Scheduled to depart from Seattle, it was the first such sailing since September of 1943, when three hundred Japanese aboard the Swedish neutral ship *The Gripsholm* had been exchanged with Americans aboard a Japanese ship at a rendezvous point in the Pacific. Now, nearly twice that number of Japanese renunciants from Ft. Lincoln, Santa Fe, and Tule Lake were listed as passengers, among them Yoneo, Kuni, and Hiro Tanaka.

Since Shiki Tanaka was not yet scheduled for repatriation, the departure of her three sons would have left her alone in America. Consequently, with the explanation that all his personal belongings had not yet been forwarded from Tule Lake, Hiro succeeded in withdrawing from the scheduled departure. Instead he remained in the barracks while others rushed out at 9:00 a.m., November 21, lugging duffel bags, suitcases, and string-tied bundles of cherished items they had managed to hang on to during their internment. In the theater building, they squatted on their haunches and waited for what they thought would be a farewell speech.

At 9:30 a.m., OIC Bill Cook stepped on the stage with an interpreter beside him. Cook had in his pocket a speech he had received from the Central Office, which he had been directed to deliver. The text of the Central Office speech tried to make it clear that no Japanese was being repatriated against his will. However, the language seemed wooden and inane to Cook, who chose to launch into his own version of the speech.

Pausing frequently to give the interpreter an opportunity to translate his speech into Japanese, Cook repeatedly invited anyone who did not wish to be repatriated to speak to any of the patrol inspectors in the audience. No one moved, and Cook went on to make it clear that neither the government nor the militant *Hokoku* would be allowed to harass those who elected not to go.

Despite those assurances, Cook counted only two or three takers among the whole group. Clearly, it dawned on him, the government's anxious solicitation had been wasted. At least he hadn't read the long official speech, which was even worse in its entreatment. Leaving the stage, he suddenly recalled the famous words of James Thurber: "You might as well fall flat on your face as bend over too far backwards."

The 174 Japanese bound for Japan left Ft. Lincoln an hour later. They went by train to Portland, then on to Seattle, where they joined up with the group from Santa Fe. On the twenty-fourth, the Army transport ship *General Randall* set sail for Japan.

No sooner had the ship left than the Justice Department announced the second sailing of repatriates had been scheduled for December 26 from Portland, Oregon. Again, Hiro Tanaka was among those listed to be repatriated. But solely responsible now for his mother in Tule Lake, Hiro again managed to remove himself from the roster of deportees, but not without the Ft. Lincoln authorities barking at him to make up his mind.

On December 26, 360 Ft. Lincoln Japanese left for Portland, this time without the official invitation from Cook to back out. In Portland, the Ft. Lincoln repatriates were joined by a huge group from Tule Lake who were likewise determined to return to Japan as Tule Lake was closed. It meant that 3,500 Japanese sailed on December 29, 1945, on the repatriation vessel *General Gordon*.

With the arrival of the New Year, the Justice Department instituted the second of its programs designed to avoid increasing objections to the existing policy of mass deportations. In an effort to give young renunciants an opportunity to remain with families in the United States, it was announced that so-called mitigation hearings would commence shortly for those who wanted to show cause why they should not be removed to Japan.

Almost concurrent with that announcement, Hiro Tanaka received a surprising telegram from his mother in Tule Lake. She had received a letter from Yoneo, who wrote from Japan that the country was in ruins. His advice for them was not to come. Remain in the United States if at all possible, he urged.

Shiki forwarded Yoneo's letter to Hiro, and informed him that she had cancelled her application for repatriation. She was scheduled to be released from Tule Lake any day. In anticipation of that, she had secured herself a domestic position as a household cook in Los Angeles. Whatever machinery was in motion to repatriate Hiro, he was to try however he could to undo it in order to remain with his mother.

On January 4, 1946, Hiro applied for cancellation of his repatriation at the Liaison Office at Ft. Lincoln. Two weeks later, the attorney Wayne Collins and his assistant Theodore Tamba visited first Santa Fe and then Ft. Lincoln, to offer assistance to any Japanese faced with deportation who wished to be added as a plaintiff in the case of *Abo* v.

Clark. At Ft. Lincoln, Collins met with Hiro Tanaka and determined to add the young *Kibei* renunciant to the suit, which would eventually include over 5,000 et als. He was not allowed to speak with him privately, however.

On March 4, as a result of his trip, Collins filed, in San Francisco, a twelve-page supplement to his original suit. After a recital of *Hokoku* terrors and duress at Tule Lake, Collins protested that those terrors were continuing at Ft. Lincoln, Santa Fe, and Crystal City Internment Camp in Texas. He also objected to continued government duress in the form of phone taps of his phone calls to Tule Lake, and eavesdropping on his lawyer-client conferences at Ft. Lincoln and Santa Fe. Then he attacked the mitigation hearings which were already underway at the various camps. He charged that they were arbitrary pseudohearings in which secret evidence was presented against evacuees who again had no opportunity to call witnesses or receive legal counsel. In no way, Collins vowed, would the mitigation hearings dissuade him from the legal proceedings he had undertaken in California to have his clients' citizenship restored.

Collins was right when he asserted that *Hokoku* influence and terror were continuing at Ft. Lincoln. Those die-hard *Hokoku* leaders who remained in camp let it be known that anything less than deportation to Japan would be traitorous. Despite their influence, some thirty Japanese reported to the Liaison Office the first day of the program to apply for mitigation hearings. But the second day no one appeared.

Cook and Will Robbins soon discovered the cause of the abrupt halt in applications: one of the hotheaded *Hokoku* leaders had placed himself out of sight of the Liaison Office, where he could intercept the would-be applicants and turn them back. It was decided then that the only way a renunciant's true feelings could be identified was to make all the Japanese left in camp reapply for repatriation. Those who had changed their minds would have an opportunity to secretly indicate that fact on the form.

Hironori Tanaka took advantage of the new system to indicate on the form that, despite his past actions, he was now reaffirming unqualified allegiance to the United States. In addition, he wanted a mitigation hearing to show cause why he should not be deported.

On February 4, Acting OIC Bill Cook announced that he expected to complete the transfer of all enemy aliens from Ft. Lincoln by March 1. The remaining two hundred Germans and two hundred Japanese waited anxiously then to learn what would be their final destination. Meanwhile, thirty-nine Japanese continued to hold fast to their renunciation-deportation hopes, but they were too small a group to have the same influence and coercion which they had wielded ever since Tule

Lake. Consequently, those renunciants who had already had mitigation hearings discussed openly what questions they had been asked, and were generous with advice on how to impress the hearing officers that they honestly wanted to remain in the United States. Most agreed that it was best to give short, yes or no answers to the hearing officers, to avoid irritating them. Furthermore, any answer that appeared to contradict testimony given at the original renunciation hearing would require a great deal of explanation and only lead to a vigorous line of cross-examination that would ultimately confuse the applicant.

While Hiro tried to prepare himself for the uncertainties of a mitigation hearing, INS headquarters announced on February 8, 1946, that those Japanese internees ordered deported by Presidential Proclamation "should be informed verbally that it has been decided by the Attorney General that he is to be ordered removed. . . but that action looking to such removal is to be held in abeyance until further notice."

The announcement was the government's way of holding open the option of deportation as it struggled to ward off legal attacks on behalf of the Japanese—from Wayne Collins on the West Coast and a new attacker from the East Coast. In New York, attorney George C. Dix sought to overturn deportation orders for 190 Latin-American internees who were threatened with involuntary removal to Germany. Many of these men were Latin-American nationals, but of German descent, who had been arrested at the request of the U.S. government. Dix had been working since December of 1945 to obtain the release from Ft. Lincoln of ninety of these so-called Latin-American German spies. Characterizing the original arrest as kidnapping, Dix explained that most of the Latin-American governments had requested the men back but were afraid to press the matter with the United States. Therefore, Dix was doing what he could. Mainly, that was to file habeas corpus petitions which, along with Collins's massive class action suit in the West, had the Justice Department scurrying to respond.

Despite the delaying tactics by Dix and Collins, on February 14 Bill Cook reaffirmed his intentions to have Ft. Lincoln closed by early March. Prior to closing, two hundred Germans would be sent to Ellis Island, he reported, and from there fifty of them would proceed on to Germany. Cook also revealed that of the 239 remaining Japanese, those thirty-nine still insisting on repatriation to Japan would shortly proceed to Los Angeles to board the USAT *General Ernst*. Finally, Cook announced, the other two hundred Japanese whose deportation orders had been or would be stayed could expect to be transferred to Santa Fe, New Mexico.

The news that he was definitely bound for Santa Fe, New Mexico, did not dispel the other mysteries surrounding Hiro Tanaka's future.

When would he have a mitigation hearing? Would his deportation order be overturned or merely stayed? Would he finally be sent back to Japan, while his mother was left alone to fend for herself in America?

Those uncertainties loomed even larger in Hiro's mind on February 18. On that Monday, in anticipation of closure any moment, reporters and photographers from North Dakota and Minnesota were invited to tour Ft. Lincoln and learn what they later called "the inside story of the camp." Permitted for the first time behind the "curtain of censorship" (*Bismarck Tribune*, February 21, 1946) which had been drawn over Ft. Lincoln, they reported the story of "Nazis and Sun Worshipers too dangerous to be loose in a world at war" (*Morton County News*, February 21, 1946). On the same day the reporters and photographers were shepherded around the camp, the thirty-nine Japanese repatriates left Ft. Lincoln. With 175 pounds of baggage each, and sixty dollars cash, the die-hard repatriates marched out the main gate and into Army trucks.

On Tuesday the nineteenth, the last Germans left at Ft. Lincoln departed for Ellis Island. Of the 149 men sent off, half were Latin-American nationals whose involuntary repatriation to Germany had been delayed by Dix's efforts. Still, most of the men, fearful that they would be deported ultimately, filed angrily and reluctantly into the trucks and buses detailed to transport them into Bismarck. One even went so far as to slip away from the guards watching over the loading. His absence was not discovered until a head count was taken once they got into Bismarck. Departure was therefore delayed until a hurried search of Ft. Lincoln was conducted and the man was discovered beneath a pile of mess hall garbage.

The missing internee was speedily escorted to the train loading point opposite the Bismarck Dairy, the same spot where almost five years earlier the first German seamen had been unloaded among a huge crowd of curious Bismarck citizens. Now, only the detail of Ft. Lincoln guards, a half dozen Bismarck residents, and Will Robbins and Bill Cook watched as the train headed east for Ellis Island. As the last car passed Robbins and Cook, Cook recognized the familiar face of the orderly who had waited on him in the officers' mess. His face pressed now against the window, the waiter stared at Cook and seemed about to wave. Cook prepared to return the gesture, but the train disappeared with no exchange between the two men except empty stares.

Driving back to Ft. Lincoln, the usually congenial Cook fell silent. "I should have waved," he thought.

On March 1, Hiro Tanaka was escorted to the second floor of the Headquarters Building at Ft. Lincoln. There, two Justice Department attorneys grilled him concerning his renunciation. As the questioning progressed, Hiro found himself trying to hold to the advice, given him by those who had preceded him, not to contradict anything he might have said at his renunciation hearing. That quickly became a critical point as the two attorneys reminded him of his past.

Hadn't he declared his intention to be returned to Japan at the time he renounced his citizenship at Tule Lake? Careful not to deny the obvious and thereby subject himself to a confusing cross-examination, Hiro admitted that he had intended just that. Furthermore, he confessed, he had remained true to that declaration right up until V J Day.

It was quite clear that the government's line of questioning was intended to establish that a war torn Japan was no longer attractive to the Japanese renunciant, and Hiro's present change of heart was a case of pure opportunism. When asked to identify anyone at Tule Lake who might have pressured him into his renunciation, Hiro declined to offer any names. Should he inform on *Hokoku* fanatics, they would seek revenge against him, he was convinced.

Finally, Hiro was presented excerpts from his recent letters to Tule Lake. Fearful that his mother would suffer *Hokoku* terror if he did otherwise, Hiro had falsely assured friends of his mother's that he remained steadfast to the Japanese cause. How did he reconcile those statements with his desire now to cancel his renunciation and profess his American patriotism?

Those were contradictions which Hiro was unable to explain away during the confusion of his hearing. No information was forthcoming which would have mitigated the circumstances of his renunciation. He was, the attorneys concluded, still faithful to Japan.

Hiro left the hearing without having explained the deeper truth that neither Japan nor America was the point. It was instead a feeling of responsibility for his mother Shiki that had first caused his desire to return to Japan, then forced him to decide to remain with her in America. Consequently, for Hiro, the mitigation hearing resulted only in a stay of his deportation order until such time as the government had parried all legal challenges to the program.

The next day, March 2, Acting OIC Bill Cook announced that the last of the enemy aliens at Ft. Lincoln—two hundred Japanese renunciants—would go to Santa Fe, New Mexico, on March 6. With their departure, Ft. Lincoln would be officially closed. For some of the remaining Japanese, news of a definite date for transfer to Santa Fe brought them closer to the promise of reunion with family members likewise awaiting deportation. In Hiro's case, his mother had been released from Tule Lake and had gone to work as a cook-housekeeper in a well-to-do household in Los Angeles. In her letters, she continued to encourage him to do all he could to remain in the United States. She even assured him that there would be a situation for him in the same household once he was released. However, for Hiro there was nothing beyond Santa Fe except the continued government promise to deport him as an enemy alien.

The approaching transfer of the last Japanese brought a flurry of activity to Ft. Lincoln. Arrangements were made for the transfer of autos, trucks, and radio equipment to Border Patrol stations within the district. Books from the Ft. Lincoln library were donated to the Bismarck Public Library. Blankets, sports equipment, and office furniture not valuable enough for the expense of transfer were given away to North Dakota welfare agencies.

On Monday, March 4, the weather warmed to nearly fifty degrees as maintenance men began to take down the fence around the empty row of temporary barracks, where first the Japanese, then Cordes and Gregeratzki had tried to tunnel out. The chain link fence was unfastened from the steel poles by sections and stretched on the ground so that from a distance it sparkled in the bright sunlight. Then it was rolled into bundles like carpeting and hoisted into waiting trucks. Next, the huge, sensitive microphones at the main gate were disconnected. Several transferred INS guards, on their way out of the Ft. Lincoln gate for the last time, stopped and shouted "good-bye!" into the dead speakers.

On Tuesday morning, while Bill Cook supervised the packing of thirty wooden boxes of internee case files for shipping to Philadelphia, North Dakota radio stations reported that the Missouri River had risen half a foot in the last twenty-four hours as a March heat wave melted the snow on the upper Missouri River. Despite the warming trend, newspapers reported that evening that no immediate breakup of ice or flooding was predicted in the Bismarck river bottom area. In fact, river ice was still forty inches thick, the accretion of a long, hard winter.

Wednesday, March 6, Hiro Tanaka and the remaining Japanese internees were awakened at dawn and directed to transfer their excess baggage for temporary storage in building T100, among the cluster of wooden bungalows which had housed the seamen officers. Loaded down with duffel bags almost their own size, they stumbled out of their barracks and along the row of elms which had once been the shade-row for *Schlageter* naps and *Wanderkameraden* strolls.

At the designated barracks, they stacked the duffel bags and then cut back through the bungalow gardens, tended proudly once by the likes of Kurt Peters but now looking like neglected little cemetery plots with fence pickets and weedstalks sticking up through the receding snow.

By 10:00 a.m., in anticipation of departure, all two hundred men had assembled in front of the east compound gate where the mob of angry Germans had threatened to storm Ike McCoy's office in 1943. Today, however, only a handful of guards, along with Bill Cook and Will Robbins, stood outside the gate.

Trucks arrived at the compound and were backed into a line just outside the main gate. Mindful of the German who had tried to escape deportation by hiding in the garbage, the Ft. Lincoln staff formed the Japanese renunciants into rank and file and counted them for the last time. All two hundred men were present and accounted for. The men marched through the main gate, which had seen 3,850 internees come and go since June of 1941. That number was in turn just a small portion of the 31,275 enemy aliens who, according to W. F. Kelly, were imprisoned in Justice Department camps during the war. Only a handful of that total had been women — interned at either Gloucester City, New Jersey, or Seagoville, Texas. Perhaps the only explanation for that imbalance lies in understanding the sexism of an era that credited men with the inherent authority to plot treason, while women were by nature deferential.

At Ft. Lincoln, among the last of the men was Hiro Tanaka, who swung his luggage up to receiving arms and was hoisted up by a guard who then vaulted in and seated himself. One by one, the trucks started up and headed into Bismarck in a convoy. Once the last truck was gone, nobody bothered to close the main gate.

The threat of deportation continued to hang over Hiro Tanaka's head at Santa Fe. Every Saturday, names were posted of those people who could leave. In the evenings, those whose names had appeared celebrated with drinking and a barracks party. Hiro attended the celebrations at first, despite the fact that his own name never appeared. Jubilant internees whose release had been announced tried to cheer up Hiro. Again and again he was told to write his mother in Los Angeles and solicit her help. He explained that she was all by herself and could do nothing. Finally, he stopped going to these celebrations, or even checking to see if his name was on the bulletin board.

With the closing of Santa Fe at the end of March 1946, Hiro was transferred to the internment camp at Crystal City, Texas. Since Crystal City was an INS "family camp," Hiro enjoyed the opportunity to be among women and children for the first time in over a year. Still, the presence of the children served mainly to prick his conscience with respect to joining his own mother as soon as he could. Therefore, in hopes of hastening his release, he wrote a short letter on July 19 to Thomas Cooley, now director of the Alien Enemy Control Unit, expressing his unqualified allegiance to the United States.

At the same time that Hiro was declaring his allegiance to Cooley by letter, attorney Wayne Collins, still pursuing his suit on behalf of the Japanese renunciants, was face-to-face with Cooley in the United States District Court in San Francisco. The government's first response to Collins's class action suit had been to move to strike the entire twenty-two-page complaint, charging that it was full of "redundant, impertinent, and immaterial matter." The oral argument was held before Judge A. T. St. Sure on July 5. It was Cooley who spoke for the government, insisting that if the issues weren't more sharply drawn, the government would insist on trying all the renunciant cases separately. The number had reached 1,500 and was going up.

Collins ignored the threat and went on to argue that the detention of Japanese American citizens was in fact a form of duress, which had ultimately coerced the renunciations from his clients. Cooley moved quickly to contradict Collins's assertions and insisted that the government was not going to concede any coercion.

Collins responded that he wasn't asking the government to concede anything. "We merely ask you to answer the allegations!"

Cooley repeated that if Collins continued to charge that government duress was an issue, "it will be necessary to split this case into individual cases and try each one.... Duress is an individual matter."

As Judge St. Sure considered the mass of written evidence in the case of *Abo* v. *Clark,* the government agreed to find some employment for the Japanese whose deportations had been stayed pending a decision in Collins's suit. Internment restrictions were therefore relaxed in order to permit renunciants at Crystal City to go to work in the frozen food plant at Seabrook Farms, New Jersey. Representatives from Seabrook Farms came to Crystal City to interview applicants, one of whom was Hiro Tanaka, and by August 1946, he was hard at work in the packing plant along with 2,600 other internees who had been hired to replace German POWs sent home.

At Seabrook Farms, Hiro was permitted to travel no farther than five miles from the barracks compound where he lived. It was in that confined Seabrook community that Hiro soon met a young, attractive Japanese American woman named Aki, who had also spent the war years under internment.

While Hiro saved his money and courted his bride-to-be at Seabrook Farms, the government continued to respond to Collins's suit in San Francisco. On September 26, government attorneys argued that, as was the case with Hiro Tanaka, parental persuasion had been present at Tule Lake. However, renunciation had not been necessary to preserve the family unit, it was argued. The renunciation hearings were fair, and the subsequent renunciations voluntarily offered. It was not until the fact of the A-bomb and Japanese surrender that any of the renunciants, again like Hiro Tanaka, appeared to have second thoughts and moved to cancel the renunciations. Therefore, the government still intended to deport them as enemy aliens.

On January 27, 1947, in support of its contention that certain of the plaintiffs in *Abo* v. *Clark* were still deportable, the government filed thumbnail sketches with the court on 112 alien enemy renunciants. Based on evidence the subjects had delivered at renunciation or mitigation hearings, the sketches were included to show that the renunciations had been voluntarily offered by dangerous enemy aliens. Hiro Tanaka was among the 112 men singled out by the government. At his mitigation hearing, the government wrote of him, he had admitted that he had been loyal to Japan from February 1943 until VJ Day and wanted Japan to win. It wasn't until January of 1946, the government pointed out, that he had cancelled his request for repatriation. Again, the government argued, opportunism was the motive, not a newfound or resurrected American patriotism.

It took Collins only two days to file a motion to suppress the thumbnail sketches. In previous written arguments of December 11 to the Court, Collins had already characterized the mitigation hearings as "star-chamber proceedings...nothing but a face-saving device designed to lend the appearance of fairness and legality" to deportation efforts.

On February 20, 1947, because of the illness of aging Judge St. Sure, *Abo* v. *Clark* was reassigned to Judge Louis B. Goodman. Appointed to the District Court by FDR, it was Goodman who would see the case through the next fourteen years of proceedings. Goodman immediately began familiarizing himself with the volumes of written evidence in the case. It was therefore not until June 30, 1947, that Goodman took his first action in the proceedings, granting Wayne Collins his habeas corpus petition. Goodman ruled that the petitioners couldn't be declared enemy aliens by renunciation alone. Consequently, Goodman wrote, their imprisonment was illegal. The government appealed the decision to the Ninth Circuit Court in San Francisco but ultimately lost. Meanwhile, 302 internees still under detention at Crystal City, Texas, or on work internment at Seabrook Farms, New Jersey, were ordered paroled into the custody of Wayne Collins.

Hiro Tanaka was released to the custody of Collins on September 6, 1947. With his release, Hiro jubilantly caught a train for the long ride from New Jersey to Los Angeles. It was a hot, September day when he finally arrived at the Los Angeles train depot. A year and a half had passed since he had left his mother alone at Tule Lake. Though he was still short and slight, his face had filled out from months of nothing more than eating and sleeping and playing mah-jongg at Ft. Lincoln. Meanwhile, Shiki's face had aged considerably from the grief of family separation. Still, they met in a crowd at the track gate and recognized each other instantly.

As he tried to set his suitcase on the platform, she hugged him and cried. Then she wondered if he was hungry.

He nodded.

With that, she led him at a brisk walk toward a Chinese restaurant, where she treated him to a chop suey dinner.

It was twelve more years before Hiro Tanaka finally got his American citizenship back. While he took up residence in Los Angeles, where he finally married Aki and started a business as a gardener, the government continued its legal fisticuffs with Collins over the final disposition of the five thousand plaintiffs he had now added to his suit. On September 27, 1948, Judge Goodman delivered an Interlocutory Order which cancelled the renunciations because they were the result of duress, menace, coercion, intimidation, and fraud. Goodman further ordered that the petitioners were native-born citizens of the United States and not subject to deportation.

Attorney Wayne Collins might have celebrated, since it was an opinion which echoed his argument of two years. However, there was a catch in Goodman's order. Perhaps, the judge wrote, the government could produce further proof that some of the plaintiffs had acted freely. Therefore, the Interlocutory Order gave them four months to designate which of the plaintiffs it intended to file further proof on.

It proved to be just the slight opening the government wanted, and on February 25, 1949, the government presented Goodman with a series of lists which singled out 3,500 individual plaintiffs, including Hiro Tanaka, whom the government intended to try individually. The names were arranged in groups, according to common circumstances which the government considered critical: Were they *Kibei? Hokoku* leaders? Had they already been voluntarily deported? One of these categories contained the names of 216 *Kibei*, including Tanaka, who had applied for repatriation, renounced their citizenship, and were still considered under deportation orders, despite court rulings.

Collins attacked the lists as sham. Meanwhile, the lists presented the very real threat of lengthy court-clogging, case-by-case trials which Goodman had been eager to avoid. Besides, Goodman wrote in a court order of March 23, 1949, none of the lists had any competency, relevancy, or materiality. He promptly ordered the lists stricken, and on April 12, 1949, Goodman issued his Final Order in the case of *Abo* v.

Clark. He blamed the government for "complete lack of constitutional authority...to detain and imprison American *Nisei* citizens...when they were not charged with criminality." All the conditions at Tule Lake, including the government duress, had produced "neuroses built on fear, anxiety, resentment, uncertainty, hopelessness, and despair of eventual rehabilitation." Therefore, Goodman ordered all effected or pending renunciations set aside. Each plaintiff was a native-born American citizen!

It was again a powerful affirmation of nearly every point Collins had been arguing since 1945. Still, the government appealed the decision to the Ninth Circuit Court on April 26, 1949. That Court, Chief Justice William Denman presiding, delivered its opinion in the matter on January 17, 1951. Now party to the suit were 4,315 plaintiffs, and the Circuit Court first agreed with the District Court that 1,004 plaintiffs who had renounced as minors (under 21) had done so unconstitutionally. Yet, the Court held that the remaining adult plaintiffs had renounced only after the Hiroshima and Nagasaki bombings had made it clear that Japan had lost the war. Therefore, the Court presumed, "simple expediency and crass material considerations, not duress," had caused the renunciations. The Circuit Court ruled that the burden of proof with respect to the involuntary nature of the renunciations lay with each internee. Though it would put a heavy burden on the courts, the cause was therefore remanded to the District Court for further proceedings.

The partial reversal of Goodman's order saddled Collins with the time-consuming task of soliciting individual affidavits from the 3,300 remaining adult plaintiffs. In October of 1951, Goodman ordered Collins to begin submitting written affidavits from individual plaintiffs, in lieu of oral testimony, on the involuntary nature of their renunciation. Collins met with the government to agree on a standard form which each renunciant would submit to the Court. If the Justice Department had nothing in its files to contradict the written testimony of the renunciant, it would not oppose a final order in favor of restoring the plaintiff his citizenship.

It took five and one-half years of patient, case-by-case processing before Collins finally directed Hiro Tanaka to submit his affidavit to the Court. In his affidavit, dated March 21, 1957, in Los Angeles, Hiro explained that in the relocation centers, it was the consensus "that eventually all the alien parents would be deported to Japan and that the *Nisei* would thus be separated from their parents. Such being the case I took steps to make arrangements for repatriation, which I did reluctantly. My mother did not want me separated from her and I couldn't let her go alone." Hiro went on to explain that fear of violence from ardent *Hokoku* members, many of whom he named in his affidavit, had also prompted his renunciation. "Never have (I) feared the nights as I had then," he wrote awkwardly, "for every shadow seemed as though someone was stalking me with a deadly weapon."

There was no government challenge to Hiro's written testimony, and Judge Goodman issued a Final Order with respect to Hironori Tanaka on January 8, 1959. It had been fourteen years to the month since Hiro had renounced his citizenship amidst the confusion and hysteria of Tule Lake. But, Goodman ordered, he was now and at all times had been a native of this country. His purported renunciation of citizenship was declared null and void. Hironori Tanaka was a citizen of the United States of America.

For Hiro, it was the end of a long ordeal. But for Wayne Collins, it would be nine more years of soliciting affidavits (even from renunciants like Kuni Tanaka who had been returned to Japan) and then waiting for the final Court order in each case before he finished with *Abo* v. *Clark*. The final court action, dated March 6, 1968, was the dismissal of the last plaintiff. Appropriately enough, the District Court let Collins have the last word in the case. "This brings to a conclusion these consolidated mass. . .proceedings, instituted on November 13, 1945," Collins's statement to the Court explained. "The abusive treatment of these citizens was halted by the commencement of these. . .proceedings in this Court. In the course of time, those who had been interned were liberated from internment and returned to their homes. With few exceptions, the purported renunciations of citizenship were ordered cancelled. . . . The episode which constituted an infamous chapter in our history has come to a close."

BIBLIOGRAPHY

Abo v *Clark.* U S District Court of Northern District of California, Federal Archives and Records Center, San Bruno, Calif., RG21.

Abo v *McGrath.* Ninth Circuit Court of Appeals, Federal Archives and Records Center, San Bruno, Calif., RG276.

"Alien Crackdown." *Newsweek,* May 19, 1941

"Aliens: Robt. Jackson's Busy Week" *Time,* May 19, 1941

The Ambrose Herald, July 31, 1941

Archibald, A. R "Alien Seamen." *U.S. Immigration and Naturalization Service,* December 10, 1934.

Biddle, Francis. "Instruction to Alien Enemy Hearing Boards." *Pacific Coast International,* January, February 1942. Institute for Governmental Studies, University of California, Berkeley.

_____ *In Brief Authority.* New York: Doubleday, 1962

The Bismarck Tribune, April 11, 12, 14, 16, May 7, 13, 29, 31, June 2, 6, 10, 13, 16, July 10, August 4, 22, September 4, October 30, December 14, 20, 1941; February 26, March 13, 14, 16, 20, 24, 28, April 1, 3, 16, July 25, 1942; July 11, 1944; February 15, December 21, 22, 23, 1945; January 8, 11, February 4, 18, 21, 22, 23, March 2, 1946; June 5, 1969.

Busch, Wilhelm *Max and Moritz.* Munich: Delphin Verlag, 1981

"A Camp for Aliens" *Time,* January 27, 1941

Collins, Wayne. Papers. File 78/177C. Bancroft Library, University of California, Berkeley

Commission on Wartime Relocation of Civilians. *Personal Justice Denied.* Washington, D.C : Government Printing Office, 1982.

Daniels, Roger *Concentration Camps USA.* New York: Holt, Rinehart & Winston, 1972

Dasch, Georg *Eight Spies Against America.* Arnold, Md: McBride, 1959

Denman, William "The Destruction of San Francisco as Planned by the Japanese," July 31, 1942. Institute for Governmental Studies, University of California, Berkeley.

"Detention of Certain Aliens" *Congressional Record—House,* May 5, 1939

DeWitt, J L *Final Report: Japanese Evacuation from the West Coast, 1942.* Washington, D.C : Government Printing Office, 1943

Ennis, Edward J. "Federal Control Measures for Alien Enemies." *The Police Yearbook,* 1943. Institute for Governmental Studies, University of California, Berkeley

_____. "Government Control of Alien Enemies." *State Government,* May 1942 Institute for Governmental Studies, University of California, Berkeley

_____. "A Justice Department Attorney Comments on the Japanese-American Relocation." *The Japanese-American Relocation Reviewed,* Vol 1, "Decision and Exodus" Regional Office of Oral History, Bancroft Library, University of California, Berkeley, 1976.

_____. "Testimony before the Commission on Wartime Relocation and Internment of Civilians." November 2, 1981. Courtesy of Edward Ennis.

_____. "Written Statement of ACLU before U.S. Commission on Wartime Relocation and Internment of Civilians." September 8, 1981. Courtesy of Edward Ennis.

Fargo Forum, February 21, 22, 1946.

Fassbender, Heinrich. "I Was a Gestapo Agent." Exhibit B, submitted to Special Committee on Un-American Activities, House of Representatives, 77th Cong., 2nd sess., 1941.

FBI Alien Enemy Case File: Albert Gregeratzki. FBI, Records Management Division, Washington, D.C.

FBI Alien Enemy Case File: Carl Kroll. FBI, Records Management Division, Washington, D.C.

FBI Alien Enemy Case File: Dr. Arthur Sonnenberg. FBI Records Management Division, Washington, D.C

FBI Alien Enemy Case File: Edgar Friedman. FBI, San Francisco, Calif

FBI Alien Enemy Case File: Hermann Cordes. FBI, Records Management Division, Washington, D.C.

FBI Alien Enemy Case File: Kurt Peters. FBI, Records Management Division, Washington, D.C.

FBI Alien Enemy Case File: Wolfgang Thomas. FBI, Records Management Division, Washington, D.C.

FBI Censorship Daily Reports. 9, No. 8507, Dr. Edgar Friedman, October 27, 1944. FBI, Records Management Division, Washington, D.C

File #4290/125: Robert Nebel. World War II Internment Centers, Ft. Lincoln, Washington National Records Center (hereafter referred to as WNRC), RG85.

File #4290/137: Kurt Heinrich Rudolf Peters World War II Internment Centers, Ft Lincoln, WNRC, RG85

File #4290/328: Edgar Friedman. World War II Internment Centers, Ft. Lincoln, WNRC, RG85.

File #4290/391: Dr. Arthur Sonnenberg. World War II Internment Centers, Ft. Lincoln, WNRC, RG85.

File #4290/395: Wolfgang Thomas. World War II Internment Centers, Ft Lincoln, WNRC, RG85.

File #4290/984: Albert Gregeratzki World War II Internment Centers, Ft. Lincoln, WNRC, RG85.

File #4290/1334: Hermann Heinrich Cordes. World War II Internment Centers, Ft. Lincoln, WNRC, RG85.

File #4290/5573: Hironori Tanaka. World War II Internment Centers, Ft Lincoln, WNRC, RG85.

File of Fred Fengler. Illinois Dept. of Corrections, Information Service Unit, Springfield, Ill.

File of Hironori Tanaka. Wartime Civil Control Administration, WNRC, RG338.

"Fingerprinting America's Aliens." *United States News,* June 7, 1940. Institute for Governmental Studies, University of California, Berkeley

"Germans Scuttle and Run from British Sea Might in the Atlantic." *Life,* January 1, 1940.

Girdner, Audrie; Loftis, Anne. *The Great Betrayal: Evacuation of Japanese-Americans During W.W. II.* New York: Macmillan, 1967.

Grodzins, Morton. *Americans Betrayed.* Chicago: University of Chicago Press, 1949.

Harrison, Earl G. "Axis Aliens in an Emergency" *Survey Graphic,* September 1941 Institute for Governmental Studies, University of California, Berkeley.

_____. "Civilian Internment: The American Way." *Survey Graphic,* May 1944.

History of Ft. Lincoln, May 1941–March 1946. Bismarck: Immigration and Naturalization Service.

Hosokawa, William. *Nisei, The Quiet Americans.* New York: William Morrow & Co., 1969.

"Investigation of Un-American Propaganda Activities in the U.S." Hearings before a Special Committee on Un-American Activities, House of Representatives, 77th Cong., 2d sess., Volume 5, *Testimony of Heinrich Peter Fassbender.*

Johnson, Phyllis. "Thoughts on the Friendship of Cordes and Gregeratzki." Unpublished manuscript. Available from John Christgau.

Kitigawa, Daisuke. *Issei and Nisei: The Internment Years.* New York: Seabury Press, 1967.

Lotze, Dieter. *Wilhelm Busch.* Boston: Twayne, 1979.

Mandan Pioneer, April 16, 1942; February 23, 1946.

Minneapolis Star and Tribune, February 21, 22, 1946.

Miyakawa, Edward *Tule Lake.* Waldport, Oreg.: House by the Sea Press, 1979.

Morton County News, January 17, 24, February 14, 21, 28, March 7, April 18, 1946.

Myer, Dillon. *Uprooted Americans.* Tucson: University of Arizona Press, 1971.

_____. "Statement Regarding the Events that Occurred between November 1–4 at the Tule Lake Center in Northern California," November 14, 1943, WRA. Institute for Governmental Studies, University of California, Berkeley.

"Nazi Eye View of San Francisco." *Time,* May 12, 1941.

The New York Times, December 6, 1939; June 1, 1940; May 8–12, 19, 1941; June 28–30, July 3, 10, August 1, 4, 9, 13, 1942.

Okubo, Miné. *Citizen 13660.* New York: AMS Press, 1966.

"Our Three Concentration Camps." *American Magazine,* January 1946.

Persico, Joseph. *Piercing the Reich.* New York: Viking, 1979.

Peters, Kurt. "Journal." August 25, 1941–April 23, 1943.

Rachlis, Eugene. *They Came to Kill.* New York: Random House, 1961.

"Records of Adjutant Generals Office–Camp McCoy, Wisconsin." WNRC, RG407.

"Records of Cook County Clerk's Office in Re: Fred Fengler, Assault with Intent to Murder" January 1933–February 1941.

Reis, Curt. "The Nazis Carry On." *Cosmopolitan,* June 1944.

"Roundup and Rally." *Newsweek,* May 26, 1941.

Rowe, James "Keeping Our Heads on the Enemy Alien Problem" *American City,* February 1942. Institute for Governmental Studies, University of California, Berkeley

Rumpf, Hans. *The Bombing of Germany.* New York: Holt, Rinehart & Winston, 1963.

San Francisco Chronicle, June 17, December 6, 1941

San Mateo Times, January 2 to March 31, 1941.

"SF Doctor Arrested by FBI." *San Francisco Call Bulletin,* December 11, 1941.

Speer, Albert *Inside the Third Reich.* New York: Macmillan, 1970

Swanberg, W. A. "The Spies Who Came in from the Sea." *American Heritage Series,* 21 (April 1970).

tenBroek, Jacobus; Barnhart, Edwin; Matson, Floyd. *Prejudice, War and the Constitution.* Berkeley: University of California Press, 1954.

Thomas, Dorothy; Nishimoto, Richard. *The Spoilage.* Berkeley: University of California Press, 1969.

U.S. Congress. House. Special Committee on Un-American Activities. "Report on the Tule Lake Riot." 78th Cong., 2nd sess., 1944.

Verrier, Anthony *The Bomber Offensive.* New York: Macmillan, 1969.

Vyzralek, Frank. "Ft. Lincoln." Bismarck: State Historical Society of North Dakota.

War Relocation Authority. "The Tule Lake Incident" Documentary Analysis Series #14.

March 27, 1944 Institute for Governmental Studies, University of California, Berkeley

War Relocation Authority Case File: Hironori Tanaka. WRA, WNRC, RG210

Weglyn, Michi. *Years of Infamy.* New York: William Morrow & Co., 1976.

Whitehead, Don. *The FBI Story.* New York: Random House, 1956

Williams, J D "Detention Camp Report" Library of Congress, April 15, 1952

"World War II Internment Centers: Central Office Files" WNRC, RG85

"World War II Internment Centers: Ft. Lincoln Files" WNRC, RG85

"World War II Internment Centers: Ft. Stanton Files." WNRC, RG85.

Zirpoli, Alfonso J. *Faith in Justice: Alfonso J. Zirpoli and the U.S. District Court of the Northern California District of California.* Oral history conducted 1982–83 by Sarah Sharp, Regional Office of Oral History, Bancroft Library, University of California, Berkeley, 1984

INTERVIEWS:

Alshouse, Frank Written response to questions, January 25, 1981

Birkefeld, Richard Telephone interview, January 14, 1981.

Cook, William. Written interview, January 8, February 8, 1981; telephone interview, November 12, 1980.

Cordes, Hermann. Interview with Phyllis Johnson, July 11–12, 1980; letter to the author, August 13, 1980.

Deneau, George Interview with the author, October 10, 1980

Ennis, Edward Telephone interview, January 15, June 30, 1982; letter, June 4, 1982

Faust, Ethel. Telephone interview, November 17, 1980

Friedman, Eddie and Liesl. Interview with the author, January 26, February 2, 1980; telephone interview, January 18, 1981.

Gregeratzki, Albert Interview with Phyllis Johnson, August 13, 1980; written statement to the author, October 15, 1980

Henzler, Alfred. Written interview, December 25, 1980.

Homan, Margaret Interview with the author, July 31, 1981

Inouye, Hisao. Interview with the author, March 31, 1979.

Kashino, Paul and Hattie. Interview with the author, November 29, 1980.

Kimmins, Boyd Written interview, December 10, 1980; telephone interview, January 7, 1981

Laidlaw, Carol Interview with the author, August 1, 1981.

Lanier, P. W , Jr Interview with the author, August 26, 1980.

Lenihan, Ray Telephone interview, May 26, 1981.

Moeller, Elmer Telephone interview, October 10, 1980

Mueller, Paul Interview with the author, September 23, 1980.

Nebel, Robert Interview with the author, July 25–26, 1981; telephone interview, September 23, 1981.

Peck, Clifford Telephone interview, December 14, 1980; letter to the author, December 1980.

Pendray, Ed Telephone interview, July 15, 1981.

Petereit, Victor Written interview, October 31, November 20, 1980, March 1, 1981.

Peters, Kurt. Interview with the author, August 23–24, 1980, August 1, 1981.

Rene, Mrs Felix. Interview with the author, August 1, 1981.

Robbins, Will. Interview with the author, August 28, 1980

Selland, E. J. Interview with the author, August 25-26, 1980.
Sonnenberg, Arthur Interview with the author, June 28, 1979, July 3, 1980.
Tanaka, Hironori. Interview with the author, May 27, 1981; telephone interview,
    August 16, 1980, July 9, 1981, July 7, 1982.
Thomas, Wolfgang. Interview with the author, March 5, 1980; telephone interview,
    June 27, 1981.

MtP 20
S^{ce}
signé